D0936609

Anglo-Irish Autobiography

James MacKillop, *Series Editor*

An eighteenth-century Adam giltwood Irish border glass mirror. The cresting is a carved lyre surmounted by an urn draped with bellflowers; the frame is carved with leaf and fluted decoration. Irish, circa 1775. Photograph courtesy of M. Turpin, Fine Antique and Objets d'Art, 27 Bruton Street, London.

Anglo-Irish Autobiography

CLASS, GENDER, AND THE FORMS OF NARRATIVE

Elizabeth Grubgeld

 Syracuse University Press

First Edition 2004

04 05 06 07 08 09   6 5 4 3 2 1

Portions of chapter 1 appeared in "Anglo-Irish Autobiography and the Genealogical Mandate," *Eire-Ireland*, 32.4, 33.1, and 33.2 (winter/spring/summer 1997–87). Copyright © 1994 by the Irish American Cultural Institute, 1 Lackawanna Place, Morristown, New Jersey 07960. Reprinted by permission of the publisher.

Portions of chapter 2 appeared in "Class, Gender, and the Forms of Narrative: The Autobiographies of Anglo-Irish Women," in Susan Shaw Sailer, *Ireland: Gender, Class, Nationality*, 1997. Reprinted by permission of the University Press of Florida.

Portions of chapter 2 appeared in "Cultural Autobiography and the Female Subject: The Genre of the Patrilineal History and the Lifewriting of Elizabeth Bowen," *Genre: Forms of Discourse and Culture* 27, no. 3 (1994). Reprinted by permission of the University of Oklahoma.

The paper used in this publication meets the minimum requirements of American National Standard for Information Sciences—Permanence of Paper for Printed Library Materials, ANSI Z39.48–1984.∞™

Library of Congress Cataloging-in-Publication Data

Grubgeld, Elizabeth.
Anglo-Irish autobiography : class, gender, and the forms of narrative
/ Elizabeth Grubgeld.— 1st ed.
p. cm.—(Irish studies)
Includes bibliographical references and index.
ISBN 0–8156–3016–6 (alk. paper)—ISBN 0–8156–3041–7 (pbk. : alk. paper)
1. English prose literature—Irish authors—History and criticism. 2. Authors, Irish—Biography—History and criticism. 3. Ireland—Biography—History and criticism. 4. Social classes—Ireland. 5. Sex role—Ireland. 6. Narration (Rhetoric) 7. Autobiography. I. Title. II. Series: Irish studies (Syracuse, N.Y.)
PR8817 .G78 2004
820.9'4920417—dc22
2003020052

To the memory of my father, mother, and brother

Elizabeth Grubgeld is professor of modern British and Irish literature at Oklahoma State University and author of *George Moore and the Autogenous Self: The Autobiography and Fiction* (Syracuse University Press), awarded the 1995 American Conference for Irish Studies Prize for Literary and Cultural Criticism.

Contents

Acknowledgments

Anglo-Irish Autobiography: Class, Gender, and the Forms of Narrative was written with the assistance of the Department of English and the College of Arts and Sciences, Oklahoma State University; the Oklahoma Humanities Council; and the Hall Center for the Humanities at the University of Kansas.

Of those who assisted this work to completion, I am especially grateful to Richard Frohock and Michael Pratt, both of whom gave countless hours of their time to carefully reading and discussing with me each chapter in multiple drafts. Barry Sloan graciously agreed to read and critique the fourth chapter, and Brendan Fleming, R. F. Foster, Heather Bryant Jordan, Leigh Partington, and James Pethica sent prompt and helpful replies to my inquiries. For their encouragement and interest in the project, I am also grateful to my colleagues in the American Conference for Irish Studies, particularly Margot Gayle Backus, Richard Bizot, Vera Kreilkamp, and Susan Shaw Sailer. Kim Marotta made it possible for me to finish this project in a timely manner, and graduate assistants Ed Adams and Aaron Gwyn checked citations and proofread the manuscript with skill and attention worthy of professional editors. My thanks also go to Jackie Mann of M. Turpin Limited who kindly reproduced glossy photographs of the eighteenth-century Anglo-Irish mirror that decorates the cover of this book.

My mother and father bequeathed a rich family lore that drew me toward the study of the family history as a form of life writing, and the engagement with which my sons hear and retell those stories reaffirms their significance to the self-making of which autobiography is a primary act. My greatest debt remains, as ever, to William Merrill Decker, who for more than twenty-five years has listened, read, and cheered me on.

Introduction

> Each door—to this my memory finds no single exception—bore
> its polished brass plate. Daughter of a professional
> neighbourhood, I took this brass plate announcing its owner's
> name to be the *sine qua non* of any gentleman's house. . . . At the
> top of the Herbert Place front steps . . . I would trace with my
> finger my father's name. This was not an act of filial piety only; it
> gave him an objective reality, which I shared.
> —Elizabeth Bowen, *Seven Winters*

$\mathcal{L}$ike so many other Anglo-Irish autobiographers, Elizabeth Bowen traces her own story over the names and stories of her fathers, assimilating the patronymic design and finding there what T. R. Henn calls in his autobiography a "family mythologem": a cultural narrative that in the telling attains the reality of a shaping myth. As members of a depleted colonial class, Anglo-Irish autobiographers draw from their family histories a sense of continuity and dissolution, influence and irrelevance, identity and nothingness. They rail against their own class, and they defend its attitudes and actions; they assert their place within an Irish nation, and they question its legitimacy. In every text, they query the nature of their identity and question the location of their true home. And against an overwhelming narrative of cultural decline, they engage in the struggle of self-making that is autobiography.

Because autobiography constitutes such a volatile meeting point of personal and public experience, I have repeatedly examined individual life stories against the analyses of Anglo-Irish life offered by historians. Autobiographical self-representations exist in a mutually influential relationship with the conversation, politics, private writings, and even architecture, material culture, and domestic practices of a society. Through culturally mandated tropes of genealogical preoccupation, loss of property, a vanished utopian childhood, and a degenerative view of history, the autobiographers of Anglo-Ireland situate their life stories within what most see as the story of their culture.

At points, it can be difficult to distinguish among the life experience, the writer's perception of it (a perception often guided by inherited patterns of interpretation), and the literary traditions that affect the transformation of experience into written text. Psychologist Jerome Bruner notes that the very process of remembering and representing experience is a negotiation among learned ways of perceiving life:

> Given their constructed nature and their dependence upon cultural conventions and language usage, life narratives . . . reflect the prevailing theories about "possible lives" that are part of one's culture. Indeed, one important way of characterizing a culture is by the narrative models it makes available for describing the course of a life. And the tool kit of any culture is replete not only with a stock of canonical life narratives (heroes, Marthas, tricksters, etc.), but with combinable formal constituents from which its members can construct their own life narratives: canonical stances and circumstances, as it were. (1987, 15)

The "canonical stances and circumstances" of Anglo-Irish life writing encompass many variants among the multiplicity of people whom I have grouped under the loose appellation "Anglo-Irish." They also differ among time periods, regions, and family background. Although the autobiographical subject finds expression within cultural discourses and generic traditions, these writers also critique the tropes they nevertheless retain. Autobiographers work within inherited forms of apprehending experience but do so as individuals capable of speaking in singular and unpredictable ways.[1]

In so constructing their lives, even those who reject the mores of the parental household often see themselves as cultural bards who pass on the stories of their group and locate the trajectory of their lives within a larger history. Elizabeth Bowen's assessment of family history's effect on the individual consciousness could be taken as the motto of all: "I am ruled by a continuity that I cannot see" (1942, 449). The sense of living in the shadow of one's ancestors intensifies when autobiography is imagined as moment in familial and cultural

---

1. Throughout his critique of theories that postulate subjectivity as fully constrained by language and other determining factors, Paul Smith argues that human beings have the power to "simultaneously exist within and make purposive intervention into social formations." Smith also points out that "interventions" are specific to individuals and not necessarily revolutionary in their motive or effect: "Such intervention . . . can take the form of a refusal as much as an intervention; it can be in the service of conservatism as much as of disruption. It may well call upon an experience of class; but more generally it calls upon the subject/individual's history: such a history is not exclusively determined by class or class membership, real, borrowed, or imagined" (1988, 5).

history. The autobiography is for many the record of a dying way of life, and the urgency to document the fall of the father's world often subsumes the desire to tell a personal story.[2]

Not every Anglo-Irish autobiographer shares that urgency, but its pervasiveness affects the way they read one another and the way we read them in the present moment. A tradition may well be, as W. J. McCormack has argued, "the (sometimes contradictory and violent) convergence of *readings*, not of texts" (1985a, 15–16). The Anglo-Irish autobiography has felt most particularly the influence of W. B. Yeats's reading of Anglo-Irish history, one that itself depends upon prior attempts at cultural self-definition and that would be adopted, adapted, and sometimes rejected in the fiction, autobiography, and history that follow it. Since the late 1600s, those who lived as a privileged minority in Ireland have produced essays, satires, political writings, fiction, and autobiography that draw from their respective generic conventions and from preoccupations passed down through centuries. Publishers and readers then interpret texts in accordance with their own ideological motives and the expectations garnered from prior texts. At times, these expectations and emphases dominate the subject matter to such a degree that they appear forced onto texts that otherwise do not fit the anticipated patterns. In the as-told-to memoir *Seventy Years Young* (1939), Pamela Hinkson imposes on the recollections of Elizabeth Fingall the motifs of social elegy, although at many points Fingall expresses a sense of entrapment within that same society and satisfaction with the probability of change. A similar disjunction arises in Joan de Vere's *In Ruin Reconciled: A Memoir of Anglo-Ireland, 1913–1959* (1990), an autobiography whose title points in one thematic and ideological direction while its content—the story of her nursing career and years in Africa—points in quite another.[3]

In the autobiographies of Fingall and de Vere, the breach between estab-

2. Mary Jean Corbett charts the fusion of personal and public histories in mid-nineteenth-century England as "the triumph of bourgeois ideology" that values the lives of middle-class individuals and their perspectives on history (1992, 98). The Anglo-Irish autobiography differs from the texts Corbett treats in what I have called its narrative of decline. Its authors uniformly express the sense of having lived in a world apart from the majority population and having now reached the end of that era.

3. A rare exception to this pattern is Marjorie Quarton's *Breakfast the Night Before: Recollections of an Irish Horse Dealer* (2000). Her family, who came to Ireland in the 1400s, declined from ownership of Bunratty Castle and the Smithwick Brewery to a tiny farm in Tipperary. But the family history is given quickly and without extensive commentary. From the title page to the final paragraphs, the story concerns itself exclusively with the author's love of dogs and horses and her development as a shrewd dealer of both. Quarton discusses the emergence of independent Ireland only in terms of Eamon De Valera's economic policy and its effect on livestock farming.

lished form and incompatible content is all too evident; in other cases, the form generates a story so predictable that it seems to fit the mold with suspicious exactness. S. R. Lysaght's *My Tower in Desmond* (1925) contains almost every motif, set scene, thematic preoccupation, and narrative pattern that can be identified generally with the Anglo-Irish autobiography. The title page gives no indication of genre, and no internal cues point to its designation as fact or fiction, although the degree of coincidence and high drama renders its factuality suspect. This representative autobiography is in truth a novel, written to a formula of expectation so popularized by 1925 that the book was praised in reviews for its historical merit and went into an American edition and a second London printing within two years. Further entrenched in their expectations by seventy-five subsequent years of "Big House" novels and autobiographies, at least two booksellers have classified *My Tower in Desmond* as autobiography in their current catalogs, suggesting that readers can still be deceived by the formulaic elements of an invented history.[4]

With the literary tradition of Anglo-Ireland in a state of perpetual invention and reinvention, we are obliged to inquire whether it is possible even to speak of the Anglo-Irish, an ambiguous category subjected to ongoing revision since the turn of the eighteenth century. If we identify a cultural narrative, presumably there must exist, or have existed, a culture that it narrates, even if, as McCormack has argued repeatedly, the terms of its self-description were formulated at the very moment that it ceased to function except as a synthetic memory.[5] Some people in Ireland did (and continue to) define themselves as different from a majority population it is now common to call the "native Irish," although that term is as contradictory and misleading as the contested "Anglo-Irish." The question of who exactly the Anglo-Irish took themselves to be will arise repeatedly as we look at different assertions of identity and the imaginative means of their projection. According to Louis MacNeice, they

4. Keochs Books (England) and Grub Street Books (Australia) both list *My Tower in Desmond* as autobiography. Although recognizing it as a novel, a 1925 review from the *Saturday Review of Literature* praises its worth as history, given that "very little history, very few memoirs that one can trust," comes out of Ireland (Canby 1925, 210). I assumed *My Tower in Desmond* was autobiography until about one-third of the way through a first reading, but I was not absolutely certain of its fictionality until biographical information about its author confirmed my suspicions.

5. In his many books on Protestant Ireland, W. J. McCormack repeats and refines his claim that concepts of Protestant Ascendancy, Anglo-Irish culture, and the symbolic "Big House" crystallized and gained force only after what they described had nearly ceased to exist. He also stresses that Anglo-Irish self-definition was various and perpetually in flux and that the idea of the Anglo-Irish as an embattled sector of the Irish population should not be anachronistically read back through the early eighteenth century. See also Hill 1989.

were marked by "nothing but an insidious bonhomie, an obsolete bravado, and a way with horses"; R. F. Foster speaks of "a certain savagery of mind" and "a ruthless but ironic pursuit of style"; and Brendan Behan reduces it all to the absurd: "a Protestant with a horse."[6] But how do the people so named characterize themselves: as a racial or ethnic group, a class, a religion, or a culture? Or does their sense of difference finally amount to an inconclusive assortment of these factors?

Judging from autobiographical evidence, it appears that most Anglo-Irish understood their differences from the majority primarily as differences in class. In part, this perception explains why I rely on the term *Anglo-Ireland* instead of *Protestant Ireland* and include Catholics as well as Anglicans and a few members of Dissenting congregations. Although most people who held positions of prestige (owning land or having access to the gentleman's occupations) were Anglican, not all were. In the late nineteenth century and first decades of the twentieth, Catholics at the upper ranks of society might be affected professionally and socially by enduring sectarian bigotry, but they attended the same house parties, struggled with the same tenants and agents, and dealt with the same loss of status and property as did their Anglican neighbors. Writers like George Moore, Elizabeth Fingall, Enid Starkie, and Hannah Lynch were Catholic in upbringing, but their social circles and their professional and financial expectations mirrored with minor variance those of their Protestant fellows. In contrast, the urban Protestant working class and the Dissenting groups concentrated in the North lived lives very distinct from the political and social privilege enjoyed by the professional classes and their rural landed cousins. They rarely identify themselves as Anglo-Irish, nor do they share similar preoccupations.[7] Even given the intraclass distinctions and snobberies ex-

6. MacNeice cited in Foster 1988, 168; Foster 1988, 176, 170; Behan 1962, 15. An exchange from Brendan Behan's *Hostage* illustrates the comic potential of categorizing the Anglo-Irish with a repertoire of stereotypes, although the speaker's choice of class as the primary identifying factor of the Anglo-Irish is not entirely inaccurate. Pat, a former Republican turned brothel keeper, explains to one of the prostitutes that an Anglo-Irishman cannot be "an ordinary Protestant like Leadbetter, the plumber in the back parlour . . . nor a Belfast orangeman, not if he was black as your boot." When she asks why, he answers, "Because they work. An Anglo-Irishman only works at riding horses, drinking whisky and reading double-meaning books in Irish at Trinity College" (1962, 15).

7. See, for example, Edith Newman Devlin's *Speaking Volumes: A Dublin Childhood* (2001), which recounts the life of an impoverished Presbyterian child growing up in Dublin around the years of World War II; John Hewitt's sketch of his upbringing as a Methodist teacher's son in Belfast, "Planter's Gothic: An Essay in Discursive Autobiography" (1987); or the numerous Protestant autobiographies excerpted in Frank Ormsby's collection, *Northern Windows: An Anthology of Ulster Autobiography* (1987).

posed in the autobiographies of George Bernard Shaw, W. B. Yeats, and William Trevor, their middle-class upbringing had more in common with prosperous Irish Anglicans and Catholics than the working-class world of either a Catholic like Frank O'Connor or an impoverished Belfast Protestant like Robert Harbinson.

Turn-of-the-century tales of class relations and upheaval are by no means unique to Ireland. The symbolism of ruined houses and diminished estates pervades English fiction and autobiography of the same period. In language that could easily describe much of Anglo-Irish literature, M. M. Kelsall remarks in his study of the English country house that "the decline and fall of the country house . . . has been one of the obsessional subjects of modern literature from the late nineteenth century onwards. . . . As pure idea, with the country house written off as a vanishing social phenomenon, there is nothing to check its growth and elaboration in the mind itself" (1993, 155, 161). A photograph from the autobiography of C. Day Lewis demonstrates the point. Seemingly a picture from Lewis's childhood as the son of a country rector near Enniscorthy, it displays young Cecil in a sailor suit with his beloved companion, a local fisherman in rough boots, cap, and a pipe. It might have served as a cover illustration for this book. Unfortunately for an author in search of cover art, the text discloses that this fisherman's nearly incomprehensible dialect was East Anglian and that he lived along the Norfolk coast where Lewis was taken for holidays. What appears to be a typical tableau of the Anglo-Irish child and a native Irish servant is in truth a symbol of a broader class dynamic.

If class privilege had not depended so much on the colonial occupation of the land they claimed as theirs, Anglo-Irish relations with the majority population might have been at least superficially no different from the relations among the classes in many European countries during the nineteenth and early twentieth centuries. Yet because more Protestants belonged to the middle and upper classes and belonged there because of a colonial legacy that awarded power and land to English Protestants while denying it to Irish Catholics, those differences of class have a sectarian and ethnic dimension that is not replicated to such an exaggerated degree in England. Many believed Anglicanism to be equivalent to a separate class and a set of behaviors and attitudes so distinct as to constitute a culture apart from that of Catholic Ireland.

Tempestuous debate has erupted over the question of whether the English and the Anglo-Irish also saw the native Irish as a different race with biologically inherited capabilities and tendencies of their own.[8] A fuller discussion

8. See, for example, the debate between L. Perry Curtis and R. F. Foster recounted in the title essay of Foster's *Paddy and Mr Punch: Connections in Irish and English History* (1993, 171–94).

will come in the chapters that follow, but in short, the evidence from the auto-biographical record suggests that the answer depends upon who is speaking, in what contexts, and for what purposes. Race turns out to be what American novelist John Edgar Wideman calls "a wild card . . . open-ended, situational, functional, predictable to some extent, but a flexible repertoire of possibilities that follow from the ingenuity of the operator privileged to monopolize the controls" (1994, xvi). Over the two centuries here examined, autobiographers share no consistent common meaning in their use of such concepts as race, na-tionality, and culture. Even an individual writer rarely uses such categories with consistency.

If class, religion, and race are all interpreted variously and generally am-biguously, culture is an equally inconclusive factor. Edward Said's remarks his 1983 *The World, the Text, and the Critic* remain important in explaining its role in the formation of identity. The idea of culture, he writes,

> is used to designate not merely something to which one belongs but some-thing that one possesses and, along with that proprietary process . . . a boundary by which the concepts of what is extrinsic or intrinsic to the culture come into forceful play. . . . [It] is the power of culture by virtue of its elevated or superior position to authorize, to dominate, to legitimate, demote, inter-dict, and validate: in short, the power of culture to be an agent of, and perhaps the main agency for, powerful differentiation within its domain and beyond it too. (8–9)

According to this formulation, Anglo-Ireland may be described primarily in terms of an opposition, much as Declan Kiberd argues that England needed "a foil to set off English virtues" (1995, 1) and "invented" the idea of Ireland in order to further define itself.[9] Whether or not Anglo-Irish life constituted a culture in the anthropological sense, its life writing suggests that those indi-viduals who wrote autobiographies perceived themselves as possessing a dis-tinct culture and used it to differentiate themselves from others.

Among autobiographers, however, the validating function of cultural self-definition seems less active than the differentiating function. Particularly as writers engage a comic approach to the life story, they represent behavioral and ideological norms as performative, artificial, even arbitrary; often, they denaturalize the norm and hold it up to ridicule. Perhaps it is most accurate to

9. In his 1916 autobiography, *The End of a Chapter*, Shane Leslie remarks: "To write of Ireland among English institutions seems a *bull* or as the Greeks called it, an oxymoron (sharp folly). Nev-ertheless, England would not be what she is without Ireland. For good or for bad, for sunshine or for rain (chiefly the latter), England and Ireland seem doomed to cross-entanglement" (133).

say that all these factors—class, religion, ethnicity, culture—combine in infinitely various interpretations and emphases to create an indeterminate but unmistakable perception of being different from the majority of the population they call "the people."

∽∾∾

I begin with an exploration of the development of this genre's major features as practiced by the Anglo-Irish: its tortuous efforts to assert claims to legitimacy in Ireland through an obsession with family history, patronym, and inherited property, as well as its efforts to avoid the entropic force of time by imagining a childhood immune from narrative and the movement of time implicit within it. Taking in several cases the very same texts from which these predominant features come to the forefront, the second chapter then trains the lens of gender analysis on the ways women—in most cases unable to inherit either name or property—both wrote and rewrote masculinist narratives to create for themselves a dynamic place within a story that would otherwise render them ciphers. The true cipher of Anglo-Irish autobiography is the mother, and the third chapter explores those few texts in which she receives sustained attention in order to read her presence elsewhere in the margins. Private discourse such as the intimate letter or diary provides a sphere for maternal self-representation, but the dominant ideology of gender and class in Anglo-Ireland also leads to the expression of "matrophobia," in which the mother's powerlessness leads to rejection by the daughter who fears to see her reflection in her mother's life. To see the mother outside her role as a supportive figure in the patriarchy, however, can result in a transfigurative textual reconciliation of mother and daughter.

The final chapters move from gender to genre analysis. Although few beyond professional clergymen produce life writings that fall firmly within the genre of the spiritual autobiography, many Anglo-Irish writers do reflect on religious identity and recount stories of religious conversion and deconversion. Because they so associate Anglicanism with conservative political and class positions, their deconversion narratives merge with ideological shifts toward socialism or nationalism, whereas writers who affirm their continued allegiance to the Church of Ireland do so as part of a broader statement of their allegiance to class values. As in the considerations of women's position in Ireland, the representations of the maternal, and the rhetoric of conversion and deconversion, the final chapter's examination of the Anglo-Irish comic autobiography reveals that it too upholds yet critiques the patterns of cultural identity set forth early in this study. Although autobiography and comedy may seem incompatible in narrative structure and rhetorical aims, the singular phenomenon of the Anglo-Irish comic autobiography appears in the late eighteenth century and endures into the present. With literary antecedents in the political and fictional discourse of the eighteenth century, the comic autobiography—particularly its parody, satire, and ironic reductionism—emerges as a characteristic form of Anglo-Irish life writing, preoccupied like its more somber relatives with ancestral houses, family history, and the literary childhood.

If there is a central character in the tradition I have proposed, it is Elizabeth Bowen. An autobiographer of unusual skill and subtlety, she manages the most astute negotiations between inherited identity and her life as a woman, and between her story as the failed heir of Bowen's Court and an arena of concern that must go beyond that narrow world. The autobiographical writing of W. B. Yeats has received so much critical attention that I have restricted mine to less studied works; although my intent has not been to evaluate and rank texts, certain treasures have surfaced from the bibliography amassed at the end of the book. Along with the autobiographies of Elizabeth Bowen, George Moore, and W. B. Yeats—whom I believe to be among the finest of all Irish autobiographers in intellectual complexity and technical brilliance—readers may wish to pursue more fully Katherine Everett's *Bricks and Flowers* (1949), Lionel Fleming's *Head or Harp* (1965), Enid Starkie's *Lady's Child* (1941), Mary Pakenham's *Brought Up and Brought Out* (1938), and the two equally engaging autobiographies *Five Out of Six* (1960) and *Within the Family Circle* (1976) by Pakenham's sister, Violet Powell. For their vitality and comic candor, G. B. Shaw's various autobiographical writings; Samuel Hussey's as-told-to memoir, *The Reminiscences of an Irish Land Agent* (1904); and Shane Leslie's *Film of Memory* (1938) are also requisite.

Not every text I have read has made its way into the discussion, nor can I claim to have located every Anglo-Irish autobiography. It has been a hit-and-miss effort accomplished through years of hand searches among the stacks of libraries distinguished and obscure. Some autobiographies proved to be novels; some were little more than military memoirs or generic religious testimonies; some were on close examination more English than Anglo-Irish. A few choices might remain controversial, like the heavily fictionalized *Thalassa* (1931) by Mary Frances McHugh or the autobiography of the distinguished British politician and activist Frank Pakenham. Yet in the latter case, the very ambiguity of national identity adds to the fascination of the text. Although my concern has not been comparative, I have drawn parallels between Anglo-Irish life writing and travel writing, particularly in relationship to audience and the representation of alterity. The comparisons between Anglo-Irish and Anglo-

Indian identities, however, expose their circumstances to be more unalike than analogous.

Most of the writers here considered possess a strong sense of the historical significance of their life writing. They frequently understand their stories as testimonies to the ruin of one way of life and the difficult birth of another. In 1916, Shane Leslie begins the first of his three autobiographies in the middle of what he calls "the suicide of a civilisation called Christian and the travail of a new era to which no gods have been as yet rash enough to give their name" (n.p.) The vast majority of Anglo-Irish autobiographies appeared during the decades following the establishment of the Irish Free State and the beginning of the Second World War, but World War I had already accelerated a feeling of rapid social transformation. Many landholding families were left bereft of heirs; a chapter of George De Stacpoole's *Irish and Other Memories* (1922) begins with cameo portraits of his five sons: all soldiers, two dead, two "horribly wounded," only one surviving intact (186–88). As the Great War ended, the war of independence in Ireland began to gather force, and although the Anglo-Irish world had been in its death throes for many decades—some historians have argued that its decline began with the great famine of the 1840s—the major demographic change in modern Protestant Ireland took place within the revolutionary period. The census of 1911 and that of 1926 indicate a 33.5 percent decline in the Protestant population of the twenty-six counties (Kennedy 1980, 151–52), and in heavily Protestant areas like Cork, the change was much greater.[10] Looking back on the era, T. R. Henn marks it as the period in which things fell apart; his autobiography, he hopes, "may throw some light on a culture that died between 1916 and 1921" (1980, 12). Others thought the end came with the Second World War; for those writing during the late 1930s and 1940s, the terrifying reality of fascist aggression tipped the balance even further toward a pessimistic view of the future.

Against this vision of entropy or apocalypse, these autobiographers attempt not only to memorialize but also to reconsider and reshape their lives. The autobiographies of Anglo-Ireland present more than a previously undoc-

10. In his study of the urban Protestant working class, Martin McGuire claims that "what appears to be a loss of Protestants in general was in fact a loss of mostly urban working-class Protestants" who left, he suggests, because of the decline of "non-essential industries" in Dublin during the First World War (1995, 201–2). His interpretation of the Protestant exodus differs from many histories of the period but appears to draw on previously overlooked data; his work supplements, rather than contradicts, the perception of the Protestant diaspora as an upper-class group driven out by land reform and nationalist agitation. For further discussion of Protestants in the Irish republic, see K. Bowen 1983.

umented fragment of a literary mosaic, more than an obscure field of interest for the specialist. They offer instead stories of the effort to reconfigure one's moorings once the ship has moved on, like the cautionary tale of Seamus Heaney's poem "The Settle-Bed." Faced with the inheritance of an old settle bed whose heavy boards weigh down his spirit with their reminders of Ulster's hard history, the speaker in Heaney's poem admonishes himself to

> . . . learn . . . that whatever is given
>
> Can always be reimagined, however four-square,
> Plank-thick, hull-stupid and out of its time
> It happens to be. You are free as the lookout,
>
> That far-seeing joker posted high over the fog,
> Who declared by the time he had got himself down
> The actual ship had stolen away from beneath him.

Anglo-Irish Autobiography

1

Place, Patronym, and the Literary Childhood

Jean-Jacques Rousseau begins his *Confessions* with an audacious assertion of selfhood: "I have resolved on an enterprise which has no precedent, and which, once complete, will have no imitator. My purpose is to display to my kind a portrait in every way true to nature, and the man I shall portray will be myself. . . . I am made unlike any one I have ever met; I will even venture to say that I am like no one in the whole world. I may be no better, but at least I am different" (1953, 17). The autobiographical occasion often turns on just such an assumption of difference, and readers have commonly privileged the successful creation of a first-person narrator as sharply characterized as the protagonist of the realist novel. The majority of Anglo-Irish autobiographers were more confident than we are today of the representational powers of language to create a text that, being utterly unique, would stand as a perfect corollary to a unique life. Such confidence may, in fact, coexist with a contradictory desire to see one's life as representative of a larger pattern in the history of one's own group: to understand one's life as both a singular experience and an exemplary one.

With varying degrees of self-consciousness, autobiographers embed the particularities of experience within an inherited form of life narrative. Since the late 1970s, the study of autobiography has taken as a point of departure Paul de Man's argument that the forms of autobiography influence or, in his more restrictive phrasing, "determine" the nature of the first-person pronoun that speaks from the page (1979, 922). Much subsequent work in autobiographical theory has drawn attention to the way generic structures are themselves shaped by forces beyond the literary. Culturally mandated forms of memory—what is remembered and how it is remembered—arguably generate the "plots" by which individuals write the stories of their lives. My purpose is to examine how inherited forms of imagining a life give design to the autobiography and to explore how these forms are adopted and adapted given the structures of class and gender in which the life is experienced and articulated.

1

To take this approach requires that we see autobiography as the product of an ongoing interaction among readerly expectations, literary models of life writing, cultural patterns of living and interpreting one's life, the particular occurrences that provide the historical basis for the narrative, and the formative imagination of the writer. As Shirley Neuman has proposed, this way of reading autobiography recognizes "a dialectic between . . . the subject as acted upon and produced by social discourse and the subject as acting to change social discourse and, therefore, its own subject position." Neither fully determined by history nor fully autonomous from it, the autobiographical speaker is thus both "socially constructed and constructing" (1992, 223).

The life writing of Anglo-Ireland provides an unusually rich field in which to explore the historical pressures and narrative forms that at once enable and constrain what an autobiographer presents as a private life. Such an exploration also necessitates an inquiry into the suppositions with which readers approach the subject: how our preconceptions as readers shape and are in turn shaped by what we find in the texts themselves. In his informal and idiosyncratic study of the Anglo-Irish, Terence de Vere White declares his own assumptions regarding the form and content of Anglo-Irish life writing when he maintains that it consists by and large of "books of reminiscences by Irishmen who went out to govern New South Wales, or otherwise achieved eminence, [that] begin with a short Irish chapter containing a joke; the next deals with a school in England; then Oxford or Cambridge. The bulk of the book is composed of chapters on London and life abroad. . . . Ireland is left like the shell of the egg out of which the chicken emerged" (1972, 168). Although some works superficially conform to this model, a more extensive reading reveals quickly the limitations of his generalization. Readers come to Anglo-Irish literature with a variety of other formal, thematic, and ideological expectations gleaned from the immensely influential W. B. Yeats, or the revisionists of his time and ours who have disputed his versions of history. The autobiographers likewise come to the narratives of their own lives with surprisingly unitary notions of what Anglo-Ireland was and what it meant; we will find these paradigms to be often strangely at odds with the details of their stories and what might be more productive ways of understanding their lives.

Also requiring reconsideration is the fundamental critical terminology of Irish literary history. Irish studies has undertaken a wide-ranging review of vocabulary formerly thought to be unproblematic, including the very terms with which this book is titled. If the indeterminate appellation "Anglo-Irish" and its even more discredited cousin, "Protestant Ascendancy," produce for the specialist more questions than clarity, to the general reader both expressions conjure an image of grand country houses in disrepair, mad uncles and decaying dowagers, an obsession with horses, and pride of lineage. Recent advertising for the reissue of Countess Fingall's 1937 autobiography, *Seventy Years Young*, describes her book as delineating the "twilight world of Catholic Ascendancy Ireland," suggesting that the phantom term *Ascendancy* might be affixed to any denominational adjective with equal imprecision as long as a work exhibits the requisite motifs of houses, horses, and the family pedigree.

I use instead the expression "Anglo-Irish," broadly and with full recognition of its origins and ambiguity. Most, but not all, of the autobiographers under consideration were affiliated with the Church of Ireland, although many families converted to Protestantism only in the late 1700s. Most drew income from rural properties, although others were dependent on earnings from their professions. Some, but not all, were wealthy or belonged to previously wealthy families. Some trace lineage to Gaelic families or the predominantly Norman "Old English" who crossed over before the Reformation; others were born of more recently immigrated English parents. Some lived at least part of the year, or part of their lives, in England; for others, England was an unknown and foreign land.

Numerous literary and social historians have argued that the Irish upper classes were less the ancient aristocracy whose image was promulgated by Yeats than, in Seamus Deane's words, "a predominantly bourgeois social formation" often urban and mercantile in nature (1987, 30). In *Vanishing Country Houses of Ireland*, the knight of Glin estimates that of about two hundred remaining "Big Houses," only twenty would be classified as "Great Houses" (McDowell 1992, 291). Mary Leadbeater corroborates such moderating views of imagined grandeur in her memoir of a small community in nineteenth-century Kildare (1862). A Quaker, she distinguishes between her own group of prosperous Protestant farmers and businessmen and the "English" occupants of "the Great House" whose social life is distinct from her own for reasons of class as well as religion. Mary Hamilton offers in her autobiography the following description of the classes in the late nineteenth and early twentieth centuries:

> Between the two extremes of titled families or county families and the poor people, came the farmers; and, on our side of Meath, a number of retired people from Dublin; a barrister and his family; a widowed colonel with a family of eleven daughters; a stockbroker and his English wife who divided their time between Ireland and England and never seemed settled in either.
>
> Then there were the rich farmers who kept themselves to themselves, and the smaller farmers, and the trainers, and horsey people of all kinds. There was the English set who . . . had come to Ireland for the sole purpose of hunting and race meetings. (1948, 184)

The variety and subtlety of class distinctions offered by Leadbeater and Hamilton contradict the more dramatic Yeatsian account of "hard-riding country gentlemen" and "lords and ladies gay" that has long been beaten into the clay by years of historical revisionism.[1] W. J. McCormack has successfully demonstrated that the rural "Big House" was often small and located in town (1985a, 111–17) and that "Protestant Ascendancy" was more a political idea than a sociological reality (1993b, n.p.; 1994, 49–91). *Anglo-Irish* is perhaps best considered a term of self-description rather than a freestanding category. Whether the term *Anglo-Irish* is invoked, the one feature shared by every autobiography here examined is the writer's sense of difference from both the English and the majority population of Ireland. This assumption of difference bases itself on perceived distinctions in class, political loyalties, denominational affiliations, or cultural practices and attitudes. Although many autobiographers offer passionate declarations of their own "Irishness," they may simultaneously refer to Catholics of the middle and lower classes as "the Irish" or "the people." George Birmingham tries to distinguish them as "Irish Irelanders," but his attempts at clarity belie the general confusion among multiple allegiances to bloodlines, class, denomination, culture, region, and nation (1919, 192).

Even if self-identification depends more on the explanation of what one is not than on what one is, the life writing of this loosely defined and now largely extinct group manifests certain generic characteristics, especially in the late nineteenth and early twentieth centuries when the Anglo-Irish were quickly disappearing as an influential factor in Irish history. With few exceptions, though with many variations, the family history provides a structural framework for the life story, encompassing a preoccupation with family houses, the specific topographies of childhood, and a narrative movement toward familial and cultural extinction that threatens the writer with increasing intensity as chapters move forward in time. Significant variations on these generic models appear in the work of women writers, the surprising number of autobiographers of both sexes who write the life as a comedy, and those who embrace a more ecumenical vision of modern Ireland; however, these forms of narrative, even when contested, constitute a specific cultural expression.[2]

---

1. In her memoir, *Crowned Harp*, Nora Robertson presents a set of distinctions that parallels Hamilton's. Her description of four "rows" of Anglo-Irish, descending from the higher echelons of peers to "Loyal professional people, gentlemen professional farmers, trade, large retail or small wholesale," is reproduced in McConville 1986 (247–51).

2. Julian Moynahan offers six characteristics of Anglo-Irish writing, at least one of which appears in almost every autobiography here addressed: (1) involvement in Anglo-Irish society; (2) thematization of the misfortunes of isolated estates; (3) interest in the lives of the "native" Irish; (4)

The Genealogical Mandate

The family history, either as a prose narrative or as a pedigree printed adjacent to the text of an autobiography, acts as the predominant structuring device of Anglo-Irish life writing. As might be expected, the autobiographers in question do more than simply recite genealogical details in prose paragraphs. Yet what they do is not necessarily predictable. The genealogical orientation may frequently serve to "propagate" what W. J. McCormack has deemed the "false sociology" of the so-called Protestant Ascendancy as a once flourishing landed culture (1985a, 88), but it even more often frustrates its own ambitions. The genealogical approach to life writing repeatedly undermines the autobiographer's attempt to inscribe a continuity between personal and social identity. Even as writers avow their families' roles in public history, class precedence, and hereditary rights to an Irish identity, their doubts about each of these claims emerge. For women, who usually inherited neither property nor patronym, the effort to affirm one's significance through these motifs is ineffectual or, at worst, debilitating. Similarly, efforts to solidify one's position within a community through the evocation of an Edenic childhood and a timeless sense of place are thwarted by the relentless historicity of the family chronicle. And in nearly all of these texts, the teleological impulse of the genealogy veers uneasily toward a degenerative version of history that endangers the vitality of the speaking subject.

Genealogy, as practiced in autobiographical writing, may encompass diagrammatic and verbal representations of lineage, a thematic preoccupation with descent, and a narrative built upon its linear and teleological implications. Anglo-Irish autobiographies frequently duplicate a genealogical chart on the endpapers or among the illustrations; family descent often provides the organizational structure for at least one chapter, if not the entire book. Its presence influences both the form of the autobiography and our readerly presumptions about the text. When a genealogy appears in fiction, it may accentuate the author's concern with biological inheritance or act as a guide to a bewildering number of characters. In autobiography, its rhetorical function is more complicated. Like an accompanying photograph, it affixes the speaker to a history outside the text. Yet just as a photograph may be chosen to illustrate those characteristics of personality explored in the text, the particular shape of the genealogy is subject to the selective and interpretive acts of the autobiographer.

---

an attitude of "research" toward the latter; (5) distinction between the self and the English reader; and (6) a consciousness of using English differently (1995, 39–40).

In her groundbreaking essay on the relationship between genealogical practices and autobiography, Julia Watson maintains that the former implies a deterministic explanation of identity in contrast to the more autogenous ambitions of the latter:

> Genealogy detects the recorded past; autobiography pursues the desire for creation of free, agentified subjectivity. Genealogy is a chronicle that can be verified through documents and records; autobiography depends on memory to dislodge the writing subject from the norms, traditions, and constraints that governed past generations.
>
> Genealogy justifies and legitimates social status, through both genealogical record and the ability to produce a pedigree; autobiography can dispute and revise the inherited past. (1996, 318)

Watson's generalizations describe the contrasting methods of each genre and the differing explanations of purpose commonly offered by their practitioners. The two species of writing overlap more than her distinctions would suggest; the genealogical orientation in autobiography frequently questions or dislodges "social status" and is highly susceptible to imaginative reconstruction and interpretation. Yet as she observes, the deterministic thrust of genealogy impedes an individual's attempt to recast the life outside the pattern imposed by a communal history. As a species of autobiography, it encapsulates that fundamental ambivalence of the autobiographical project: in Paul John Eakin's words, the "motive for all autobiographical making, a tension between acceptance of the constraints of contingency and surrender to the irrepressible claims of desire" (1992, 45). By its very form, the family history concedes the influence of historical contingency on that creation of desire, the autobiographical speaker. Conversely, the desire to create the self anew struggles with the historical constraints of genealogy.

The association of self with a defined historical moment appears as one of the primary tendencies of much late-eighteenth- and early-nineteenth-century life writing. Deriving from the testimony of trial and redemption, the titillating confessions of notorious criminals, and the exoticism of travel writing, autobiographies depict lives of unusual adventure designed to excite or edify their readers. Titles like Captain Neville Frowde's *Life, Extraordinary Adventures, Voyages, and Surprising Escapes* (1767), Thomas Cloney's *Personal Narrative of Those Transactions in the Co. Wexford in which the Author Was Engaged During the Awful Period of 1798* (1832), and Anne Lutton's *Memorials of a Consecrated Life* (1883) indicate that early Anglo-Irish life writing closely follows such precedents. Like many memoirs appearing during and after the Land

Wars, William Trench's *Realities of Irish Life* (1868) proceeds from a more complex motive. In addition to entertaining and informing the reader, Trench seeks to justify the actions of the Anglo-Irish and to merge more fully the historical record with a more intimate personal one. His story, he declares, is unique and thrilling: "From youth to manhood, and from manhood to the verge of age, it has been my lot to live surrounded by a kind of poetic turbulence and almost romantic violence, which I believe could scarcely belong to real life in any other country in the world" (viii-ix). His purposes are those of the historian, and he presents his life as representative of a historical moment. Addressing his work to an English and American readership (an elaborate folding map of Ireland is included in the first British edition), he explains his wishes "to give the English public some idea of the difficulties which occasionally beset the path of an Irish landlord or agent which is desirous to improve the district in which he is interested" (vi-vii). Although he says that were his tale too personal "I should simply give a history of my life, and this could scarcely prove generally interesting" (viii), he portrays his familial surroundings and school days with warmth and skill, blending the personal with the historical more fully than do the stories of adventure or the standard military and political memoirs that precede his work. Like John Hamilton's *Sixty Years' Experience as an Irish Landlord* (1894) or Samuel Hussey's *Reminiscences of an Irish Land Agent* (1904), Trench's book integrates the features of travel writing, history, and a personal narrative to impart significance to the individual life.

In his examination of the relationship between autobiographical and historical writing during the Victorian period, A. Dwight Culler affirms the observation of many literary historians that "by far the most pervasive paradigm . . . is the parallel between the life of the individual and the life-cycle of civilizations." Culler suggests that "the discovery of the parallel was often the means whereby the individual overcame his alienation and reconciled himself with the world" (1985, 280). After the First World War, the proportion of space given to the psychological development and personal history of the writer greatly increased. However, in Anglo-Irish autobiography this more intimate representation of the self remains fully enmeshed with what the author puts forward as the history of a group. Cultural nationalists like Samuel Ferguson had been arguing since the early 1830s that Protestant alienation might be overcome by a concerted effort to recover and identify with the Celtic past (Lyons 1979, 27–55), but most chose, instead, family history as the vehicle through which to assert position and class, establish nationality, and substantiate an ambiguously defined cultural identity.

If many exploited genealogical records as evidence of social prestige, not all Anglo-Irish assumed that a recourse to family history would establish their place in the community. On one hand, Mrs. Morgan John O'Connell, who in 1887 edited the journal extracts of Attie O'Brien, a well-to-do Catholic girl from County Clare, observes, "It gives great interest to a lonely country life to know the story of every old castle you see pass in your rides, and I have often seen how the consciousness of ancient and honorable descent, has helped on many an Irish country gentlewoman, in an uphill struggle for culture and refinement among the prosaic surroundings of rural housekeeping" (3). On the other hand, her contemporary, Sir William Gregory, says with self-satisfaction that family history "is a subject in which I never took the smallest interest" (1894, 13), a sentiment echoed by Lennox Robinson's father who, while solemnly displaying to his young son a parchment inscribed with the family tree, reminds him that "no gentleman ever boasts of his birth" (1942, 12). Writing in the early eighteenth century, Thomas Prior makes his disdain for the genealogical preoccupation even more explicit. In his 1729 polemic against absenteeism, he declares that "the Pride of Names and Families, is despised by all People of Sense, and is rarely to be found but in poor Countrys, or Persons of reduc'd Fortunes, and is generally accompany'd with the Want of real Merit" (1991, 899). To O'Connell, the family history is an aid to the pursuit of gentility, particularly for women; to Prior, it is the obsession of those individuals without gentility. For O'Connell, it consoles the loneliness of being the sole possessor of "culture and refinement"; for Prior, an interest in it betrays one's lack of real importance within a community.

The paternal grandfather of Maria Edgeworth comes closest to describing the ambivalence surrounding the genealogical preoccupation when he admonishes whichever son shall succeed him not to engage in ungentlemanly talk about his pedigree, to recall that real breeding reveals itself in actions not boasts, yet to recognize that knowing his ancestry can "inform my son of what stock he really is, that he may not . . . suppose himself to be a mere upstart" (Butler and Butler 1927, 5). In other words, a good pedigree should ensure both status and character, but such traits are manifested by the silence that the well bred observe on the subject of their own breeding. Despite the centuries dividing these autobiographers, their comments expose the pervious borders of a predominantly bourgeois society; moreover, they acknowledge that the genealogical preoccupation may be motivated by a feeling of isolation from the class one finds desirable. The family history can both answer and fail to answer the need for community and status, and its own tropic properties both preserve and threaten the autobiographical subject who embraces them so earnestly.

Given an ever diminishing role in the life of the emergent nation, it is unsurprising that so many Anglo-Irish use the autobiography as a place to avow their ancestors' Irish credentials as nationalists or humanitarians.[3] As if to reinforce their legitimacy in the always contested matter of whether a family is actually "Irish," descendants of Anglo-Irish families who came to Ireland after 1700 tend to skim over family history prior to the few generations preceding their own. Their narratives often obfuscate the brevity of the period in which the family accumulated its wealth, generally during the Napoleonic Wars or in the years before the Great Famine. In a scenario common to many of these texts, the servants—presumably Catholic and often represented as speaking in an exotic dialect—display a respectful interest in the genealogy of their employers. Mary Hamilton remarks that the "older Irish of the cabins and the little farms" bore them no grudge but valued them as the "'rale ould stock' " (1948, 181); the elderly servant Mary Frances McHugh remembers from childhood dismisses the "wealthy late-comers" as incomparable to "the old stock that are the real genthry" with whom, says McHugh, the servants felt themselves to stand "shoulder to shoulder against the world in fortunes good and ill" (1931, 45).

In her 1949 autobiography, *Bricks and Flowers*, Katherine Everett recalls, "We thought our family important, and this idea was based partly on what we had to write out and learn of the section in 'Landed Gentry' devoted to our family" (1). She reflects:

> It was not snobbishness on my mother's part to value her ancestry so highly; it was the fashion of her day. Indeed, for long after that time profound interest in genealogies continued, more especially in Ireland. At any social occasion you might hear a remark such as, "Wasn't the wife of Maurice O'Meara of Ballyduff the daughter of Tom Cassidy of Castle Cassidy? and that would make her our cousin to Sir Timothy. . . ," etc., and the topic would be followed up in all its ramifications with the eagerness of hounds on a hot scent.
> Even the servants were interested in such discussions. (9)

The genealogical consciousness of both her mother and those individuals who appear to be landowners of Gaelic ancestry Everett attributes to "the fashion of her day." Like Hamilton and McHugh, she may be accurately reporting a phenomenon that crossed class and ethnic boundaries. Hamilton and McHugh characteristically use the widespread interest in genealogy to bolster their own assertions of social standing, but many landowners were uncomfort-

---

3. Vera Kreilkamp notes a tendency in Anglo-Irish historical fiction to render ancestors, particularly females, as martyrs to the famine (1998, 263). Because women were often directly responsible for nursing and feeding servants and, less frequently, tenants, there may be a historical basis for such representations in fiction and autobiography.

ably cognizant of the familial histories that supported native claims for the lands they now possessed. Perhaps for this reason, Everett hesitates to explore the motivations of her neighbors and servants.

Not until much later does an autobiographer like Lionel Fleming, in his 1965 *Head or Harp*, explicitly address doubts about his ability to interpret the sentiments of "the people" regarding his family history. Just what is he hearing, Fleming wonders, in an elderly country woman's song about his ancestors, the Flemings of Newcourt? "The old woman now sitting in the back seat of our car—how many of her relatives fled to America, what really had her parents told her about their Fleming landlord? Why should she sing of a life that had so little to do with hers?" (14). Fleming made a decisive break with Ireland in the late 1930s after coming to the conclusion that "Protestants continued to be hopeless and apathetic, and Catholics impervious, and the North bought over by England" (177). Perhaps because of that break, he interrogates the typecast scene by which numerous others argue their right to be regarded as an integral part of Irish life. Most of the autobiographers who came of age before the era of independence base their claims to belonging on their ancestors' participation in Irish history and the loyalty of their Catholic tenants and neighbors. Fleming, however, openly questions the reverence of the servants toward the "'rale ould stock.' "

Race or Nation?

When they explain their differences from the majority population, the Anglo-Irish tend to distinguish themselves through categories of politics, class, and religion rather than by terminology that bases ethnic distinctions in hereditary bloodlines. In the eighteenth-century recollections of Sir Jonah Barrington, the Irish poor are said to resemble "Indians" or "Asiatics," and an old cook is cast as a "squaw" (1967, 13). George Moore's *Parnell and His Island* (1887) portrays the tenants as dark, hairy brutes a step above their simian ancestors. Yet this racialist terminology is never applied to "native" Irish of a higher caste. Both writers, especially the Catholic-bred Moore, react to the strangeness of the rural poor, whose customs, clothing, and language seem incomprehensible and repellent. It is the poor who appear a different race, and because the poor are "native" Irish, the declaration of difference takes on a more racial orientation than the context warrants.[4]

4. David Hayton cites two much earlier comparisons between the Irish and American Indians: John Dunton's *Dublin Scuffle* and Thomas Dinely's *Observations in a Voyage Through the Kingdom of Ireland*, both published in the late seventeenth century (1988, 10). See also Constantia

As alternatives to race, some autobiographers either substitute categories such as religion, class, or birthplace or invoke a mixed origin as a means of asserting their shared nationality. Mary Hamilton, born in 1872, recalls, "My family were Unionists; their tenants were Nationalists; we were brought up as Protestants; our tenants were Catholics. . . . Yet if any of us, rich or poor, had been accused of not being Irish, we would have been indignant" (1948, 183). In Samuel Hussey's *Reminiscences of an Irish Land Agent* (1904), the elderly autobiographer exhibits little interest in questions of race and nationality. The product of a mixed marriage whose Catholic patrilineage is directly traceable to Norman immigrants in the thirteenth century, Hussey proclaims: "It's the proudest boast of my life that I am an Irishman, and the compliment which I have most appreciated in my time was being called 'the poor man's friend,' for I love Paddy dearly though I see his faults" (140). Hussey begins his autobiography with the declaration of his identity as a Kerryman and explains at length his deep roots in Ireland going back at least six hundred years, but he is equally emphatic about the difference between himself and "Paddy." He also distinguishes himself from the "Saxon" to whom his work is addressed. "Paddy" and he represent different social and economic classes within a shared nationality, as do the English workman, "John," and the assumed "Saxon" reader of his memoirs. As a derogatory term in the popular press, "Paddy" carried considerable racial implications absent from the normalized English figure of "John." However, Hussey's coupling of "Paddy" with another term implying only a class designation suggests that if intimations of racial distinction underlay the Anglo-Irish sense of difference, those intimations could be subsumed by a greater concern for class boundaries.

Similarly, line-drawing illustrations in William Trench's *Realities of Irish Life* (1868) exaggerate stereotypical physical characteristics in order to underscore class conflict. Only when the tenants take a threatening role in the narrative do the illustrations portray "simian Paddy." Drawings of the tenants in more placid scenes parallel the depictions of the narrator as tall and slender, with narrow features and light hair. In his critique of L. Perry Curtis's studies of the anti-Irish caricature, R. F. Foster points out that on the pages of *Punch*, "representation of all working-class types was dark and brutish; all enemies, especially class enemies, tended to the monster. . . . [G]enteel journalism, on both sides of the Atlantic, saw the Irish as a threatening underclass rather than a colonized subrace" (1993, 192). Although Foster's analysis targets only En-

---

Maxwell's *Stranger in Ireland* (1954). Further citations and discussion of the debate may be found in Curtis 1996 (ix-xxix) and R. F. Foster 1993 (171–94).

glish representations, the illustrations in *Realities of Irish Life* suggest that his conclusions may be applied to the Anglo-Irish as well. It is equally accurate to say of *Realities of Irish Life*, as Foster does of *Punch*, that "class and religion were more central preoccupations in constructing an alien identity for the Irish. . . . [T]he whole process may relate more to resentment of the Irish attack on property and the Union" (193). However, the transformation of the tenants' features into bestial types recognizable to English readers as a specifically Irish threat attests that the concept of racial difference in Ireland could quickly emerge from a latent state when aligned with more generalized fear of lower-class revolt.

Although Hussey and Trench are concerned with differences of class and culture, those writers more preoccupied by so-called racial distinctions share much of the same vocabulary. It is sometimes exceedingly difficult to know which frame of reference is the more dominant. Clearly, when W. B. Yeats denounces George Moore as the product of the "coarsened" blood of Catholic ancestors, he articulates but one instance of his obsession with eugenic explanations of history. But are we in the realm of religious difference, cultural snobbery, or racial prejudice when Violet Martin wonders in a letter to Lady Gregory how it is that Moore's talent comes in an "earthen vessel"? "Paris, on top of R[oman] C[atholic] Mayo ancestry can produce these things. . . . The second rate R. C. with the French admixture is a blend peculiar to itself & betrays itself sooner or later" (Frazier 2000, 370). Martin appears to be speaking in terms of bloodlines, especially when we call to witness her description of the residual inheritor of a severely declined Galway family as "a strange mixture of distinction and commonness, like her breeding," marked by generations of "living with country women, occasionally marrying them, all illegitimate four times over" (Somerville and Ross 1978, 313). Martin shares with many of her class a preoccupation with "breeding," one that Vera Kreilkamp speculates could derive from preoccupations with the breeding of racehorses and hunting dogs as well as the more obvious motives of authorizing lines of succession (1998, 125). Yet the Martins were themselves Catholics who had come to Ireland before the Reformation and whose relatively recent conversion occurred when Violet's paternal great-grandfather sought to marry Elizabeth O'Hara, whose own family was also newly Protestant. The genealogical terms by which she denounces Moore and the old Galway family may be an effect, rather than a cause, of class anxiety. Those she saw as usurpers of a different class and religion often came in through the bedroom door. Maria Edgeworth understood a century before that Anglo-Irish families declined less from sexual misalliance than from fiscal irresponsibility on the part of landlords and fiscal ingenuity on the part of the Jason Quirks of Ireland. But Edgeworth's astute recognition was perhaps too self-damning for many to accept. Given the general interest in eugenics current in the later nineteenth and early twentieth centuries, Violet Martin, like Yeats and many others, turned to a Gothic horror of miscegenation to explain what had long been the terror of class instability.

As the language of race became increasingly confounded with nationality, a descriptor such as *Irish* became increasingly confusing for the Anglo-Irish, all of whom employ it as a term defining both what they are and what they are not. Those definitions are frequently unclear and self-contradictory. Is a national identity based upon its distinction from another country? Or is it rooted in shared experience, language, politics, or religion? Or does it depend on birthplace, the ownership of land, or ancestry? The earl of Dunraven refers to the "Irish" as "they," yet without recognizing any contradiction in his usage of the term recounts that as a young child he would pronounce to any listening, "I am an Irishman," later jumping up on the tables of his father's tenants to declare to their applause, "I am Irish bred and born" (1922, 1:1–2). In this account, whether one is or is not "Irish" has little to do with religion or political allegiances, nor does Dunraven's later interest in land reform and his father's conversion to Catholicism make him any more or less Irish. He is not Irish because of ancestry, class, and culture, while at the same time, precisely because of ancestry and the location of his upbringing and birth, he is "Irish bred and born."

Margot Backus has explained that in the nineteenth-century Irish novel, "intersectarian marriages enact reconfigured national social contracts through which historically hostile or estranged groups are symbolically reconciled, and historical wrongs, palliated" (1999, 262). In the autobiographies of the many whose ancestries were mixed, the story of an intersectarian inheritance functions in a similar way. Frank Pakenham, who spent nearly all his life in England, nevertheless looks to genealogy to classify himself as a "Celt," thereby substituting in place of culture a loosely conceived idea of race and arguing that "whoever accuses me of lacking Celtic blood on my Irish side is foxed by the authenticity of my Welsh credentials" (L. Pakenham 1953, 14). After a lengthy recitation of ancestors famous in British history, he concludes, "Nor shall I treat this as an occasion for . . . disentangling my Irish and English strains. I will say only that there has never been a moment of my life when I was not proud of being an Irishman" (15). In *Green and Gold*, Mary Hamilton proposes that because her ancestry is mixed, she is particularly at home in Ireland. Tracing her father's descent from Cromwellian planters, she remarks that her ancestors "like many other such families had been given grants of land in Meath, married Irish women, and, in the course of time, became Irish both in their characteristics and in their love for that country" (1948, 12). Like many of her contemporaries, she emphasizes intermarriage so as to bring to the fore earlier correlations among marriage, property, and legitimacy of claim. Although it is marriage in *Green and Gold* that acts as a vehicle of assimilation, Hamilton's terms seem to be primarily cultural. Yet within the context of early-twentieth-century interest in eugenics and its association of behavioral and attitudinal traits with biologic descent, the word *characteristics* may imply the same racialism as Frank Pakenham's *Celt.*

W. J. McCormack has established that the hybrid term *Anglo-Irish* came into currency only near the end of the 1700s (1993a 181; 1993b, n.p.). From that point on, however, the autobiographical writing of Anglo Ireland voices a compulsion to amend one's declaration to nationality by a prefix that conveys both the exclusivity of an identity determined by bloodlines and, conversely, a national identity that could be adopted within a century's residence in Ireland. The meaning of a word like *Anglo-Irish* varies, according to the intentions of the writer and the expectations of the reader, as to whether *Anglo* is to be set apart from *Irish* or joined to it. By implying a distinction between the writer and "the people," the hyphenated descriptor accommodates the autobiographer's role as an interpreter of Irish life for the English reader to whom many of these works are clearly directed, mixing as they so frequently do the genres of autobiography and travel writing. But by implying a union between two lines of descent as equal parts of a common nationality, *Anglo-Irish* refutes the ever intensifying conceptual conflation of nationality and race seen in Ireland and throughout European thought at the turn of the century.[5] For a few individuals, like W. B. Yeats, the hybrid term paradoxically marks a pedigree so pure as to be susceptible to the "pollution" of "mixed blood." But for most, mixed blood could bolster claims to a legitimate presence in Ireland.

In an increasingly nationalist and eventually independent Ireland, racialist thinking had the potential to exclude those individuals without clear ties to Catholic Ireland from full participatory citizenship. Among the Anglo-Irish, recognition of this possibility exacerbated the anxieties ensuing from changes in land ownership and management after the famine, disestablishment, land legislation, the apparent failure of the Home Rule movement, and the perception of wholesale anti-Protestant sentiment during the 1920s. Lionel Fleming candidly assesses his elders' interest in family history as a defensive response to

5. A nativist work like John O'Hart's *Irish and Anglo-Irish Landed Gentry* (1884) evinces a similar confusion of race and nationality buttressed by the genealogical preoccupation. Omitting the peerage and claiming to trace the origins of the "Old Irish" and "Anglo-Norman" families, it was hailed by Irish and Irish-American newspapers as a "heroic" nationalist gesture that would help Ireland assert itself as a nation in coming years.

the undermining of their security. Of his parents' generation, he wrote in 1965, "by and large, the whole world of the Anglo-Irish gentry was beginning to disappear at about this time—to be replaced, in so many cases, by a rather nostalgic world where silver was treasured if it had the crest on it, where family trees were meticulously composed, and where nobody even thought of himself as being 'middle class' " (17). Anglo-Irish autobiographers turn to one of the few aspects of tradition that could not be burned or sold and that was conveniently susceptible to imaginative reconstruction while bearing the rhetorical authority of public history.

Familial descent could come to a dead end, and the majority of the autobiographies in question were written after the First World War, a war that in many cases concluded the patrilineal line. Yet the story of lineage could still be told. Records of descent stretch back, sometimes improbably back beyond Elizabeth or Cromwell into branches of the family said to be descended from ancient Irish kings (and in these charted exercises in longing, the ancestor is invariably royal). Or, as in Nicolette Devas's imaginative borrowing of the Celtic stories of the half-human silkies, one's antecedents could extend to the most indigenous beings of all, the seals that played off the rocks near her paternal grandfather's properties in Clare (1966, 14–15). In a strange turn that illustrates the ever shifting directions in which the confluence of culture, nationality, and lineage can meander, Lord Inchiquin confesses in a 1994 collection of interviews about Irish class identity his bewilderment at the way his English accent, Eton schooling, and title, granted to his Gaelic ancestors by Henry VIII in 1543, prohibit his compatriots from recognizing his Irish lineage (O'Dea 1994, 169–88). Neither his patronym, Conor O'Brien, nor the record of his family's descent from ancient Gaelic nobility holds force against the markers of class differences that came to be associated with ethnicity and nationality.

The "Vicissitudes of Families"

Richard Lovell Edgeworth's 1820 recitation of the burnings, attacks, betrayals, and psychological torments his family suffered at the hands of their tenants presents his misfortune as a series of singular events, not a pattern of group decline. But as in the genealogical sketch offered in the recollections of the earl of Desart, later accounts of the acquisition of familial lands, names, and in some cases titles betray a vocabulary of persistent class anxiety. Desart's memoirs display a frequently echoed repertoire of terms: *possession* and *occupation*, *attainment* and *restoration*, *displacement* and, invariably, *extinction*. Efforts to bring about a sense of belonging through family history never seem satisfactory, couched as they are in the terms of a defensive gesture. The further back one can go—particularly if to the Elizabethan or Cromwellian eras—the more the defensive posture is maintained and the more likely we will see unfold the tragic plotline implied in the word *extinction*.

Sir Bernard Burke, the most prolific chronicler of family histories, laments the loss of the "Milesian" and "aboriginal" dynasties, but he saves his strongest expression of grief for the way in which, according to his view, the Encumbered Estates Court exacerbated the process of "confiscation, civil war, and legal transfer" to tear "asunder those associations between 'the local habitation and the name,' which have for centuries wound round each other" (1859, 10–11). Of the tales of loss that make up *Vicissitudes of Families*, he asserts that the Irish family histories are so sad that he can bear to recite only one: "No cases of vicissitude would be so pathetic, no episodes of decadence so lamentable as those that could be told, in connection with the transfer of land in Ireland, but the wounds are too fresh, and the ruin too recent, for me to enter on so painful a theme" (11). Writing in 1859, Burke here anticipates a century of autobiographies structured as family histories of exile from the Garden, a model far more pervasive in Anglo-Ireland than any of the other familiar patterns of British autobiography.[6]

The family history thus frustrates what it sets out to attest: a correlation between its writer's life and a shared national history, a place within the social structure of the community, class status, and a hereditary nationality. If a troubled uncertainty about the future prevails in late-nineteenth- and early-twentieth-century autobiography more generally, for most Anglo-Irish writers that anxiety takes the form of a conviction that one's world is about to disappear or has disappeared already. The perception of being caught in a devolutionary process beyond one's personal control exerts a gravitational pull even on Nicolette Devas's reclamation of an alternate pedigree, one matrilineal and French rather than patrilineal and Irish. In the first of her autobiographies, *Two Flamboyant Fathers* (1966), Devas examines the way family history haunted her rebellious father, driving him to play the wild rake in opposition to the patriarchal prototype of his father, the earnest landlord and Protestant gentleman. Although rejecting his father's estate and social role, Francis MacNamara could not ignore the ancestral image. In his daughter's eyes, he wasted money, talent, and reputation in relentless sexual exploits and hard drinking

---

6. The Edenic model of Anglo-Irish autobiography differs from the paradigm of English literature in that the Garden is perceived as flawed even prior to the Fall. See Fleishman 1983 and Henderson 1989 for a full discussion of other structural patterns in autobiography such as the exodus, the pilgrimage, and the crisis, conversion, or awakening.

with the small farmers of Doolin, where he built his own house as a taunting challenge to his father's. Having recounted how familial ghosts distorted her father's life, Devas removes herself from his line and becomes in her second autobiography "no longer the individual Nicolette" or the daughter of the doomed MacNamaras but the inheritor of her maternal grandfather's line of French Quakers (1978, 177). The matrilineal genealogy alone decorates the endpapers of *Susannah's Nightingales*. Realizing through the recovery of her French ancestors that "the blood of all those dead people ran in my veins" (175), Devas concludes her book with a somber recognition that the Majolier line has died in herself, "without issue, the end of the line" (177). She ends with images of the Quaker cemetery, the demise of traditions, and what she names the "tranquility" of having no future for which to fight. *Susannah's Nightingales* unsuccessfully resists the degenerative movement explicit in her father's story; even the matrilineal history brings with it the associations of decline ascribed to the family narrative.

"Childhood in a Colony": Childhood Spaces and the Invasion of Time

Autobiographies of childhood present other forms of resistance by attempting to step out of the pervasive awareness of historical time endemic to the autobiography founded on the motif of genealogy. With its epiphanic moments, powerful sensory experiences, and vivid limning of natural landscapes, the autobiography of childhood diverges from the linear propulsion of the family history. As Louis MacNeice suggests in his autobiographical poem "Carrick Revisited," recollective immersion in the consciousness of childhood can undermine the historian's quest for perspective:

> Fog-horn, mill-horn, corncrake and church bell
> Half-heard through boarded time as a child in bed
> Glimpses a brangle of talk from the floor below
> But cannot catch the words. Our past we know
> But not its meaning—whether it meant well.
>
> Time and place—our bridgeheads into reality
> But also its concealment! Out of the sea
> We land on the Particular and lose
> All other possible bird's eye views. . . .
>
> (1967, 224)

Under the pressure of the genealogical mandate, the most autobiographically significant of "bird's eye views" is chronological perspective. Yet autobiographers repeatedly address the incompatibility of childhood experience and the structure of linear time. W. B. Yeats begins his "Reveries over Childhood and Youth": "My first memories are fragmentary and isolated and contemporaneous, as though remembered some first moments of the Seven Days. It seems as if time had not yet been created, for all thoughts connected with emotion and place are without sequence" (1965, 1). In her 1899 memoir of a Dublin childhood, Hannah Lynch reflects: "I have always marvelled at the roll of reminiscences and experiences of childhood told consecutively and with coherence. Children live more in pictures, in broken effects, in unaccountable impulses that lend an unmeasured significance to odd trifles to the exclusion of momentous facts, than in story. This alone prevents the harmonious fluency of biography in an honest account of our childhood" (4–5). And Mary Frances McHugh begins her autobiography with a comparable observation: "As grown-up people we live distractedly, half our being either projected into a longing for some future ineffable bliss, or drawn backward away from us into a passionately remembered past. But as children—we are simply children, soulless and exquisitely absorbed in the passing moment of happiness or grief— opening to the sun, darkening to every cloud, trembling to each passing wind" (1931, 1–2).

Cognitive psychologists exploring the structures of autobiographical memory confirm these characterizations, arguing, as does John A. Robinson, that "sensory and affective elements predominate in early memories. They are isolated from a temporal series of related events, and lack a clear sense of self " (1992, 228). In his encyclopedic study of more than one hundred European and American autobiographies of childhood, Richard Coe concludes that recollections of childhood consistently differ in both content and form from recollections of adulthood, particularly as they center around an impression of ecstatic presence whose foremost temporal feature is that of recurrence (1984, 189–90). "The experiences of childhood," he observes, "take place in a dimension, whether material, spiritual, or linguistic, *different* from that of the adult. . . . [T]heir remoteness and their "Otherness" constitute their unique role" (241). Where, then, is the point of contact between two of the most prominent yet contradictory aspects of the Anglo-Irish autobiography: an obsession with family and national history and an equal obsession with a seemingly timeless world of childhood?

Despite itself, the childhood autobiography invariably encounters the impermanence of time. Paul John Eakin has taken issue with the idea that autobiography—even of childhood—could ever be conceived outside the structures of narrative, or narrative conceived outside the consciousness of historical time. Grounding his argument in historiographical theory and language-acquisition research, Eakin contends that at the most rudimentary level, our self-articulation is founded in narration. It is, he says, the principal device by which human beings articulate their self-existence and must be seen "as a manifestation of the fundamental temporality of human experience" (1992, 193). If the discontinuous moment is pervasive in the literature of childhood, through the very neologisms by which writers describe it they also admit its relation, however resistant, to temporality: the Wordsworthian "spots of time," Virginia Woolf's "moments of being," or even Mary Frances McHugh's "passing moment" and Hannah Lynch's "broken effects" lie invariably within time, as they do within the larger continuity of a plot itself structured by linear time.

Attempting to explain the essence of his childhood through a present-tense recounting of its sensory experiences—the texture of leaf mold, the hum of insects, the smell of water, the feel of one's knees pressing into small stones by a pond—Francis Stuart predicts the failure of his effort: "Mysterious, emotional, fantastic childhood! Apart from dying, being a child is the only human experience that cannot be told, written about, from first-hand knowledge. For after the lapse of years the knowledge that we have from memory is no longer true and accurate but conditioned and tempered by too much in between" (1934, 13). The "lapse of years" renders childhood irrecoverable. We cannot remember accurately, and present knowledge causes us to revise what we once thought. As adults, we live within an inescapable consciousness of time, in years rather than in moments of what Coe calls "ecstatic presence."

In *The Film of Memory* (1938), Shane Leslie echoes Stuart's understanding that one's childhood apprehension of timelessness is unsustainable. The spatial and sensory organization of Leslie's childhood memories endures only a few pages until the adult's cognizance of historical change subsumes events into its pattern. Vividly recalling the noise of rooks, the weird light of the oil lamp against the great tree trunks surrounding his house, strange sounds in the dark, and, ironically, the mystery and pleasure of a cuckoo clock, he remarks, "I had a fixed sensation . . . that there was no Time: that everybody remained precisely as old or young as we had always been. The passing of days made no difference to me. . . . I would have wished no change and was willing to continue life amid the same grown-ups, the same servants, the same trees and the same rooks. All these symbols of my past life have gone or changed except the rooks" (1938, 13). From the retrospective angle of the autobiographical speaker, the diachronic constraints of history envelop the child's perception of timeless synchronicity.

The memory of Anglo-Irish childhood often merges with the image of a prelapsarian national life. As Seamus Deane observes, "writers are compelled, in their confrontation with the obduracy of existing conditions, to create alternatives to them. . . . The most exploited alternative is the Edenic one, the imagined time in which present strife and rupture did not exist and the question of the self's relationship to the society was not even at issue" (1991, 380–81). Writers of the Irish Revival period, proposes Declan Kiberd, associate their

> childhood with that of the Irish nation: those hopeful decades of slow growth before the fall into murderous violence and civil war. In their subsequent autobiographies, childhood was identified as a kind of privileged zone, peopled with engaging eccentrics, doting grandmothers and natural landscapes. What they were describing, of course, was childhood in a colony. . . . Disenchanted with the growing murderousness of their land, they sought relief amidst the scenes of childhood memory, only to discover that the very act of dreaming that dream was itself tainted with the politics of Anglo-Irish relations. (1995, 101, 105)

Accounts of the Anglo-Irish childhood thus differ dramatically from the best-known Irish autobiographies wherein, from James Joyce to Edna O'Brien and Frank McCourt, childhood is a terror-ridden period of repression, guilt, and disillusionment.[7]

Kiberd's hypothesis that colonial privilege accounts for the idyllic representation of childhood is partially corroborated by the parallels that at least two Anglo-Irish autobiographers themselves draw between Ireland and India, and between their world and that of Anglo-India. Having returned to the landscapes of her childhood for "relief" after her divorce, Theodora Fitzgibbon muses that in Ireland, she had found "the same kind of magic as I had found in India . . . two countries which had cast a never-to-be-forgotten spell over me with their mysticism, fatalism and religious strength. . . . Now they both had their independence from the British Empire. Was it because of all these similarities that the colours of the Indian flag were the same as those of Ireland?" (1985, 169). Reflecting on the way his curate father was snubbed by landlord society, C. Day Lewis remembers that "proud and poor, the Anglo-Irish exalted their snobbery into a tribal mystique, living . . . the same enclosed, garrison life, for all their deeper roots in the country and their more easy-going relationship with the native Irish, as the Anglo-Indians in India" (1960, 17).

---

7. For further analysis of the unhappy childhoods of Irish autobiography, see Coe 1982, 46–58.

Such parallels, however, demand a close examination, as do other applications of a postcolonial framework to questions of Irish history. On one hand, the parallel seems accurate. Irish nationalists, including Michael Davitt and liberal Protestants like the Quaker Alfred Webb, discern resemblances between the English occupation of India and the English occupation of Ireland. The younger sons of the Anglo-Irish and their wives inundated the British colonial service, and children like George Buchanan and his brother, growing up the sons of an Anglican clergyman in a small town along the Antrim coast, pretended they were Indian princes as part of their daily play (1959, 27–29). Mary Procida has demonstrated how Anglo-Indian life writings draw upon genealogical tropes to emphasize a family's duration in India, beginning "with quasi-Biblical recitations of ancestral connections with the Raj," whereas "those who had no ancestral links with the Raj often felt compelled to manufacture a mystical connection with India" (2002, 137, 138). These writers also exhibit pride in their familiarity with Indian culture and languages and relish the distinct patois of their colonial community.

On the other hand, the analogy between Anglo-Indian and Anglo-Irish experience is not as clear as these examples would suggest. Despite a legacy of colonial souvenirs—from tiger-skin rugs to relatives remaining in Africa or Asia—few writers make analogies between themselves and the English in India, as do Fitzgibbon and Lewis. Second, Anglo-Indian life writings, according to Mary Procida, are almost without exception apologetics for the imperial government. In contrast to the many Anglo-Irish autobiographers who openly question the British presence in Ireland or whose stories are devoid of overt political reference, Anglo-Indian autobiographers see themselves as producing important contributions to the work of empire and "the upholding of British prestige in the East" (130). And although they might declare an attraction or a repulsion to Indian ways of life, just as the Anglo-Irish express a similar range of reaction to what they call the "native" Irish, at no time do Anglo-Indians claim to be Indian in nationality as every autobiographer encompassed in this study claims to be Irish. However, given the dilemma of determining exactly what late-nineteenth- and early-twentieth-century writers intend when they claim to be "Irish," the meaning of this claim is debatable.

The emergence of Irish identity among Protestants from the middle of the eighteenth century onward took many divergent tracks. David Hayton has explained the "two concepts of Irish nationality" current among Irish Anglicans at the turn of the eighteenth century: "one defining only the indigenous Gaelic and Catholic Irish as 'the Irish' and the Protestants as 'the English interest'; the other regarding all the inhabitants of the island as 'Irish' and on occasion going so far as to talk of the Protestants as the true Irish nation" (1987,

149). Historians like Hayton, S. J. Connolly, and Patrick McNally have made clear the differences between the sense of Protestant Irish "patriotism" in defending settler interests against English domination that developed through the eighteenth century and a modern sense of "nationalism" as the expression of ethnic and cultural unity (Hayton 1987; Connolly 1992; McNally 1999). The idea of an "Irish" identity among people of English extraction has deep roots; only with radical simplification can it be paralleled with the Anglo-Indian position. Even C. Day Lewis's comparison of the two betrays the dangers of drawing rough analogies between very different situations. His characterization of his own family, who under Kiberd's definition would also be "colonists," as distinct from the landholding group he compares to Anglo-Indians, hopelessly muddles the analogy he attempts.

The autobiography of Lady Glover, a descendant of Cromwellian settlers, provides yet another example of how uncertain the categories of colonist and native can be. Her memoirs of an Irish childhood do display features endemic to colonialist travel writing, such as the portraiture of "natives" as childish and humorous and the identification of Anglo-Irish soldiers as "sons of Britain." The text of her book is also followed by pages of advertisements for the travel memoirs of Britons in exotic places. But like those eighteenth-century Anglo-Irish (or "Hibernians," as some named themselves) whose multiple and usually contradictory allegiances have been carefully traced by recent historians, Lady Glover will not fit easily into a simple colonial category. Despite her intermittent residence in England, her disdain for the Catholic working class, and the relatively recent arrival of her ancestors in the 1650s, even this unusually chauvinistic autobiographer classifies her family and associates as "Irish," and—like some contemporary Northern Protestants—labels the rest of the population "Fenians," "Sinn Feiners," or "tenants" (1923, 25–30, 38–39, 309). Rendering the interpretation of colonial analogies even more difficult is T. R. Henn's comparison between the way the Anglo-Irish identify themselves in terms of extended family and similar thinking among East Indians (1980, 193).

For many Anglo-Irish children, living at an Irish rural estate was by the 1880s an experience less "colonial," along the Anglo-Indian model, than one akin to visiting relatives in the country. To some children, the Irish ancestral home, even when occupied by their parents year-round, was a summer vacation spot and a respite from the harsh schools to which they were sent from an early age. What Kiberd calls the experience of "childhood in a colony" is perhaps a less likely explanation for the representation of a "privileged zone" than matters of class, religion, and even literary antecedents for recounting childhood. A benign portrait of childhood may be the product of the privacy afforded by large houses and small families, the freedom to play rather than work outdoors, and an education that, at least during the early years, took place at home rather than in the oppressive atmosphere of a school.[8] Anglican religious instruction was also by most accounts less frightening than the schooling of the Irish Catholic Church and many Dissenting Protestant sects. And just as T. R. Henn recalls his childhood as if it were a series of illustrations to the poems of W. B. Yeats, so other autobiographers draw from Rousseau, Wordsworth, Blake, and the writers and pictorial artists who follow them in portraying children in emotionally evocative rural settings, surrounded by animals and the kind, elderly poor. The lament for a lost golden age has been echoed in the literature of the United States and Western Europe since the Industrial Revolution and cannot be attributed solely to a colonial experience.[9]

The argument for a causal connection between colonial privilege and attitudes toward childhood is more persuasive when we analyze the unity of land and self these texts frequently postulate. The childhood autobiography attempts to bring together into a metaphysical unity the remembered self and specific natural landscapes. More than a Wordsworthian trope and the fitting emblem of a privileged childhood, it is a gesture as defensive as the genealogy's insistence on duration within a place. In one of the few studies to examine Anglo-Irish autobiographies as genre, Michael Kenneally argues that concern for what he calls "historical and mythic place" "manifests itself in a stress on familial connections with the land; it is as if such individuals still possess vestigial feelings of alienation, of being an outsider if not a trespasser, and so strive to legitimize their claim to national identity by establishing the bond between self and setting, the historical plexus of genealogy and place" (1989, 126). W. J. McCormack reads the texts of Anglo-Irish literature in general as "markers of an intellectual constellation in which endangered property is a common denominator" (1985b, 73). Similarly, Terence Brown remarks that through "topographical claims" conjoined with "familial and dynastic piety," Anglo-Irish poetry makes "insecure assertions of an Irish identity" (1985b, 182–83).

8. In their study of female inhabitants of English country houses, Trevor Lummis and Jan Marsh describe the sudden widespread availability and understanding of birth control among the English upper classes and the subsequent fashion for small families near the end of the nineteenth century. Because of the extensive contact between English and Anglo-Irish families of the upper classes, it is a reasonable hypothesis that the smaller families observable among the Protestant upper classes in Ireland were the effect of deliberate attempts to control birth through contraception (1990, 193–95).

9. Avrom Fleishman argues that the depiction of the fall from the garden of childhood is a primary structure of Victorian autobiography (1983, 111–20). See also P. Brown 1993 and Walvin 1982 for detailed histories of the representation of childhood in nineteenth-century English literature and social discourse.

In the autobiographies of Anglo-Ireland, landscapes take part in human emotion and participate in human consciousness: Elizabeth Bowen describes the demesne of Bowen's Court as having "received" the visual "imprint" of the many generations of Bowens who gazed upon it; Lady Anson prizes her first name, "Clodagh," given after the river near her family's home; Maud Wynne maintains that the outcroppings of rocks along the coast of her Connaught home "had played with us and . . . loved us to sit and idle with their golden heads of lichen" (1937, 282). W. B. Yeats recounts his hopes that the land itself would provide images to unify all classes into a common national consciousness (1965, 131). In describing her house and estate, Augusta Gregory repeatedly employs what John Wilson Foster calls "a species of pathetic fallacy, [whereby] feelings were thought not only to be kindled by the landscape but also to reside in the landscape": a device he notes as being used by Anglo-Irish landscape poets interested, like Gregory, in reifying emotional ties to rural places (1991, 18). The house and grounds are sites of sensual pleasure: not only the natural beauty of the woods but also the management of the woods and the architecture and furnishings of the house. Sir William Gregory's books, collected from all over the world (which, she discretely refrains from reminding us, were never at any time her own and, like the house and woods, passed from Sir William to her son, Robert, then to Robert's wife as custodian of her little boy's property), reflect the history Lady Gregory takes as her legacy, and they are apprehended sensually as an interaction between her body and the body of her house: "They have felt the pressure of my fingers," she writes in *Coole*. "They have been my friends" (1971, 21). A statue imported long ago from Italy rests "as if exhausted by such travel" (39). The garden animals are "company"; the trees, too, are "my comforters" whose "companionship has often brought me peace" (38). Such anthropopathy removes the house and its demesne from the specific conditions of their creation and renders the estate a transcendent entity deserving the reader's affection.

The conscious effort of such analogies of intimacy may reveal, against the writer's intent, just how much he or she is not at home in the surrounding material world. As Elizabeth Bowen writes in her 1938 novel, *The Death of the Heart*:

> Only in a house where one has learnt to be lonely does one have this solicitude for *things*. One's relation to them, the daily seeing or touching, begins to become love. . . . After inside upheavals, it is important to fix on imperturbable *things*. . . . Their imperturbableness, their air that nothing has happened renews our guarantee. Pictures would not be hung plumb over the

centres of fireplaces or wallpapers pasted on with such precision that their seams make no break in the pattern if life were really not possible to adjudicate for. . . . In this sense, the destruction of buildings and furniture is more palpably dreadful to the spirit than the destruction of human life. (1986, 139, 207)

The books, animals, trees, and statuary draw Lady Gregory's solicitude and her love. Her affections may be hyperbolic because she finds herself victim to the knowledge of dislocation endemic to Anglo-Irish self-description, saved from being, like Hannah Lynch, "a hopeless wanderer" only by old age and death. By the time Lady Gregory's memoirs were completed, these objects were marked for destruction and served as a sign of how much "the break in the pattern" had already occurred. Although her stoic reserve prohibits her from overt lament, the identification forged between her house and her own being impels her story into the apocalyptic mode in which her friend W. B. Yeats openly cast it.

Completing a similar process through the engineering of a truly topographical "autobiography," Emily Lawless built a garden that represented the Ireland of her youth and then records its creation in *A Garden Diary* (1901). Although she describes her psychic bond with the landscape as if it were a thing of the past, the evident emotion with which she describes the County Clare coastline of her earlier years betrays the perpetuation of her feeling:

> In those days only upon the largest combination of sea, sky, mountain; seascape, land-scape, cloud-scape, did it seem possible adequately to exist. As for a mere rustic landscape, as for a confined one, as for a humdrum English one, above all as for a landscape within fifty miles of London, why the mention of such things merely moved my commiseration! Those were the days when to be called upon to leave what is sometimes uncivilly called the ruder island, and to repair, even temporarily, to the more prosperous one, seemed a fall and a degradation hardly to be measured by words. When the contraction of the horizon seemed like a contraction of all life, and of all that made life worth having. (8–9)

Exiled by old age and financial need to a hated England, Lawless plants the living relics of her earlier life into a garden whose bushes, rocks, and flowers replicate those portions of Ireland she most mourned: "Thus I have a Burren corner, a West Galway corner, a Kerry corner, a Kildare corner, even a green memento or two of the great lost forest of Ossory" (125). She apologetically dismisses her efforts as "childishness," but this fusion of a life history—and a family history—with topography epitomizes that tension so resplendent in Anglo-Irish autobiography between an enervating recognition of human temporality and a stubborn hope that specific landscapes holding human meanings, often places of childhood, might be immune from time's power to change or destroy them.

Whatever its origins, the "privileged zone" is insufficiently privileged to withstand the historical consciousness that viewing one's life as a moment in family history must bring to the autobiographer. Whether dated before 1798, the famine, Gladstone, the First World War, or the Irish Republic, the idea of a historical Eden is reconcilable with the chronicity of the family history, but the fall of Eden also accentuates the motif of decline underlying the genealogy, clouding its vision of a fundamental unity of self and place. Eden is finally a place from which one is exiled and can never be successfully remembered except in terms of the expulsion that follows the period of idyll. In his intently felt description of the "Eden" of his childhood (the family house was named "Paradise"), T. R. Henn permeates his recollection with his belief in time's capacity to imbue a landscape with accumulated human meanings and to finally efface those meanings. Scornfully, Henn avows that no sudden infusion of "foreign money" in the old houses could possibly substitute for "the building of what was, in effect, a family mythologem: woods named for men or women . . . a springing well, where a girl had meditated; even a rustic bridge, named for a forgotten guest who, at the last drive on a winter's evening, had fallen through the handrail into the little stream below" (1980, 216).

That "family mythologem" of which T. R. Henn speaks is built in time and deteriorates in time; his autobiography, *Five Arches*, is overwhelmed by elegiac regret and a feeling of displacement in modern England as well as in modern Ireland. Although intoxicated by a romanticism he could not see as ironically as Yeats himself could, Henn acknowledges that although his vision of childhood might intimate eternity, the illusion is rooted in historical contingency and temporary prestige:

> [T]he Anglo-Irish race to which I belonged had been sliding downwards for a very long time. . . . So long as I could remember there had been agrarian troubles. When a ruined cottage beside the mail road was pulled down, a pistol and pike were found concealed in the thatch. . . . There might be, and was, friendship, great loyalty, an age-old concern with blood and race; but inescapably the Big House was built on wealth, privilege, and the large revolutions of politics and religions. (215)

As in so many other texts, a yearning for the universe of childhood and a politically neutralized topophilia clash with an acute consciousness of historical class relations, however confused here by notions of race.

In this way, the Anglo-Irish country house is eulogized differently from its English counterpart: almost always more historicized and inadequate even at the height of its power.[10] Although Katherine Everett idealizes a relative's English country house as a site of social harmony and prosperity for the surrounding community, she draws no similarities between it and the Irish country house, remarking only that its pigs enjoy better lives than do the tenants in Ireland (1949, 34–40). The dream of an Edenic period in the life of the individual or the nation is severely circumscribed, despite the nostalgia of the dreamer. The devolutionary implications of an autobiography sprung from the family history are rarely eluded. Instead, we see the final irony of the genealogical mandate: to escape the nullifying power of the rhetorical structure whose purpose is to vindicate one's legitimacy within a social community, the writer has to regenerate family history into an openly figurative metaphor and, most important, a metaphor at the service of concerns other than status and nationality.

Alternatives

Justifying in 1894 the decision to publish her late husband's memoirs, intended by him for family readership alone, Lady Gregory explains in the preface, "[M]y hope in publishing them is that his name, which was known, and kindly known, in many countries beside his own, may be kept alive a little longer, and that for his sake a friendly hand may sometimes in the future be held out to his boy" (S. W. Gregory 1894, iii). Her hope to preserve the memory and influence of something valued is not uncommon or surprising, but there are two striking features—and problems—to this avowal of purpose. First, she acknowledges that her motives are pragmatic and confined to the benefits of the family, particularly its youngest member. Second, her language reveals her conviction that "his memory" will be alive only "a little longer." Although Lady Gregory's statement can be read as a characteristic gesture of public modesty, her assumption that both memory and the act of remembering will soon disappear betrays her concurrence with Yeats's similar predictions and his indictment of the "unremembering hearts and heads / Base-born products of

10. The contrast between the depiction of Irish and English country houses is discussed at length in Gill 1972 and Kelsall 1993.

base beds" whom he dismally forecast as the inheritors of Ireland. The degenerative pattern appears again precisely because the stated agenda of her edition
fails to extend beyond the family, nor does it look toward a vision of a livable
future.

Others also write their lives through the structure of the family history, yet
by extending their vision beyond it are also able to reach beyond the narrative
of eclipse. In concerning himself with local history and architectural preservation, Hubert Butler carries on a preoccupation long associated with English
and Anglo-Irish women, but he does so with a difference. His consuming interests begin in the local yet are greater than the local; they shape a lifetime of
writing and thinking, not the idle hours of one who has power and material
goods to commemorate. His many essays on the history of his family and region forward his conviction that all social units—from the familial to the international—are best served by a devoted cultivation of regional ecology and
culture. In the introduction to his collected personal essays, *Independent Spirit*,
Butler reflects that "the strength to live comes from an understanding of ourselves and our neighbours or the diaspora that has replaced them. If we could
focus on them all the curiosity and wisdom that we disperse round the world,
as we focus all the rays of the sun through a burning glass on a pile of dead
leaves, there is no limit to the warmth and life we could generate" (1996, 8).
Butler concedes that "all this sounds misleadingly nostalgic" (5), and the international publication of his essays might open him to the charges that David
Lloyd has made against those writers who he believes celebrate regionalism as
a product to be consumed by the international marketplace (1993, 36–37). But
Butler's collection of "dead leaves"—his familial narratives and his participation in the public life of Kilkenny and its historical preservation—finds its own
motive in revitalizing the local for the sake of its inhabitants.[11]

Stephen Gwynn's 1926 *Experiences of a Literary Man* resembles Butler's essays in that Gwynn, too, assumes a new place for himself in twentieth-century
Ireland. Like many others, Gwynn includes in his autobiography anecdotal
portraits of the working people who populate his childhood memories. As the
residue of autobiography's origins in the literature of scientific exploration and
colonial domination, such anecdotes historically entertained the reader with

---

11. Butler's 1956 essay, "The Sub-Prefect Should Have Held His Tongue," presents an instance when the urge to withdraw from his local community must have been a powerful one. As
Butler tells the story, his public protest of the brutally enforced "conversion" of Orthodox Croats
to Roman Catholicism resulted in his removal from the leadership of the Kilkenny Archaeological
Society of which he was a principal founder (1996, 452–64).

the amusing or exotic details of alien beliefs, customs, and language patterns. However, Gwynn's stories of the Catholic and Protestant small farmers among whom he grew up are never crudely anthropological or exploitative of these individuals as sources of humor. The chapter titled "Family," for example, sets out to depict the community of which his father's rectory and farm were a part. The story of his nursemaid and her family moves quickly from his childhood recollections to an exploration of her own early life, her hopes and ambitions, and the agricultural conditions that kept her husband from ever turning a profit despite his diligence, inventiveness, and the intelligent application of his readings in agricultural management. The portrait of the Coyles, like few others within the genre, reveals its author's grasp of the economic and social lives of those servants and tenants who worked in the houses and on the lands of the middle and upper classes.

As in his story of the Coyles, Gwynn's foray into his family history again echoes but also differs from many other Anglo-Irish autobiographies. He unearths the same kind of ancestral hybrid as does Mary Hamilton: a Welsh patrilineage of ancestors present in Ulster since the siege of Derry, and a matrilineage originating in the old Gaelic dynasties that turned Protestant under Henry VIII and produced such figures as Gwynn's grandfather, the rebel nationalist William Smith O'Brien. The unwinding of lineage to indicate longevity in Ireland and the proudly told tale of a patriotic relative reiterate typical motifs of the genre. Gwynn's stated purpose, however, is different. He seeks to identify himself not only as an Irishman but also as a modern European with a place in twentieth-century life: a man comfortable in London or in southern France, with Gaelic speakers in Connemara, Orangemen fishing along the River Bann, or those middle-class members of either sect he meets in government or university circles. Finally, although the richness of his memories enables him to write affecting reminiscences of a past era, he expresses delight at the changes brought by widening democracy, the relaxation of social caste, feminism, and the decline of European colonialism. His optimism about the new Ireland recalls Scottish novelist George McDonald's definition of "home" as "the only place where you can go out and in. There are places you can go into, and places you can go out of, but the one place, if you do but find it, where you may go out and in both, is home" (Auden 1971, 184). Because he is able to imagine a home as a locality and a way of life available to the present, to which one can "go in," Gwynn's autobiographical narrator finds himself at home in the new state.

However fanciful or factual, the family history has served as the deep structure of a culturally inscribed life story of degeneration and extinction.

Butler and Gwynn write their way out of such constraints, but few autobiographers avoid the contentious debate over ethnicity altogether. A handful of works, like Monk Gibbon's *Inglorious Soldier* (1968), are so focused on other subjects, in his case World War I and the author's conversion to ardent pacifism, as to forgo the question. Yet even Gibbon, whose other autobiographies trace his romances and hunting experiences, is compelled to answer the query, "Am I Irish?" in a contribution to *The Crane Bag* (1982). Since the late nineteenth century, Anglo-Irish autobiography has persistently been attached to a defense of nationality, almost invariably ending with the perception of having been marginalized to the point of nonexistence. In *Anomalous States* (1993), David Lloyd proposes that colonial and postcolonial conditions impelled Irish writers to advocate an exclusivist nationalism at the expense of other structures of identity. As Declan Kiberd has demonstrated, the writers and theoreticians of the Revival years actively pursued the hope that *Anglo-Irish* could pair with *Gaelic-Irish* as two equally acceptable variants, fused culturally if not theologically into "Protholics and Cathestants" (1995, 418–27). Kiberd indicts Irish governmental policies as having made this aspiration unreachable, but the sharp demarcations resultant from a genealogical orientation toward identity may also have contributed to its failure.

Those autobiographers who de-emphasize ethnic or national identity tend to be women, many of whom found themselves able to experience broader lives away from their families in Dublin, England, and the Continent. Others include persons who lived primarily in England. Frank Pakenham's declaration of his "Irish credentials," for example, is only one detail in what is actually a genealogy of his liberal perspective. His Irish ancestry, he says, is consequential primarily in that it led him to support Irish nationalism as an extension of his conversion to Catholic socialism and his commitment to worldwide independence movements. And although each of George Moore's many autobiographies incorporates stories of the Moores of Moore Hall and the author's youth in Mayo, he takes every autobiographical occasion to argue the irrelevancy of the world of his fathers and to repudiate family and nationality in order to reinvent himself as a European writer.

Still others, like Lionel Fleming or Stephen Gwynn, devalue a separate Anglo-Irish identity because they believe that the success of modern Ireland requires an ongoing blending of cultural influences. Unlike Mary Hamilton, who cites her mixed pedigree as a sign of her citizenship, Fleming and Gwynn turn from biological metaphors to ones of cultural hybridization. If Moore relates the family history only to commit autobiographical parricide, and Butler escapes the debilitating ironies of genealogy by altering its motifs to advance his wider concerns for ecological well-being, Fleming and Gwynn interrogate its meaning but finally dismiss any power it might have once had to define an identity. Given the racialist tenor of so much twentieth-century nationalism, the abandonment of the family history as a claim to national belonging was their contribution toward an inclusive view of citizenship that seemed to become more critical with each passing year.

2

The Daughter and Her Patrimony

Women are perhaps most responsible for the species of fiction that has come to be known, not without dissent, as the Big House novel. At the same time, female autobiographers shape the conventions of place, patronym, and the literary childhood that so dominate the life writing of their class in the late nineteenth and twentieth centuries. Yet when we examine Anglo-Irish autobiographies as gendered texts, they reveal just how much identities of gender compete with identities of class. Women write and simultaneously unwrite the masculine emphasis of the Anglo-Irish family chronicle. And on this volatile textual ground, so often dismissed or sentimentally appreciated as the self-elegy of a doomed colonial elite, is fought out the very viability of the speaking self.

In the life writing of Augusta Gregory and Elizabeth Bowen, the two best-known female writers of Anglo-Ireland assert a close identification of the autobiographical "I" with the property each woman inhabited or, as in Bowen's case, inherited as the result of marriage or birth. Despite significant differences between them, both women chose to build their life stories upon the framework of the family property. Because Lady Gregory could never actually own Coole and Bowen depicts herself as a weak link in the chain of primogeniture, their work emerges as the site of a particularly explosive intersection of literary practices with specific class and gender identities. Most women never gained ownership or any degree of control over the family property, and their autobiographies exhibit a profound dissonance between the familiar motifs of Anglo-Irish self-representation and factors unique to their position as women. Out of print and generally forgotten since their initial reviews, these texts compel a rethinking of the conventional wisdom regarding the Anglo-Irish, one that holds ramifications for the broader consideration of the relations among gender, genre, and class.

Beyond religious testimonies, excerpts of diaries, or the incidental self-descriptive remarks that accompany travel literature, little autobiographical writing appears to have been published by Anglo-Irish women during the nineteenth century, although many of their male counterparts produced life writings of a wide variety, and the practice was not uncommon among English women.[1] The overwhelming majority of autobiographies by Anglo-Irish women were published during the 1940s and early 1950s. Having experienced the dislocations resultant from two world wars and a prolonged period of violence within their own country, these women had to adapt to extensive changes in class relations and gender roles, while seeing their parents undergo a precipitous loss of status and property in Irish society.

Enid Starkie speaks for many in explaining that in addition to her desire to explore the "sticky lump" of her family's emotional dynamics, she wishes to write a memoir of "those years when no one dreamed of the possibility of war and also those, somewhat later, when a first World War had swept away much of the life in which I was born. . . . In August, 1939, with a further tornado gathering strength, I wished to recapture, while there was still time, what was left of that early life before it was completely buried in the debris of a second World War" (1941, 11). Starkie assumes the roles of chronicler and analyst and, to a much lesser degree, elegist. The latter role has been perpetually associated with Anglo-Irish writing, yet it is probably the least prevalent among women autobiographers. Although "that early life" is commonly the focus of recollection, the majority of these writers condemn it as a stultifying if not aggressively destructive atmosphere. They evoke memories of the house and lands on which they were brought up, particularly as structural devices by which to organize the narrative, but these memories frequently clash with other elements that undermine the privileged place of the familial property within the life story.

Women's autobiographies thus necessitate a rethinking of the relations between identity and property. Although Anglo-Irish women may compose their lives as narratives of cultural decline and dwell in detail upon country houses and the historical transference of familial property, they often engage such motifs with intense irony or use them mechanically to frame a life story otherwise unrelated in emphasis. Although they almost always offer the autobiography as an insight into a past era, the values of the past are held up less as guideposts for the future or relics of a superior way of life, than as part of a story exemplifying how to live with change at once terrifying and emancipatory.

1. Davis and Joyce (1989) suggest that Queen Victoria's having become an author allowed many aristocratic women to consider the publication of memoirs within the realm of respectability and may account for the surge of published autobiographies by English women during the later nineteenth century.

This approach to women's autobiographies admittedly emphasizes aspects of Anglo-Irish identity founded upon readings of masculine texts, and alternate issues for analysis, such as figurations of maternity and women's friendships, will be treated separately in the subsequent chapter. In both chapters, I will ask of a specific body of writings those questions raised more broadly by Sidonie Smith as to how women's autobiographies produce a "hybrid form," negotiating between the as yet unspoken, unheard life and the social and literary models that a woman attempting a life writing finds already "installed" in the expectations of the genre in which she works (1993a, 4). The Anglo Irish woman's use of the little studied genre of the family history inspires several questions of significance to readers of Anglo-Irish literature and to the study of autobiography as a genre shaped by the discourses of gender and class. What happens to a woman's life writing when she chooses as her autobiographical mode a patrilineal history offered also as a microcosm of the history of an imperial culture? In what ways does viewing such a work of "cultural autobiography" as a gendered text alter what we see therein?[2] More generally, is it possible to write one's subjectivity within the generic protocols of an openly patriarchal form, yet critically step outside, or even beyond, the constrictions of that form to a new construction of the speaking self?

As might be expected, these autobiographers adopt, adapt, and sometimes abjure culturally assigned identities. To a degree greater than any other woman here under consideration, Augusta Gregory writes of her own life as emblematic of what Smith calls a "collective social" identity: in her case, one formed by the values of nineteenth-century Protestant Evangelicalism and the self-descriptions of Anglo-Ireland that evolved during her own lifetime. Aside from her most private diaries and occasional letters to intimate friends, her life writings consistently explain her role as a public figure and rarely admit doubts as to the continuing national importance of her life, her late husband's, or the estate with which both lives were interwoven. Yet she relates those aspects of her experience that she believes to hold the greatest interest for her readership—her involvement in politics, her work in the theater, her friendships with famous people—without many engaging anecdotes or moving descriptions. Constrained by social mores and personal reticence from publicly discussing

---

2. The term *cultural autobiography* is derived from Caren Kaplan (1992, 130–32). For the sake of concision I use the term *women* as a general category, but with recognition of T. L. Broughton's caution that "any argument based on similarity of content across a range of women's autobiographies runs the risk, however innocently, of eliding differences between women's lives, of obscuring cultural specificities in the name of an *ad hoc* separate women's 'tradition.' Suggestions of gender specificity lurch precariously towards assertions of gender *generality*" (1991, 77).

the human beings who stir her emotions, Gregory writes with greatest feeling concerning the landscape surrounding Coole and the house itself; it is in the passages concerning Coole that her autobiographical writings are most vivid and persuasive.

Considering that the ideology of a hereditary culture grounded in house and land is so fully a part of her autobiographical position, she writes surprisingly little of Roxborough, the estate that had been in her family since the late 1600s and where she lived until her marriage at nearly twenty-eight years of age. The early versions of *Seventy Years* make clear that while Lady Gregory originally portrayed her youth as an unhappy one, her revisions, as Mary Fitzgerald has summarized, "toned down the bitterness of her recollections of early childhood, eliminating sketches of her odd and unhappy tutors and of the colder aspects of the Persse home" (1987, 52). Fitzgerald justifiably reads these changes as the thoughtful gestures typical of a woman ever concerned with the feelings of others. However, given Lady Gregory's stated desire to posit the ancestral estate as a center of "the spiritual and intellectual side of our country" and to confirm her own position within that estate, the dissenting evidence of Roxborough's oppressive, even humiliating, atmosphere may have seemed incongruous (L. A. Gregory 1978, 15). In the same vein, she suppresses the awkwardness of her peripheral position there as a plain girl who did not attract admirers and whose strong, speculative intellect isolated her from her peers.

Lady Gregory may have occupied only a peripheral position at Roxborough, but widowed after only twelve years of marriage, she took on the responsibilities of managing Coole with fervor and skill. The centrality of her place at Coole and the centrality of Coole within its environs are prevalent motifs in her autobiographical writing, and uniquely so. Rather than the monotony and entrapment (or, conversely, instability and exile) that the landed estate so often represents in the life writings of Anglo-Irish women, a sense of order and importance exudes from Coole, as it does from the country house in English memoirs of the interwar decades.[3] Having textually suppressed the memories of another country house in which, as a disfranchised daughter, Augusta Persse held no power, she builds a totalizing vision of Coole as a place from which the world emanates in concentric circles.

As if confirming W. B. Yeats's tribute to her in "Coole Park, 1929" as "a compass-point" around which scholars and poets "whirled" in formation, Gregory imagines Coole to be a place whose importance belies what was historically her own precarious position as a woman born in the Anglo-Ireland of

3. See M. M. Kelsall's *Great Good Place* (1993) for an extended discussion of the representation of English country houses in literature after World War I.

1852. Perhaps because of distinctions in both circumstances and age, most other women did not so imagine their homes. With only a few exceptions, they were born considerably later than Lady Gregory and wrote during or after the Second World War. None besides Elizabeth Bowen held a position of authority in regard to the family property, and all contest much more directly the ethos of class and gender identity that renders their positions equally insecure.

Cultural Autobiography and the Feminine Subject: The Autobiographies of Elizabeth Bowen

In the case of Elizabeth Bowen, that contestation involves adopting the form of the patrilineal history while indirectly questioning its tenets. Explaining her decision to write the chronicle of her family's past, Bowen suggests that such a history acts as a metonym for her private and present moment: "I am ruled," she affirms, "by a continuity that I cannot see" (1942, 449). Writing during the Second World War in "the savage and austere light of a burning world," Elizabeth Bowen, like many others of her time, turned to autobiography in search of the continuities of private life that the impersonality of fascist nationalism and the random effects of war threatened to extinguish or, at the very least, render irrelevant. "Outwardly," she writes, "we accepted that at this time individual destiny had to count for nothing; inwardly, individual destiny became an obsession in every heart. . . . Every writer during this time was aware of the passionate attachment of men and women to every object or image or place or love or fragment of memory with which his or her destiny seemed to be identified, and by which the destiny seemed to be assured" (1950, 50).

As she here implies, private consciousness was inseparable, at times indistinguishable, from the context of its social being. Its continuities were collective, as were its shattering dislocations. Elizabeth Bowen was a celebrated novelist and an integral part of London literary circles; she was also a woman of passionate attachments to friends and lovers. Yet her autobiographical writing locates its subject neither in narratives of her public career nor in introspections upon her personal life. With a keen sense of the instability of the subject that Shari Benstock has found endemic in the fiction and autobiography of other women writers of her generation (1988, 21), Bowen disperses what she calls "the uncertain 'I' " between two kinds of autobiographical writing, both of which, despite fundamental differences, shun any assertion of the ego as a purely private construction.

In her childhood memoir, *Seven Winters*, written immediately following the completion of the first draft of *Bowen's Court*, she portrays the child primarily as a responsive medium, receiving on her consciousness the imprint of exterior sensations and impressions. In *Bowen's Court*, she speaks as the last of a family, relating the history of her ancestors and her father's estate in County Cork in chronological sequence illustrated with genealogical charts, photographs of the family house, and portraits of her predecessors. Despite a decided emphasis on her sensory, emotional, and historical environment, she acknowledges the need to consciously shape oneself. In *Pictures and Conversations*, she observes that a "main trait of human nature is its amorphousness, the amorphousness of the drifting and flopping jellyfish in a cloudy tide, and secret fears (such as fear of nonentity) . . . prey upon individuals made aware of this. There results an obsessive wish to acquire outline, to be unmistakably demarcated, to *take shape*. Shape—shape is the desideratum" (1975, 58–59). She provides shape by sketching the world around and through the perspective of the speaker; the speaker is drawn as if in outline.

Bowen's ideas parallel the view of her friend and contemporary Virginia Woolf that it is "the invisible presences" that "keep in position" the subject of the memoir. Rather than posit a firm sense of self and speaker, it becomes much more important for the autobiographer to sketch those moments— faces, incidents, bits of speech—that press upon her consciousness. Woolf explains, "If we cannot analyze these invisible presences . . . how futile life-writing becomes. I see myself as a fish in a stream; deflected; held in place; but cannot describe the stream" (1985, 80). Bowen justifies her minute description of "the stream," that is, the history of her ancestral estate in County Cork, by suggesting that it is the means by which she delineates her autobiographical speaker: "The land outside Bowen's Court windows left prints on my ancestors' eyes that looked out: perhaps their eyes left, also, prints on the scene. If so, those prints are part of the scene to me" (1942, 451). As her own gaze imprints the scene and is likewise reflected by it, its contours manifest both the speaker and the continuous family past in which she locates herself.

Bowen attributes even the solipsism of the child to cultural traits. In *Seven Winters* and the posthumously edited and published *Pictures and Conversations*, she relates with the novelist's specificity the generic features of the childhood: the exaltation of physical motion, the egotism of one's own group, the enormity of landscapes and rooms, the startling sight of a dead animal, the view from the nursery window, the scalding experience of discovering oneself ugly in a mirror, the smell and feel of the mother's body. Her emphasis is upon sensory experience, epiphanic recognitions, and visual rather than narrative perception. This world of significant trifle, this world of "difference" so seemingly devoid of the narrative elements of a history, nevertheless proves crucial to the emplotment of a life. What Virginia Woolf calls "moments of being," those "shocks" of ecstasy or horror, penetrate through the "cotton

wool" of the forgotten past. They reveal, according to Woolf, either the horror of nothingness or a vision of cosmological unity in which the self is embraced within the whole (1985, 71–72). In a peculiar but characteristic gesture,
Bowen attributes such moments to her family inheritance. Because during the
war years one of Bowen's most important links to the world of "the whole" was
the myth of ancestry, she reflects that the powerfully "subjective, shifting . . .
visual" memories she describes were the product of having been born into a
family of dreamers in which "they each ruled their private kingdoms of
thought . . . a home at once unique and intensive, gently phenomenal" (1962,
9). In *Bowen's Court* she identifies this inward-looking, isolated mode of being
as the most definitive aspect of the Anglo-Irish character.

At every opportunity, Bowen offsets the private nature of the child's consciousness by an acknowledgment of its formation in dialogue with literature,
family traits (often defined by Bowen as typically Anglo-Irish), and the pat-
tern-seeking of the remembering adult author. Not only is the present self inseparable from its social inheritance, but its past is also inaccessible except as
an aspect of the remembering mind. She notes in a 1938 review of a contemporary autobiography, *Unforgotten Years:*

> One cannot surprise one's past: the very quickest look back makes everything
> fall into order—if only into a momentary order, the order of a mood. . . . Be-
> fore any deliberate retrospection starts one has already rejected, with an un-
> conscious violence, what is untoward, what might not fit in the pattern. For
> that pattern, whatever may be its nature, is an intimate part of one's self-
> esteem, and one's idea of survival is closely bound up in it. . . . Ultimately,
> one's own emotional taste must be the censor of memory. Thus the memoir,
> the reminiscence takes it place half-way between aesthetics and pathology.
> (1950, 129–30)

The past, Bowen argues, is the product of the present search for it; as she asserts in her essay "Out of a Book" (1946), a past experience cannot be distinguished fully from narratives borrowed from the world outside the self,
particularly the world of literature (1950, 265–69). Childhood experience is itself so colored by childhood reading as to be inaccessible apart from it—even
to the child who lived the experience: "We have relied on our childhoods, on
the sensations of childhood, because we mistake vividness for purity; actually,
the story was there first—one is forced to see that it was the story that appar-
elled everything in celestial light" (269). Taken together, her writings present
both the recollecting narrator and the recollected past self as the most tenta-
tive of entities.

Such destablizations of the subject have become commonplace since the 1980s for critics and autobiographers alike. The question remains as to how Bowen's vision of autobiographical practice relates to her chosen mode of the historical family narrative with its records of financial dealing and cross-dealing, lawsuits and countersuits, architectural construction and destruction, and the ongoing, turbulent transferences of property. To seek one's place in such a chronology may be to find an antidote to the anxiety attending a loss of faith in the speaking subject, yet it may also prove for the woman writing auto-biography an especially dangerous undertaking.

The answer to the question begins to emerge from *Seven Winters*, where Bowen explains that her nursemaid's habit of drugging the milk "unnaturally widened for me the infant sleep-zone," so extending the period before the recognition of difference that "tore across some veil and first made me realize that I was I" (1962, 14–15). The "I," however, lacks centrality and authority: a sudden awareness of the Russo-Japanese War "was my first vision—I mean, the first moment in which I conceived of reality as being elsewhere than in me." Shut up in a darkened nursery for naps, the child remains tense with the agony that the city of Dublin outside her window "rose to a climax—a climax from which I was withheld" (26). The child here feels "reality elsewhere" while paradoxically discovering herself most acutely. Similarly, the chapter of *Seven Winters* titled "Brass Plates" encapsulates a fusion of the child's emerging iden-tity and the collective identity—in this case, a patrilineal ethnicity—in which it will come to consciousness. Bowen concisely portrays the child's recognition of her place within the carefully demarcated ethnic and class structure of Anglo-Ireland in its urban setting. "All here stood for stability," she declares, and that stability is manifest in the brass plate upon the door, a sign of patriar-chal inscription equated with being itself: "Just as the tombstone says 'Here Lies,' the plate on the front door (in my view) said 'Here Lives.' Failure to write one's name on one's door seemed to me the admission of nonentity." Naively scornful of any household without a doorplate, the child pities the "nonentities" who inhabit the anonymous houses of London, concluding that "Dublin has chosen to be smaller than London because she is grander and more exclusive. All the important people live in Dublin, near me." As a child, Bowen writes, "I would trace with my finger my father's name. This was not an act of filial piety only; it gave him an objective reality, which I shared" (34, 35).

In this extraordinarily rich passage, the "I" expands socially and geograph-ically beyond the circumference of a child's body at the same time that it is built upon a snobbish exclusion of those people without doorplates. Bowen gently mocks her childish egocentrism while simultaneously affirming it as the ethnocentrism of the collective Anglo-Irish minority. The little girl projected by the adult autobiographer finds her subjectivity in the inscription of her father's name, which was even more impressive, she says, because she could not read it. Bowen refrains from explaining in this essay that her mother purposely kept her illiterate until the age of seven in fear she would, by tiring her brain, incur the mental derangements of her father's family. Elizabeth Bowen never became mentally ill; nevertheless, she did take on the role of heir to her father's family, reading and writing her name in an autobiographical representation of that plate whose very existence in the once elegant neighborhood of eighteenth-century houses marked a metahistorical tragedy of class she chose as her own paradoxical metaphor of permanence amid a world at war. If the narrative implicit in one's own inscription upon the "brass plate" is in fact a narrative of class (and, in her terms, "racial") decline, then "Here Lies" must surely be conjoined to "Here Lives." To write the daughter's name upon the father's is to mark the failure of both.

As a locus for that narrative of decline, Bowen's Court is the material manifestation of an adult conflict rather than a matrix of sensation for the child. It is also the domain of the patriarchal history from which, as a girl, she was plucked at the very moment of her birth and from which her father's mental illness required her and her mother to live in exile. Childhood remains the realm of her mother, but *Bowen's Court* articulates her identification with patrilineage. Despite the nearly thirty years that separate her two volumes of childhood memoirs, they resemble one another far more than either resembles the family history written in the years between. Associative and spatial in organization and impressionistic and sensory in their methodology, they differ greatly from a family chronicle dependent upon sequential narration and documentary materials. Yet both kinds of autobiography display that "harmonious merger and identification with a collective consciousness" that Mary Mason has discovered as a common feature of numerous autobiographies by women (1980, 231). Though perhaps a gender-inflected feature, it also reflects the specific ideology of class identity. Bowen projects the "harmonious merger" as mystically inclusive, but it is equally a highly exclusive vision of a culture originating in inherited property and reified by declarations of genealogical and sectarian distinction.

It would be all too easy to designate Bowen's autobiographical writings the feminine corollary to W. B. Yeats's use of Coole Park as an emblem of a splendid Anglo-Irish world now lost to the "filthy modern tide," and many studies of Bowen invoke epigraphically Yeats's poems on the demise of the Ascendancy. In the work of both writers, the loss of property becomes symptomatic of familial and cultural collapse. Yet most Anglo-Irish women have not written their autobiographies along such lines. To Katherine Everett, Daisy Fingall,

Hannah Lynch, Edith Gordon, and numerous others, the ancestral house is a troublesome reminder of their own inadequate status as trespassers on the property of their husbands, fathers, brothers, or uncles; their identity as Anglo-Irish is bound up in the behavioral restrictions that each feels compelled to challenge.

Elizabeth Bowen chose to emphasize her relation to house and property and to remake the terms of that relation. The past, however, was not altogether a blessed inheritance. In *Bowen's Court* and more explicitly in the later *Pictures and Conversations*, she makes reference to the "constant, underlying, watchful anxiety" with which her mother examined her for signs of her paternal ancestry (1975, 11). Patrilineal traits were all hazardous: freckles on the hands, overwork, sleeplessness, and the sum of them all, a paralyzing and delusive melancholia. If paternal forebears were dangerous, the lives of her grandmothers are barely mentioned; the feminine is a nugatory concern within her book of the past. Revisionist literary histories of modernism like Shari Benstock's *Women of the Left Bank* (1986) and Sandra Gilbert and Susan Gubar's *No Man's Land* (1988) have demonstrated at length that the nostalgia for an imagined world before the Great War was in fact peculiar to males of the middle and upper classes, and not necessarily part of women's responses to world events. In the essay "Feminist Fiction and the Uses of Memory," Gayle Greene observes that "the good old days . . . [were] also the time when women knew their place, and it is not a place to which most women want to return. As Ostriker suggests, 'Prufrock may yearn to be Hamlet, but what woman would want to be Ophelia?' Nostalgia is not only a longing to return home; it is also a longing to return to the state of things in which woman keeps the home and in which she awaits, like Penelope, the return of her wandering Odysseus" (1991, 296).

Bowen's revisitation of the past casts herself not as Penelope but as an impossibly thwarted Odysseus. Her history of the demise of the "Big House" also takes its place within a subgenre overwhelmingly the domain of female novelists. The narrative of familial and historical decline was (and remains) for Anglo-Irish women a compelling form in which to write fiction, as well as autobiography, and W. J. McCormack has made the tantalizing recommendation that we "consider the use of domestic setting by Irish women writers as a preemptive strike against continued male monopoly in the ownership of the landed estate" (1992b, 36). McCormack's suggestion leads to the question of how the claim of ownership, the claim to the status of Odysseus, reconfigures the female autobiographical subject. And conversely, how does the female autobiographer change the shape of the subgenre in which she works? Particularly important are the broad queries raised by Sidonie Smith as to "the ways in which specific subjects not only resist provided subjectivities but also comply with those that affect their exclusion from history" and, in addition, "the ways in which the laws of genre lock the autobiographical subject into certain forms of compulsory gender identity and how the autobiographical subject seeks to unlock the genre and thereby unlock those compulsory identities" (1993b, 396, 405).

The "laws of genre" controlling the patrilineal history affect Bowen's autobiographical writing in at least three ways: the context of values within which she places herself, the bifurcation of experience into maternal and paternal spheres, and the sense of her life as a microcosm of the world beyond her. There is no question that adapting the myth of Anglo-Irish inheritance brought Bowen to valorize style, verbal agility, and a personal reserve—even haughtiness—coupled with genuine courage. She depicts herself, even in childhood, as the retainer of such traits with which the Anglo-Irish liked to associate themselves: "It was," she explains, her mother's "great wish (survival, perhaps, of the expectations she had formed of Robert) that I should not be muffish" (1942, 406). Her mother's desire that she, the female child, act as the bearer of cultural traits is predicated thus in the expectations surrounding the never-to-be-born male heir, Robert. Even more significant, the expression of these attitudes comes most eloquently as she addresses the loss of all she, by accident of birth, inherited. The elegant, austere reserve of the sentences in which she describes the decline of the property and the destruction of her house, as well as the death of her mother, her widowhood, and her childlessness, is in fact a powerful stylistic articulation of an ethic she believes to be at the core of her lineage as Anglo-Irish.

As the author of *Bowen's Court*, she must use the language of the male heir whose birth she usurped in order then to describe his losses as her own. The role of inheritor forces Bowen's autobiographical subject to draw a psychic distinction between Bowen's Court and the "pavilions of love," as she calls the rented villas along the southern coast of England where she and her mother lived following her father's mental breakdown (1975, 29). As I have noted, the structural and stylistic approaches to the one world differ greatly from those of the other. To become the inheritor is to embrace the world of the father, a place whose resonances were as tragically historical as the others were maternal and ecstatically sensual.

It is also to attempt the role of the lost son. Mary Mason has suggested that women frequently project the autobiographical self in collusion with a more empowered "double" (1980, 221–32), and Bowen's here is "Robert," the family name awarded to the uncle who, unlike her father, was suited to the role of landlord but died young, killed by a horse at the beginning of his military career. Although Bowen does not herself make the association, even his mode of death seems to have been in keeping with Ascendancy traditions. His photograph was so much reproduced that "one must have hung in every Bowen's Court room. He has a broad forehead, short upper lip and sweet straight candid indolent eyes. He remains the image, this second short-lived Bowen, of what *the* Bowen of Bowen's Court might have been; his unborn sons and daughters seem to congest the place" (1942, 368). "Robert" was also to be the name of the child whose arrival was joyfully anticipated until the moment when it became evident that "Robert" was actually "Elizabeth" and that for the first time a male heir had "failed for the County Cork property" (1983, 4). Her resolve not to be "muffish" may be part of an effort to absorb the identity of the lost son, but it is a futile effort. In this book whose chapters are titled according to the names of the inheritors—John, Robert, Henry in alternating sequences—the last chapter is not titled "Elizabeth." It is called, tellingly, the "Afterword," and it begins: "So, Henry VI died, and I as his only child inherited Bowen's Court. I was the first woman heir: I had already changed my father's name for my husband's, and I have no children." As a form of consolation, she adds, "there are, however, three male Bowens of my own generation" (1942, 448). In the 1964 revision, written after her house had been sold and subsequently destroyed, that consolation is eradicated, and the sentences bear an even greater finality through alterations in pronouns and tense: "I was the first woman heir; already I had changed my father's name for my husband's. We had no children" (1964, 448). As the insufficient shadow of "Robert," she gives her life as a series of negations, her name never to be etched in the brass plate on which she traced her father's.

Bowen's elegance in dress, manner, and prose style may derive from the sangfroid she felt to be part of her role as an Ascendancy heir, but the inheritance could also be disabling, leaving the female autobiographical subject a barren shadow. "Family myth," as she writes in a review of Sheridan Le Fanu's *Uncle Silas*, might be a "demonic power" (1950, 4). However, the role of heir also further enforces her profound sense of the individual—and, in particular, herself—as microcosmic: a self whose being is always contextual and in whom the surrounding world is concentrated. In a passage from *Seven Winters* reminiscent of the "brass plates" sequence, she recounts with droll irony the error that misapprehended the sign of England's colonial power as a token of its marginality in relation to the assumed centrality of her own world:

[T]he Anglo-Irish slurred, hurried way of speaking made me take the words "Ireland" and "island" to be synonymous. Thus, all other countries quite surrounded by water took (it appeared) their generic name from ours. It seemed fine to live in a country that was a prototype. England, for instance, was *"an ireland"* (or, a sub-Ireland)—an imitation. Then I learned that England was not even "an ireland," having failed to detach herself from the flanks of Scotland and Wales. Vaguely, as a Unionist child, I conceived that our politeness to England must be a form of pity. (1962, 13–14)

A misreading of the vocabulary of power originates in the dialect of her own group and becomes a source of her ethnocentrism, a trait that she identifies as having given the Anglo-Irish some of their best qualities as well as procuring their downfall. In *Bowen's Court* she writes that "the preoccupation of Irish country people with their own affairs may be found either mystic or irritating. Each member of each of these isolated households is bound up not only in the sensation and business of living but in the exact sensation of living *here*. . . . Their existences, like those of only children, are singular, independent and secretive" (1942, 19–20). She argues that this very inwardness made the Anglo-Irish fail to respect, even to acknowledge or see, any world outside their own. Yet she takes this sense of being at the world's center to rather different ends.

Seeing one's house, one's land, one's culture, even oneself as representative need not require recasting the world in one's own image or reducing it to one's own terms. Bowen articulates the very premise of the ethnocentric history she offers as her own, but she alters fundamentally its conclusions. In his analysis of English and Irish autobiography of the 1930s, Gerard Barret notes a repeated appropriation of the imagery of fascism and genocide to describe the adolescent conflicts that consequently seemed to demand an escape into the womblike refuges of a book-enclosed solitude. He sees a tendency during the period to "define autobiography as an attempt to escape from the meta-narrative of events, a refuge from history" (1992–1993, 22). Bowen, however, makes clear that she works in the realm of synecdochical rather than equalitative metaphor: the war is neither equated with the personal nor put into service solely as a metaphor for the personal. Instead, the familial story focuses an international trauma otherwise too large to grasp. As a story explicitly grounded in political history and social transformation, *Bowen's Court* provides no refuge from these forces.

Neither does it attempt to escape the "meta-narrative" of change through the apocalyptic potential of its own narrative of decline. In defining the "cultural autobiography" as a form of women's autobiography in which "narrative inventions are tied to a struggle for cultural survival," Caren Kaplan may not have in mind the highly literate record of a colonizing planter society (1992, 130). Yet Bowen is most concerned with the survival of what she defines as Anglo-Irish values, and survival on terms that are—at this point by necessity as well as choice—more reasoned and tolerant than the terms of her ancestors. At the same time, she must as autobiographer either transform the terms by which her subjectivity finds its locus at Bowen's Court or remain a cipher. If the title of her last chapter bespeaks an autobiographical subject who has failed to fulfill the line of descent that her book takes as its narrative structure, it also succeeds at opening a new way for the female subject to transform her allegiance to a particular place beyond a futile effort toward domination. Bowen's hope for the "cultural survival" of the Anglo-Irish becomes intermeshed with her vision of the survival of the world, and nowhere is this more apparent than in the quiet fervor with which the "Afterword" is written.

In the 1942 "Afterword" she explains her motives for having written *Bowen's Court*, arguing that

> the urgency of the present, its relentless daily challenge, seems to communicate itself to one's view of the past, until, to the most private act or decision, there attaches one's sense of its part in some campaign. These days, either everything matters or nothing matters. The past—private as much as historic—seems to me now to matter more than ever: it acquires meaning; it loses false mystery. In the savage and austere light of a burning world, details leap out with significance. . . . War is not an accident; it is an outcome. One cannot look back too far to ask—of what? (453)

Seamus Deane has suggested that with Elizabeth Bowen's work "the last remnant of social faith disappeared from Irish fiction—that is, faith in the enduring power of contemporary society to confer meaning on the individual life" (1986a, 206). As this passage implies, Bowen also feels it is the responsibility of the individual to confer meaning upon the society in which she lives. For Elizabeth Bowen, the will to peace could exist only if individuals could see its possibility through some vision of their own.

Characteristically, her private vision is also the foremost symbol of her culture. She writes: "I suppose that everyone, fighting or just enduring, now carries one private image—one peaceful scene—in his heart. Mine is Bowen's Court. War has made me this image out of a house built of anxious history" (1942, 457). There is little question that her vision is deeply conservative and self-contradictory, yet it is much more complicated and, finally, humane than is suggested by a claim that it merely "represents a conservative, elitist retreat from the problems of war."[4] Bowen does forward the unsustainable suggestion

4. Kristine A. Miller also accuses Bowen of having created "structured illusions of her nostalgized past" (1999, 143). Her conclusions derive from a comparison of Bowen's own home with the

that property such as Bowen's Court allowed "my people and people like them" a way to exercise the hunger for power that otherwise would find an outlet in the fascist aggression that threatened the world. Her correlation of the mental instability of her father's family, Ascendancy overbuilding, and European fascism as all products of the same "heated brain" diminishes and obfuscates the profound differences among these personal, regional, and global disorders. Yet recognizing this vision of exquisite peace to be "a magic mirror, reflecting something that could not really exist," she also stops short of viewing the demise of Anglo-Irish power as a sign of the degradation of Europe in the face of democracy. She blames the demise of Anglo-Ireland—very pointedly in the 1964 revision—on "the quarrels, the lost law-suits, the father-and-son conflicts, the spasms of *folie de grandeur*" that mark her family as typical of its class (458). At the same time, she offers her house as a metonym of a vision of peace for which others must find expression within the symbolism of their own experience.

By the final version of the "Afterword," Bowen can no longer assert that the Anglo-Irish must and will have an influential role in the life of their nation, as she did in the earlier edition of *Bowen's Court* or in her wartime essay "The Big House." However, the burden of being both the first woman heir and the first heir who could not sustain the house does not so much alter the purposes of the first "Afterword" as it leads her to underscore what had been its original direction. The terms of "cultural survival" become more fully metaphoric as the house comes to function not only as a sign of the destructive "spasms" of the past but also as an enduring symbol of the aspirations toward peace. Defending in the revised "Afterword" her choice to retain the present-tense descriptions of a building since destroyed, she explains: "And so great and calming was the authority of the light and quiet round Bowen's Court that it survived war-time. And it did more than that, it survived the house. It remains with me now that the house is gone" (457). She would later revise the passage, but the sense of these words written during the war is sustained: "The peace of the image can never be realized: staying human, as we must stay human, we

---

Mount Morris of her wartime novel, *The Heat of the Day*. Miller contends that although the figuration of the London protagonist's domestic space effectively challenges gender restrictions, Bowen's failure to overcome her class biases (evident in the depiction of the Irish estate, Mount Morris) deflates her capacity to challenge "traditional gender ideology" (138–39). Although her point is convincing and meaningful, Miller overstates the resolve of Bowen's position and does not acknowledge how rigorously Bowen questions the origins and the stability of both Bowen's Court and Mount Morris.

shall still fumble and blunder. . . . But we did once see peace, in the heart of war-time. That is the peace to remember, seek and ensue" (1942, 457).

Mary Pakenham reflects in her 1938 autobiography that in anticipation of the possible burning of her own ancestral house during the Irish civil war, "I brought myself to think of everything I valued as being only a temporary loan. This I succeeded so well in doing that I have never re-acquired the feeling of ownership. Even my clothes feel lent" (55).[5] Bowen recalls in a 1952 preface to a new edition of *The Last September* (1929) that during the civil war, she had taught herself to imagine Bowen's Court in flames, thus to imaginatively project a loss in order to protect herself from despair should it come. In the "Afterword" to *Bowen's Court*, however, the knowledge of the vulnerability of her house has an effect that extends beyond the self. "This month," she writes, "the belt of fire has met right round the earth. Islands in oceans suffer; meditative and passionless stretches of country are being torn up. I must not think of the trees at Bowen's Court without thinking that upon an equal innocence on the part of nature, elsewhere, bombs fall" (1942, 457).

The fallen house emerges as an image that compels one to seek peace, a metaphoric means by which to feel the need of others for peace. Elizabeth Bowen's transformative blending of the genres of autobiography and the patrilineal history comes thus to its full expression. Although *Bowen's Court* risks nullifying its female subject, she develops beyond the solipsistic child or the tragically inadequate inheritor. She has shown how fully contextualized her female subjectivity has been within the often contradictory material circumstances and historical myths of her class, but she has also laid claim to the most potent symbol of her class, taking it out of its familiar (and familial) associations with the past and rendering it an emblem for her anxiety concerning the future.[6]

In one sense, she echoes what W. J. McCormack has defined as the attempt of writers like Mann, Joyce, and Kafka to "deal with the consequences of bourgeois decay, seeking forms of order which do not re-impose the totalitarian imperatives of race or bureaucracy, of fideism or instrumental rationality" (1992b, 51). Her imaginative transformation of Bowen's Court is conditioned

5. Bowen favorably reviewed Pakenham's autobiography in the *New Statesman and Nation*.

6. Kathleen Woodward (1988) maintains that anxiety over future loss is a distinctively "female model," whereas the "male model" of narrative more frequently projects the desire to recover that which has already been lost. Although such a universalizing theory of female subjectivity lacks necessary historicity, it is a useful point of inquiry from which to examine specific relations with the past, particularly in conjunction with feminist revisions of modernism.

by literary modernism and the masculine displacement that informs it, but the gesture also becomes the lifeline through which she, as woman autobiographer, can articulate her subjectivity outside of the terms of failure by which the patrilineal history has defined it. By self-consciously utilizing a genre that almost destroys her as autobiographical subject, she can—perhaps precisely by declining to title the last chapter with her own name—critique the form of discourse from which she has hitherto spoken.

Daughters of a Fallen House

For most women, a family history based on property and patrilineage allows little space for feminine representation, and the struggle of Elizabeth Bowen to speak within such a generic structure is echoed with multiple variations in the life writings of other Anglo-Irish women. Although Bowen self-consciously titles each chapter of *Bowen's Court* with the names of Bowen patriarchs, that way of seeing family history appears as a mere reflex in other autobiographers incapable of imagining the family history as anything but a story of men. The extensive family history given in Raymond Brooke's *Brimming River*, for example, records the deeds of his Elizabethan male forebears, the Irish Protestant girls they married, and the Irish lands they gained by various means. Brooke offers a tale of ongoing male acquisition, although the wealth derived from the acquired women and properties is lost to gambling and an ambitious illegitimate son, only to be regained and retained despite marriage with a family whose fortune had been reduced through an elder son's seduction of "the Duke's illegitimate daughter" (1961, 32–33).[7] The family history is a masculine story of loss and profit in which women play the part of either a money lender or a temptation requiring the services of a money lender. With such models, how can women assimilate the family history to their own life writing?

In a resilient effort to offset displacement by mocking that which displaces them, women more frequently note the trails of illegitimacies and point out the injustice of being turned out of one's house to make room for a distant male

7. A. P. W. Malcomson (1982) argues that, at least prior to the famine, "the pursuit of the heiress" was much less common in Anglo-Ireland than has been popularly imagined, although not the recurrent fear that family fortunes might be lost through entanglements with lower-class women. Although he demonstrates that "settlements and financial negotiations" were "concomitants" rather than "causes" of most marriages, the prevalence of the theme in Anglo-Irish fiction from Edgeworth on nevertheless suggests that the idea—real or imaginary—was very much alive in the nineteenth and twentieth centuries.

inheritor. Additionally, women express the peculiarity of their family's positions within a community by highlighting eccentric behavior, a common practice among autobiographers both male and female, and reading such behavior as a sign of failure within Anglo-Ireland more generally: betrayed by "toxic fantasies," concludes Elizabeth Bowen; full of "indiscriminate magnificence," says Edith Gordon; and marked by the "irresponsible poverty of the landed gentry," according to Nicolette Devas.

Many women also imply that there never existed, nor would there exist in the future, a psychological, social, or geographical locale in which they could truly be at home. The romance novelist Dorothea Conyers, whose 1920 autobiography consisting of some 284 pages of hunting and fishing anecdotes most resembles works written by altogether too many English and Anglo-Irish men, articulates the perception that life had not deteriorated so much as it had been set adrift—if it had not in fact always been adrift. At the end of a chapter recalling the sale of her late father's house and estate, she remarks, "Everything was sold except one cream-colored hack, and the problem which I have to try to solve ever since, how to live on what you have not got, was written on the page of life to be worked out" (21). Although Conyers refers to her income, she also intimates here the condition of actual and attitudinal nomadism that more than anything else characterizes the autobiographies of Anglo-Irish women.

For some women, the sense of placelessness results directly from a real or threatened loss of property. Houses deteriorated from lack of ready income or were sold to creditors or the state; according to newspaper reports, approximately two hundred were burned during the years between the Easter Rising and the end of the civil war. Elizabeth Bowen and Mary Pakenham recall training themselves to imagine their houses in flames, but their accounts are unusual in commemorating an initial sense of ownership. For many women, lack of ownership was most keenly felt within the father's (or brother's or husband's) house. Numerous women resented their inability to inherit entailed property and openly protested the traditions that led to the surrender of the family house to some distant male relative. Joan de Vere, for example, writes that "from an early stage I was keenly aware of being cut out of the inheritance because of my sex. . . . I loved Curragh Chase dearly and, ironically, in later life became the only person in the family who continued to really care about it" (1990, 46). Violet Powell remembers her mother's disappointment "at having produced four daughters, three of them in sequence. She gloomily noted that four girls were a formidable tribe to be coped with if they did not marry" (1976, 39). Her mother frequently reminds the girls that they are not to become too attached to Pakenham Hall, for "though Pakenham might seem to be our home, it would pass to Edward on his coming-of-age" (44). In *The Gilt and the Gingerbread*, Anita Leslie recalls that "females were wanted in very small quantities by the upper classes. They had to be married off and that cost money" (1981, 88). Ignoring the erosive effects of land reform and rising taxation, Leslie argues that families destroyed themselves solely through their fixation upon male inheritance. She complains with disgust that "the Great War of my childhood had wrecked many homes simply because social usage decreed that houses and estates must go with a name and the name went with men only. . . . All around us echoed this chant concerning slaughtered heirs" (88–89). To Anita Leslie, the whole system was preposterous, and her autobiography unmasks with acid humor the hypocrisies of a society that—like Rossmore Castle, where once elegant ceilings now spouted growths of mushrooms—showed signs of dry rot throughout.

Other women developed variant strategies to separate themselves from the decline explicit in the stories of crumbling estates. In some cases, for the greater part of her autobiography, the writer ignores the question of family history or the fate of the ancestral house. Elizabeth Hamilton, for example, makes no attempt to see herself as typical of a group, and while *A River Full of Stars* portrays her father through features that mark him as a class type—a military officer and a dignified and courteous landowner in brown boots and tweeds, carrying his gun into the woods while followed adoringly by his dogs—these characteristic markings are his rather than hers. "Like many of his generation," she writes, "he had family pride and an interest in his ancestry" (1954, 17). Her story, however, records her quest for education and her experiences as a teacher rather than her genealogy. In her autobiography, *Another Book* (1937), Lady Clodagh Anson has little to say about her genealogy or her family property, and even the Irish civil war passes with minimal comment. She gives her attention instead to her reading, her interest in the suffrage movement, and her work as a poor people's advocate.

Although the house often acts as an extension of the self in Anglo-Irish literature, in the life writings of many women it can also represent a threat to one's autonomy. The self might be rooted in the parental household, but it also develops in opposition to all the house represents. In the 1899 *Autobiography of a Child*, Hannah Lynch is more concerned with evoking the consciousness of a child than demonstrating a specific class or gender identity, but she nevertheless finds her experience to exemplify the circumstances of Anglo-Irish girls in general. Lynch, who became in adulthood "a hopeless wanderer," depicts the house of her wealthy parents as a nightmarish site of enclosure and punishment. Of her own youth and the fortunes of the young women she knew, she asserts that Ireland was "the very wretchedest land on earth for woman, the one spot of the globe where no provision is made for her, and where parents consider themselves as exempt of all duty, of tenderness, of justice in her regard, where her lot as daughter, wife, and old maid bears no resemblance to the ideal of civilisation" (196).

More than a century before, but with similar vehemence, Dorothea Herbert's *Retrospections* expresses a similar horror at the memory of the family home. Written between 1770 and 1806 by a less prosperous relative of the Herberts of Muckross, this early diary depicts the inner life of a woman overwhelmed by unrequited love. As if glossing the events of Maria Edgeworth's *Castle Rackrent*, she tells a tale of women locked up in the house for speaking out, failing to give up their property, or rebuffing the advances of callous suitors and brutal husbands. Of the parental home, Herbert spends several pages in detailed description, ending thus:

> Above there was a great low Garret a perfect Wilderness of Antique construction that made the blood run Chill with Horror—My father was forced to take down the whole Roof and rebuilding it cost no small Sum—Indeed the whole Place underwent a New Modelling and was Modernized into a Commodious and handsome Dwelling Which kept my Mother at her Wits End many years to supply the Exigencies of a falling House and growing family. (1929, 21)

Unlike Herbert, Maud Wynne never directly attributes blame to the familial house itself. In light of its unusual beauty, revealed in the photographs accompanying *An Irishman and His Family* (1937), she says relatively little regarding the actual house in which she grew up as the daughter of Lord Morris of Killanin. But family life at Spiddal, in Maud Wynne's judgment, provided "little or no outlet for any of us, and especially for Himself, whose volcanic temperament required openings and outside interests, much the same as a Zoo bear requires nuts and buns" (36). Her mother was mild, if oblivious to her children's needs; her father wild, and equally oblivious; and the isolation of the house from the surrounding community exacerbated the tensions within it.[8] As in retrospective adulthood Katherine Everett comes to blame her mother's

8. Violet Martin's account of her visits at the Morris home give a sense of its isolation and melancholy aspect. In an 1888 letter to Edith Somerville she writes, "Yesterday was given over to our expedition to Spiddal. Nothing could explain the length of those 11 Irish miles, or the loneliness of the road. It was like mid ocean and a slight mist tended to increase the unboundedness of the stretches of moor and bog. . . . The wind blew tremendously up in those altitudes, and the grey hilly country and the mist were at last a sort of intolerable nightmare. . . . Civilisation in Siberia could not be more surprising" (Somerville and Ross 1989, 98).

melancholia on the conditions of Anglo-Irish life into which she was placed, so Maud Wynne diagnoses the roots of her father's depressions in his social position. A wealthy Roman Catholic of social and professional distinction, he was scarred by memories of the Great Famine and his ongoing inability to relieve the chronic poverty around him: "The remembrances seem to have left him with a kind of secret dread or fear of what Life could and might bring. It was an undercurrent, and its presence subconsciously influenced him and his children" (39). The life of Spiddal is fully renounced by Wynne, despite the zest with which she depicts the sharp-edged, often irascible family conversation and her passion for the sea, land, and sky of the Atlantic coast.

The very cultural values Elizabeth Bowen defends—conversational agility, irony, formal manners, and suppression of the personal—Wynne indicts with fury: "We lived in a miasma of books and talk, without anything to clear the atmosphere. . . . Was it starvation? I think so, though utterly unconscious of it at the time. That it was dangerous and that this eclectic atmosphere brought tragedy to the family I am sure of, for not all of us could live by stones alone, some must have wanted bread, and they did not find it until too late, if at all" (21). As the only survivor of a large family whose children fell to suicide, mental illness, or the retreat offered by convent life, Wynne pivots, like so many other Anglo-Irish women, between seeing her life in terms of what was taken away by the changes in Irish society and seeing her life in terms of what she escaped and came to be instead. Spiddal was burned by incendiaries, and Wynne and her husband chose permanent exile in response to this and other outrages. Yet it was the life within Spiddal that she blames for the disintegration of her family, not the alterations in the world around it.

For Maud Wynne and numerous other women, bitterness and regret at the destruction of the ancestral house adjoin an even greater emotion of relief at having escaped. After recounting the follies of her parents and grandparents, Katharine Everett ends her first chapter on the somber reflection that "of the thousands of acres once owned by the Herberts in County Kerry, not a single one is held in their name to-day" (1949, 4). Yet in addition to distancing her family by use of the third-person pronoun, she never again mentions loss of property and status. The next chapter, titled "Our Home," is followed soon after by a fourth chapter pointedly called "Escape," and the rest of the story concerns aspects of her life unrelated to Cahirnane House or her family. Despite the hardships of the years during which she accepted onerous jobs in order to support her two sons, she takes pride in her career as the designer and builder of homes and gardens, her own and other people's. She disapproves of her widowed mother's choice to live in a Dublin town house rather than at Cahirnane, not from any filial affection for Cahirnane but because the town house is ugly, overpriced, and chosen only for its proximity to the church with which her mother is childishly obsessed. The one person most closely associated with familial houses is Herbert's cousin Olive Ardilaun, the widow of Sir Arthur Guinness and a woman of immense wealth. Although Everett takes pains to emphasize her cousin's kindness, she repeatedly illustrates the ways in which Lady Ardilaun's wealth and position paralyze her. Living alone in her three ancient, cavernous houses and unable because of her social position to even work in her garden or to take trains or buses, she fears to walk alone within the walls of her property during the civil war. Noting that Olive Ardilaun's elaborate herb garden has gone to weed, as lost to the present era as its owner, Everett imagines her friend so coterminous with family status and lands that she has been trapped by them in ways that the uprooted Everett never is.

Like Everett, several other women took to building houses, and the story of these successful efforts counteracts their inadequacy within the ancestral home or the social eclipse symbolized by its disappearance. Overwhelmed and never really at home in the massive, ancient structure into which she marries, Elizabeth Fingall occupies herself by building and managing houses for Horace Plunkett, her life's primary attachment and a man whose efforts she supported with her own enthusiastic Irish nationalism. Edith Gordon also enjoyed building, and much of *The Winds of Time* (1934) recounts the various houses she constructed on her own. Condemned, she felt, to a life of uselessness as part of a useless class, she discovered a sense of achievement in this work. After experimentation with spiritualism and social work led to little but futility, she recalls, "I had got to the stage which sooner or later we all reach, when one pauses to take stock of oneself and to ask wildly of Heaven what one is to do with one's life. I felt I must get away from everybody and everything if I were not to become like the lady in the Divorce Court who, on being reprimanded by the judge for the frequency with which she committed adultery, flippantly remarked: 'Well, what else *can* you do between tea and dinner?' " "Fortunately for my morals," she continues, she acquired property from a remote relative and "started building, being the ninth member of my demented family to do so in Kerry" (24–25).

Unlike Everett or Fingall, Gordon directly attributes her feeling of being adrift in the world to her Anglo-Irish inheritance and identifies her passion for building as the enactment of a hereditary madness. Yet her self-evaluation is inaccurate: unlike her female ancestors, she owned the property, designed the building, labored on the building itself, and controlled the life within it once erected. Elsewhere in the texts, similar discrepancies appear. In the introduction to *The Winds of Time*, Gordon writes of the "class to which I unhappily belong—a class now almost extinct, and which, in a few more years, will have passed completely out of memory—namely, the Irish 'landed gentry.' . . . It can be said of us," she observes, "that we went down with our backs to the wall, which, as a matter of fact, had collapsed—as walls do in Ireland—long before its owners; holding on, in spite of gunmen and incendiaries, to our dilapidated houses and our wind-swept lands with a persistence which we find it often difficult to explain" (xii). Elizabeth Bowen also writes of the inexplicable efforts she and others of her class endured to "maintain life in a draughty barrack, in a demesne shorn of most of its other land" (1950, 198), and both women explain the feelings shared by many and expressed repeatedly in Anglo-Irish fiction. Yet Gordon's houses were built by herself and were neither dilapidated nor draughty. She explains her own life as a type, yet the details of her life contradict the type.

Gordon's explanation of her motives for writing is similarly deflating. She seeks "to place on record, for anyone likely to be interested," the existence of her class. But "whether the world, or even Ireland, will be the poorer or not for our disappearance is a question which will have to be decided by our successors. . . . I imagine their verdict will be that we were a half-baked lot and not worth preserving: a point of view with which I am inclined to agree, without being at all impressed with the superiority of their own qualifications" (1934, xii). When her explanation of autobiographical intent stands beside the explanation of the poet and eminent Yeatsian T. R. Henn, the divergence in tone is striking. He wishes, Henn writes, "to do no more than to recall a story that may throw some light on a culture that died between 1916 and 1921, a peculiar and perhaps ambivalent relationship to 'country' and to wild things, some little experience of wars, and a life that has been a happy one" (1980, 12). Henn is self-depreciating yet somber, even stately in his resignation. Like Augusta Gregory and Elizabeth Bowen, he takes Anglo-Ireland with steadfast seriousness and dignity; the derisive tone of Gordon—or of Pakenham, Powell, Everett, Leslie, or Wynne—has no place in his story.

Meeting the New World

As they record the wartime loss of fathers, brothers, sons, and friends, these women also ponder the greater freedom of speech and behavior arising out of wartime conditions. Although they may—as they often do—bewail the coming of automobiles and the weekend out, they do not mourn the decline of the authoritarian parent, formal manners, or the rigidity of class and gender roles.[9] Maud Wynne vehemently scorns any such sentiments, recalling that "as we grew up it was only to enter a world of late Victorian hypocrisy, prudery and smoke screens" (1937, 22). In a chapter titled "Somebodies and Nobodies," she mocks the old system of knowing which was which, while expressing some reservations about the present confusion. She quips, "In 1890 a Somebody had a string of grandmothers to count up," whereas in the 1930s, "it is much the same as in the underground, you can miss your station and take the Otis lift to your situation" (222). Lady Anson recalls that her mother's generation was "too helpless for words" (1932, 265), being unable to fix their own hair, dress, board a train, or even take walks alone. "Even smart people," she adds, "had extraordinarily little to do" (271). To Anita Leslie, who was only a small child during the war, the new freedom in behavior lifts the screen of pretense from what she describes as the sheer idleness, consumption, and hedonism symptomatic of her class. In place of the glorification of the "ancestral houses" where in Yeats's poem "Meditations in Time of Civil War" "life overflows without ambitious pains" and "slippered Contemplation finds his ease" (1983, 200–201), she diagnoses a fundamental unhappiness in those individuals who were discouraged by the social expectations from seeking useful occupations. Although Leslie's rebellious marriage to a Russian émigré ended soon after it began, neither she nor anyone else appears to regret the passing of the arranged marriages, inadequate education, and sexual ignorance of their mothers or the young women they once were.

Unlike the eighteenth-century Dorothea Herbert, who, like her mother, was trapped in "a falling house," modern women could respond to their circumstances with a greater range of choices. Even Hannah Lynch, born in the mid-nineteenth century and whose recollection of a wealthy girlhood near Dublin is excruciating in its lonely misery, was in later years able to live independently in France and the United States and achieve a moderately successful career as a travel writer and novelist. Despite the insecurity and in many cases isolation precipitated by the decline of Anglo-Ireland, women express not only their anxiety but also their determination to make the most of the societal upheaval they witness. Dorothea Conyers and the elderly Edith Somerville are,

9. Tracing the inversion of the Gothic theme of degenerative intermarriage in Anglo-Irish women's fiction, Margot Backus finds that women novelists see the disappearance of the family line and property as paving "the way, at least potentially, for the emergence of new, less deadening forms" (1999, 194). Her conclusions parallel the patterns of reaction I have discovered in Anglo-Irish women's autobiography.

to my knowledge, alone in concluding their memoirs with the resolute expectation that everything would return again as it once was: the hunting, the parties, and all the trappings of Anglo-Irish country life. In the preface to *"Happy Days!" Essays of Sorts* (1946), Edith Somerville cheerfully insists that the days of hunting and tea parties had returned after being merely "shadowed or hidden for a time" by World War II. But Somerville was ninety-one years old at the time of publication, and the book is overtly geared toward an American and English readership seeking tales of "rollicking Irish fun." The sentiments expressed are the consoling optimism of an elderly woman who also recognizes the expectations of her readership.

More realistically, the title of Enid Starkie's 1941 autobiography, *A Lady's Child*, underscores its argument that, by the time of composition, the title represented an anachronistic concept. Her book resonates with sadness at her beloved father's inability to find a place within an independent Ireland. W. M. J. Starkie was a fellow and tutor of classics at Trinity College but was refused a professorship, he believed, because he was a Catholic. But he was also resident commissioner of education for Ireland under British rule, and his daughter remarks that "revolution and new systems of government have subsequently swept away almost all that he achieved with so much labour, effort, and sacrifice" (11). At first marginalized because of his denominational affiliation, he was later equally marginalized by having been once an officer of the colonial government. Like Sybil Lubbock, Starkie writes her autobiography as a memorial to her father, and it is the fathers who were most profoundly disoriented by the alterations of the war and the new independent Ireland. In *A Page from the Past*, Lubbock observes of her father,

> [S]omething broke in him when Desart was burnt, something that could never be repaired, though at the time he rallied with his usual courage. Only a fortnight later he wrote in answer to a letter of sympathy from my daughter: "The wound is deep and there is no cure for it. Sometimes I think that I cannot bear it." . . . In the same letter he writes: "I feel most deeply for all those who, whether for business, honour, or profession, are tied to the miserable future of Ireland—and perhaps to some dreadful form of ruin or death. It is simply appalling to think of." (Lubbock and Desart 1936, 222–23)

The earl of Desart, like Enid Starkie's father, served as an official of the British government and had expected to end his life in the house of his boyhood, a property given to his ancestors by Cromwell as payment for their part in his invasion of Ireland. The new state completely displaced both men, but the conditions and mores of postwar Britain had already displaced their way of life.

Although daughters frequently wrote in opposition to their father's will or under his control, Starkie and Lubbock are but two examples of women who wrote autobiographies in part as testimonies to the diminished lives their fathers endured in their later years. These women rarely portray conflicts between their lives as daughters and their ambitions as writers, perhaps because their autobiographies fall so strictly within the genre of family history and not at all within the genre of the bildungsroman. Although Enid Starkie gained a considerable reputation as an interpreter of French poetry, she never mentions her later career, nor does Anita Leslie allude to her prolific work as a biographer, Elizabeth Hamilton to her religious and travel writings, or Sybil Lubbock to her poetry and short stories. In the autobiographies of this generation of women, the life story chronicles the family's role in national history; the demise of that role transformed daughters into its historian. However, the daughter of Sybil Lubbock devotes one chapter of her autobiography to her father's family in the United States and another to her mother's family in Ireland, but then drops the subject of family history or public life. Announcing that she finds "it difficult to feel much concern for these traditions" except as they affected the lives of the grandparents "whom I both knew and loved," she concerns herself with her experiences in Italy and her work there as a writer and farmer (Origo 1970, 18). Older women may also have omitted from their autobiographies professional concerns or details of their adult lives because of a conservative literary climate that still associated the tale of a woman's career with the scandalous memoirs of madams, royal mistresses, and actresses. Because the psychological analysis of their parents merges in these texts with the historical record of public families, such topics may have seemed extraneous to a species of autobiography that already mixed elements of public and personal.[10]

The historical transitions that these autobiographers document cast their fathers into tragic roles, but they also allowed women like Enid Starkie, Elizabeth Hamilton, and Lady Anson to develop what Starkie's parents called "English bad manners and blue-stocking intellectualism" (1941, 272): in other words, freedom from debutante restrictions, opportunities for education, and an identity that could develop beyond one as the tragic remnant of a declined family. The opportunity to pursue her own interests allowed Daisy Fingall to

10. Mary Jean Corbett provides further discussion of the absence of the bildungsroman among nineteenth-century women's autobiographies (1992, 56–82), and Julia Bush addresses the need to appear "the modest altruistic lady author" as it constrained early-twentieth-century autobiographies of upper-class English women (2001, 47). Of Anglo-Irish women, only Lady Gregory depicts the growth of her authorship, and perhaps only because she conceives of authorship as service.

develop a life distinct from her role as wife of the eleventh earl of Killeen and, in so doing, overcome at last her feelings of inadequacy as the mistress of one of the oldest continuously inhabited residences in Ireland. Although she devotes a chapter of *Seventy Years Young* to the history of the castle and her husband's family—"that little world of his"—nevertheless both her life and the story of her life are centered elsewhere, and most particularly on her relationship with Horace Plunkett. Houses became most important as places where she could work and where friends lived. Her deep regret at the dismantling of Carton House, for instance, focuses on the disappearance of the intimate possessions of her adored friend Hermione. She dwells with pained attention on the lost artifacts of the "small white room with a narrow bed like a girl's," the refuge for a woman who did not love her husband and was not loved by him. Similarly, her greatest pleasure at Killeen is in her tiny tower room at the top of a turret, "a fortress . . . in which no one else may enter." "Even Fingall," she adds, "could not enter my fortress" (1939, 152). This feminine space is far different from, if contained within, the more masculine space of the ancestral house. It figures as a countervention against that house, aggressive in its assertion of a distinct and gendered privacy.

Like the tower room enclosed within the massive edifice of Killeen, Daisy Fingall's autobiography reveals a tension found in nearly all: a jarring dissonance between its contents and the forms of narrative in which they are placed, even if such forms inspire the book's title, organization, or frontispiece. *Seventy Years Young* concludes long before its narrator reaches the age of seventy in a tense scene during which she and her husband wait through the night, coats and jewels in hand, for the incendiaries who are rumored to be on their way to Killeen. The two helplessly await an unknown future in a new Ireland. With such an ending, one would think the whole book had been about Killeen and that Daisy Fingall had not been herself such an active figure in nationalist politics and cultural life. *Seventy Years Young*, however, presents special difficulties for the study of relations between narrative structure and autobiographical self-presentation. Unlike the other works here examined, it is the product of a professional writer to whom Fingall orally recalled her life. We have no way of knowing how much of the composition was Fingall's and how much was Pamela Hinkson's, the daughter of Katharine Tynan and a widely published novelist and travel writer. Hinkson never wrote an autobiography with which *Seventy Years Young* might be compared, but her *Irish Gold* (1947), which combines reminiscence with travel description, is openly marketed toward English expectations and highly conventional in its Irish tableaus. It is entirely possible that the ending is more Hinkson's choice than Fingall's, particularly given that during the episode in which she and her husband await the Irish Republican

Army, she meditates with considerable relief upon the small, warm, and convenient house to which she can move after the destruction of Killeen. Here Fingall's thoughts collide with the cataclysmic conclusion that the anticipated destruction is meant to have in her narrative, thus placing her life and the expectations of the genre into obvious conflict.

A similar miscue is given in the title of Joan de Vere's memoir, *In Ruin Reconciled* (1990). Joan de Vere did write a book on the history and architecture of Curragh Chase, but despite a chapter on the history of her father's family, de Vere concentrates here on her nursing career, botanical writings, and life overseas. The fire that destroyed Curragh Chase in 1941 was apparently accidental, and the place of the house in her story, except as the dreamy locale of a solitary child, does not warrant the foregrounding of it as a ruin. Maud Wynne also ends her 1937 autobiography with the melancholy evocation of a burning house, suggesting that although politically motivated arson was at one time a genuine threat, this preoccupation may also be a literary closure device whose dramatic function is superimposed upon a life narrative with which it may be little integrated. Like procrustean beds, fictional models shape the forms of autobiography practiced by women of their class. In his study of the English country house, Richard Gill notes that several late-Victorian novelists (including Hardy and Meredith) conclude their tales of declining households with consuming fires, and Elizabeth Bowen's widely read novel *The Last September* (1929) introduced the burning Anglo-Irish country house as the focus of a dramatic final paragraph.

In what may be either another literary convention, an expression of genuine feeling, or some combination of both, a number of autobiographies also finish with the observation that the demise of the landed estate concludes a long-overdue reconfiguration of political and economic status in Ireland. These observations tend to be brief and incidental to the narrative. Joan de Vere comments regarding the sale of Curragh Chase to the Forestry Department that "history has returned to the people the land taken from them in earlier days" (1990, 107), and Alannah Heather, aghast at the "incredible conceit" of her Protestant ancestors who lived through the famine and Fenian movement "with eyes shut," reflects with satisfaction that the sale of the ancestral home near Clifden signifies "a new era has started and a large family has brought back life and happiness to what was always such a warm and friendly home" (1993, 210). When Daisy Fingall indignantly tells her son that an Irish American with "the romantic desire to possess an ancient and inconvenient Irish Castle" has offered to buy the "place where your ancestors are buried and which has been in your family for eight hundred years," her son slowly and thoughtfully replies, "Well. . . . Surely if we have had it all that time, it's somebody else's turn now" (1939, 350). The remark is left without further comment. W. J. McCormack has suggested that Anglo-Irish literature has figured class decline as a "traumatic historical process in which the House finds a moral purpose simultaneously in destroying its social position" (1992b, 41), and although this perspective may form the structural and thematic basis of fiction from Edgeworth to Trevor, it appears in Anglo-Irish women's autobiographies as a casual aside rather than the focus of the narrative.

In a discussion of the relationship between women's autobiography and reader expectations, Sidonie Smith argues, "When a woman chooses to leave behind cultural silence and to pursue autobiography, she chooses to enter the public arena. But she can speak with authority only insofar as she tells a story that her audience will read. Responding to the generic expectations of significance in life stories, she looks toward a narrative that will resonate with privileged cultural fictions of male selfhood" (1987, 52). Although Smith goes on to claim that foremost of those fictions is the self's transcendence of culture, in the case of the Anglo-Irish it has most often been that of the self's complete identification with culture and, finally, victimization by culture. To the degree that women have felt this identification and victimization, they have utilized the familiar tropes of its best-known narratives. As they have inscribed as well their stories as disinherited daughters, they have diminished or disclaimed those very tropes.

In childhood, Violet Powell knew only that "the Irish question" meant mealtime arguments during which the amusing expressions of those family members overcome with emotion led her invariably to break down in childish giggles, resulting in banishment to the nursery before the pudding course. Although it would be tempting to compare this scene with the famous dinner-table discussion of politics in *A Portrait of the Artist as a Young Man* as evidence of Anglo-Irish estrangement from Irish affairs, the parallel would be inaccurate. The elders at the table in Powell's description are far from indifferent to Irish politics; it is their passion that causes the child to react with laughter. Her comically reductive handling of the topic crafts through humor a refusal to accept the devastating effect "the Irish question" could have on a woman writing autobiography. If she fully associates her being with house and family, the autobiographical self might also become a negation were the estate to fail. Because Anglo-Irish fiction and poetry so authoritatively expressed the architectural ruin as a metaphor of the ruination of a class, Anglo-Irish women had to negotiate with this enervating version of the self. The effects of their negotiation among generic expectations, class identity, and factors of gender are manifest in the battery of strategies with which they attempt to hold back the nullifying conclusions of a narrative of decline. From their writings, the loss of the house emerges not as a source of one's displacement nor a tale conferring tragic meaningfulness, but as the disappearance of a place to be at home that was never there to begin with, forcing women to make their lives elsewhere—in purposeful work, in other houses.

3

The Unwritten Mother

*S*ome of the best-known Irish autobiographies are also biographies of a mother who, resourceful or feckless, loving or callous, remains a ballast through the turbulence of childhood. Frank O'Connor's *Only Child*, Sean O'Casey's *I Knock at the Door*, and, at the end of the twentieth century, the autobiographies of Christy Brown and Frank McCourt are but a few of the many books that present the mother as the central figure of the childhood memoir.[1] Given her preeminent role in life writings by Catholics of the lower and middle classes, the absence of the mother from Anglo-Irish autobiography is a conspicuous one. It is also a telling sign of how differently groups of people in Ireland conceived their lives and of how very divergent were the narrative models for writing those lives.

Such a major distinction in the way experience was represented reflects equally profound differences in the way people lived. In many Anglo-Irish families, boys boarded at school from a young age, and a battery of servants frequently separated both sexes from their parents. Traditional fixations on the transfer of property and patronym focused the family history on patrilineage, and an Irish Anglican upbringing lacked the theological attention and emotional attachment to the Virgin Mary that for Catholics placed a maternal figure at the heart of religious experience. Perhaps because fathers occupied positions of power, the ineffectual and emasculated, if often bullying, fathers Declan Kiberd finds ubiquitous in modern Irish literature are generally lacking in Anglo-Irish autobiographies.[2] Even when alterations in economic and

---

1. The same central mother figure also appears repeatedly in *No Shoes in Summer* (Ryan, Browne, and Gilmour 1995), an anthology of the oral and written recollections of elderly Irish men and women who did not consider themselves writers and whose memories were edited or transcribed by a group of Dublin college students in the early 1990s.

2. Kiberd claims that the emasculated father is a common feature of the literature of colonized peoples more generally (1995, 380–94). By including in his discussion an extended treat-

political life diminished the father's prominence, sons and daughters alike generally express regret and sadness at their father's displacement, rather than reproach. Despite English sentimentalization of mothers as the heart of middle-class domesticity, in Irish Protestant homes a confluence of factors discouraged attention to the mother as a figure of reverence, or even interest.

Unsurprisingly then, among autobiographers like W. B. Yeats, his critic T. R. Henn, George Moore, Lionel Fleming, Stephen Gwynn, the earl of Dunraven, Shane Leslie, and many others, the mother is a ghostly figure barely glimpsed at the circumference of the life's development. The powerful influence of John Butler Yeats or George Henry Moore pervades the autobiographies of their famous sons, but of Susan Yeats or Mary Blake Moore, we hear little. Early childhood appears to have been frequently a world without mothers, even in a less prosperous home like George Bernard Shaw's. Shaw analyzes his mother extensively apart from her maternal role, but of her relation to his childhood he writes:

> I hated the servants and liked my mother because, on the one or two rare and delightful occasions when she buttered my bread for me, she buttered it thickly instead of merely wiping a knife on it. Her almost complete neglect of me had the advantage that I could idolize her to the utmost pitch of my imagination and had no sordid or disillusioning contacts with her. It was a privilege to be taken for a walk or a visit with her, or on an excursion. (1970, 189–90)

Violet Powell remembers that she and her siblings saw their mother at breakfast and in the evening when she read aloud to them, but the world belonged to Nanny and the servants, with whom the children practiced for their occasional performances before their parents (1960, 18–21). "We saw our parents very little when we were children," Enid Starkie recalls, "and they seemed to belong to another world, a world separated from ours by a great, insurmountable China wall" (1941, 36). "When we were small we were somewhat shy of my mother . . . and we did not associate her with our everyday life, since she did not play with us or romp with us" (45).

---

ment of J. M. Synge's work as illustrative of this mentality, Kiberd introduces some unresolved problems into his argument. Synge belonged to the colonizing class rather than its opposite, and although his father died a year after Synge's birth, his traditions were patriarchal and his older brother Edward functioned as a representative of landlord power. His plays depict the generally successful struggle of a young and unempowered man against some masculine figure of authority, but these plots more likely enact his rebellion against the power of masculine authority rather than his sense of its absence.

This elision of the mother—from the life, the autobiography, or both—appears to have been characteristic of most European families of at least middle-class status, as Richard Coe observes in his study of childhood autobiographies, *When the Grass Was Taller* (1984). Nearly all the works he studies are authored by men, and although Coe does not analyze his data in terms of gender or class, the portraits of mothers as passive ciphers correspond to similar representations in the autobiographies of Anglo-Irish men. Those mothers and daughters who wrote their lives—in particular, Augusta Gregory, Enid Starkie, and Elizabeth Bowen—struggle with the difficulties of representing the maternal. Despite the textual repression of mother and daughter relations attributable to inherited ways of seeing and writing the self, a number of women attempt to explore the role of mothers in their life writings.

Private and Public Representation

Women's autobiographies would presumably offer a fuller consideration of the relation between mother and child. Well-off girls were in many cases educated at home and had closer contact with their mothers than did boys. However, fewer writing daughters discuss their mothers and fewer writing mothers discuss their children than in our own time, when life narratives so often derive their structure and subject matter from the Freudian family romance. Although maternal imagery was ubiquitous—even obsessively so—in public discourse throughout the second half of the nineteenth century, the life writing of middle- and upper-class women contained little space for maternal representation except in the species of writing that has become known as the domestic memoir. In her pioneering history of such life writings, Linda Peterson argues that publishers in Victorian England resurrected the early modern family chronicle so as to reinforce specific domestic values. To be acceptable to publishers and a reading public, life writings—including diaries and letters as well as formal autobiographies—needed to relay, in the words of the editor of Lady Ann Fanshawe's 1828 *Memoirs*, "instances of conjugal devotion, of maternal excellence, and of enduring fortitude under calamities" (Peterson 1999, 23). Although a vehicle for writing about domestic experience thus existed in English tradition by the mid-nineteenth century, the terms for writing about one's family were so sentimentally circumscribed that they did not allow for the greater realism sought by later writers. And because the family histories produced by Anglo-Irish women after the 1890s are so often damning of the family as an archaic and repressive colonial vestige, the mode of domestic representation made possible in Victorian England was thoroughly incongruous with the needs of these writers.[3]

In contrast, Victorian working-class women, at least those English representatives whose views have been recorded and analyzed, speak more frankly and with less prescribed sentiment about their lives as mothers or daughters and their experiences of birthing and child rearing. Their interlocutors in all likelihood saw them less as individuals entitled to the bourgeois luxury of privacy and more as representatives of their class; accordingly, they were asked (and they answered) pointed questions about their travails as mothers and daughters within an economic and gender hierarchy that threatened their health, their prospects, and in some cases their lives. Working-class mothers express satisfaction simply that their children survived; daughters are effusive in their gratitude toward the mother who protected them against poverty and frequently abusive fathers and brothers. Many of the poor women who were interviewed or wrote frankly about their birth experiences transgressed social etiquette regarding the privacy of the body in order to effect a change in conditions for women. Those women with higher-class status who collected stories from working-class women about their experiences as birth mothers, laborers, or prostitutes crossed through boundaries of silence, even if it must be acknowledged that they asked poor women questions they would have been unlikely to ask their neighbors or answer themselves.[4] The very physicality of the relationship between a mother and her infant must account in part for the silence on the subject of birth and early childhood among women of more privileged classes. Even for women who did not nurse their infants and who employed servants to clean and dress them, mother and child relations originate in sensory experience. Gestation, birth, and the contact of flesh between

3. Linda Peterson (1999) draws a distinction between the family memoir of the early modern period, in which upper-class women recorded the public lives of their families, and the Victorian domestic memoir's myopic concentration on the details of wifely duty and maternal tenderness. In the work of writers like Joan de Vere, Elizabeth Fingall, Katherine Everett, and Sybil Lubbock, public and domestic lives merge as each relates her parents' stories to the narrative of cultural decline. Missing from their life writing, however, is much mention of their own lives as mothers, although presumably the historical transition that forms the basis of their narrative plot structures would have also affected their maternal experiences.

4. See the oral and written autobiographies of English working-class women in Gagnier 1991, Rendall 1997, Roberts 1984, and Ross 1993. Gagnier notes that as women moved toward middle-class status, they were cut off from traditional sources of information about their bodies and the birth process. Upward mobility was accompanied by a "conspiracy of silence, even between mother and daughter . . . adopted from middle-class respectability, in which, however, it was a mark of status rather than ignorance" (61).

mother and child constitute a language of the body rarely articulated in British and Irish life writing during the late nineteenth and early twentieth centuries except in personal diaries never intended for publication and working-class testimony published for reformist purposes.[5]

The line between private and public experience varies among cultures and fluctuates over time; even within a single culture and a relatively short time period, notions of what a well-brought-up woman may say or not say about the body in public, or even in private, differ depending upon the mode of discourse through which experience is represented. Such a consequential event as the forced separation of a mother and her infant secures little attention in these life writings, despite functioning as a dominant motif of English popular melodrama, war propaganda, and arguments for changes in the law or in health, housing, or labor conditions. The autobiography of Joan de Vere, for example, barely acknowledges the abandonment that must have decisively shaped her character. Deserted in infancy and kept ignorant of her origins, she was first known only as "the Castle baby" (1990, 5). The de Veres of Curragh Chase, who adopted her in infancy, left her in the care of nursemaids while they lived abroad for long periods in the colonial service. Despite her deep attachment to the de Vere home, about which she wrote *The Abiding Enchantment of Curragh Chase* (Jones 1983), she was prohibited from inheriting it. Even without this information, a contemporary reader might find oddly undeveloped de Vere's brief comment concerning her acquiescence to her husband's wishes that she join him in Africa during the fall of 1937, leaving their infant of six months with her mother in County Limerick: "To ask any mother to be parted from the child that she has been breast-feeding and watching develop goes against the most fundamental instincts, but nevertheless I took off, this time by the *Elder Dempster* from Liverpool. . . . There was plenty of time to get to know fellow passengers, many of them young wives who had also left children behind" (1990, 101). The outrage of "the most fundamental instincts" is undermined by the terse "nevertheless," and the reader is left to imagine the unspoken. In that she mentions the issue at all, her remark signifies change, however slight, in the boundaries between private and public.

Joan de Vere was born in 1913 and completed her autobiography shortly

---

5. Cynthia Huff's survey (1985) of fifty-eight English women's manuscript diaries indicates that women recorded in their diaries the time and method of birth, as well as fear of death or contracting an infection, and relief when the dreaded possibilities did not occur. They also note nursing difficulties and children's weights and measures as part of a wider tradition of keeping records of family illnesses. According to Huff, female relatives regularly read one another's childbirth entries.

before her death in 1989. Augusta Gregory lived and worked in a much more conservative milieu and writes nothing at all about having been taken by her husband, apparently against her wishes, on protracted tours of Europe and the Middle East beginning just two months after the birth of her only child. Her later diaries express her anguish at Robert's removal to a boarding school at the age of nine, her happiness at his return, and her intimate knowledge of his interests, pets, and games. But neither her autobiography nor the diaries she prepared for publication address what her husband's letters and a few despairing comments in her journal suggest was a difficult separation (Jenkins 1986, 264–66). Many other Anglo-Irish autobiographers were also mothers, but none discuss birth, only a handful mention nursing or the physical care of children, and few write at all about their children during infancy and early childhood, the period when an intimacy unavailable through conversation or shared activities might have formed through physical proximity.

While taboos against expressing the sensory intimacies of mother and child worked against their exploration in autobiographical writing, so did nineteenth-century narrative models.[6] Valerie Sanders has hypothesized that literary women infrequently discussed their mothers or children because "the female moment" was less significant to these women writers than the discovery of their vocations (1989, 21). Similarly, Mary Jean Corbett argues that the increasing fusion of personal and professional identity during the second half of the nineteenth century shaped the form and subject matter of autobiography so as to privilege professional experience over the domestic and to render the discovery of vocation as the primary autobiographical trope (1992, 17–55). As Corbett explains, readers at the end of the century became more interested in British women's domestic memoirs as documents in the history of the larger national life, but this shift did little to encourage the literary exploration of

6. Although Anglo-Irish women's autobiographies almost never depict the close physical contact of mother and child, such physical intimacy was a frequent feature of advertisements and numerous late-nineteenth- and early-twentieth-century photographic portraits of upper-class English women, particularly those pictures taken by female photographers such as Alice Hughes and Imogen Cunningham. Describing, for example, a 1904 photograph of Pamela, Countess Lytton, with her son Antony, art historian Anne Higonnet observes, "His mother smiles at his naked, wriggling warmth, holding him gently and proudly, enjoying the touch of his little hand on her bare shoulder. . . . [N]othing about the subject is out of the ordinary." According to Higonnet, "A mother's pleasure in her child's body was a standard feature of photographic portraiture at the highest echelons of society" (1998, 129). In Molly Keane's novel *Good Behaviour*, the cold and self-absorbed Lady Grizel displays on her dressing table portraits of her infant sons as "lush cherubs with folds of muslin dropping off eatable shoulders" (1981, 39), suggesting that in Keane's memory such portraiture bore little relation to genuine affection for children.

more exclusively feminine concerns such as birth or the nurturing of young children (98). Such writing mothers as Nicollete Devas, Katherine Everett, Daisy Fingall, and Alannah Heather address their work, family histories, and their family's place in the national history, but they mention their children only incidentally and then only after they have grown to adulthood.

While the discourse of motherhood appears to have been perceived as inferior to the story of vocation and unrelated to the larger historical events in which lives were most frequently cast, domestic conversation was also frowned upon in fashionable circles as a topic of discussion through the middle of the twentieth century. Anita Leslie re-creates in *The Gilt and the Gingerbread* the exasperation with which the London society of the 1920s received her flamboyant American "mama's" tales of her children's behavior: "money, servants, illness and children," she observes, "were considered conversational anathema" (1981, 24). Professionally, Leslie found a gold mine in family intimacies, writing numerous biographies of her famous relatives, including the best-selling *Jennie: The Life of Lady Randolph Churchill* (1969) and *Edwardians in Love* (1974). However, these familial revelations are in keeping with the generic features of the celebrity autobiography and biography popular in the late nineteenth century, and her discussions of domestic life are more concerned with sexual peccadilloes than the association of mother and child.[7] In her own autobiography, Anita Leslie represents her relationship with her mother through a sardonic reductionism that disguises its emotional complexity. She never writes of family matters except with a tone of cool detachment. In Elizabeth Bowen's novel *The Last September*, Lady Naylor's acid pronouncement on an English woman's "tendency, common to most English people, to talk about her inside" suggests that conversational self-reflection was itself antithetical to notions of good behavior (1983, 46). W. B. Yeats recalls his mother's similar disgust at the "lack of reserve" shown by the English in displays of affection, and another relative's dissatisfaction with a man who " 'Englishman-like' told him all his affairs" (1965, 21). Whether maternal experience was perceived as excessively dull or excessively private, the attention to which Anglo-Irish autobiographers gave this important feature of women's lives was severely limited.

Nevertheless, a careful reading of Anglo-Irish women's life writings reveals that maternal absence—an absence from the life, from the life story, or from both—constitutes a crucial, if most often repressed, plotline within the patrilineal narrative of familial and class decline that most commonly forms the autobiography's main thrust. Jo Malin has argued in *The Voice of the Mother*

---

7. For the history of life writing by female celebrities, see the fourth chapter of Corbett 1992 and Peterson 1999 (27–42, 146–72).

(2000) that women's autobiographies across cultures often embed a conversation of some kind with the mother and, even more frequently, a mother who has become inaccessible through abandonment or death. Numerous psychoanalytical readings of women's narratives have sought to explain the origins of what Bella Brodzki calls "motherlack" through Lacanian theories of mother-infant relations (1988, 246).[8] With the exception of Elizabeth Bowen, none of the writers here under discussion suffered the early deaths of their mothers, nor were they abandoned. But none lived with their mothers in quite the intimate exile that Bowen experienced during the later years of her childhood. As one who experienced both presence and absence at their uttermost, Bowen most fully writes what I have called the "unwritten" maternal narrative. Yet the story of the mother hovers at the edges even of those texts that suppress it. Class and culture separated mothers and daughters, and demarcations between private and public discourse and generic models of life writing forestalled discussion of the maternal experience in autobiography. But a cognizance of both absences—from life and from writing—produces a text counter to the autobiography's announced concern with such familiar topics as family history and class decline, love of place, or the quest for a profession and public voice.

The Unwritten Mother: The Letters and Diaries of Augusta Gregory

That many women did write about their mothers and their children in their letters and diaries suggests that their relative silence on the topic in their formal autobiographies has little to do with ambivalence as to whether the maternal lies within the realm of language. It speaks more of their doubts as to whether one's experience as a mother or daughter was a topic sanctioned for public usage. For much of women's experience, the "formal modes of autobiography," as Valerie Sanders argues, "were alien and inappropriate." As a result, women sought other genres of life writing to represent their domestic lives.[9] Thus, Sanders continues, "women are found pushing the retrospective

---

8. Overviews of Lacan's writings on the mother-child relations are available in most recent writings on the subject, as well as in feminist revisions of Lacan. A particularly useful critical review is offered in the first chapter of Homans 1986.

9. Some readers of women's diaries have claimed that in its "resistance to wholeness, unity and formal closure," focus on detail, relative privacy, and lack of structural or thematic hierarchy, the diary is the form of women's writing most reflective of women's experience. For a review of such arguments, see Hogan 1991 (95–107).

impulse to one side of their writing lives: concealing it in travel memoirs, disguising it in autobiographical fiction, releasing fragmented memories into manuals or essays that profess to be about Shakespeare or household management, confining themselves to the private and short-term retrospect of diaries and letters, weaving together their more public letters into 'recollections,' mostly of other people" (1989, 19).

Letters and diaries were frequently shared by family members and even read aloud, but because their assumed audience was predominantly an intimate and female one, the experience of mothering or being mothered could enter into their pages. In the case of one of Anglo-Ireland's most famous writers, the personal diary and the subterfuge of fiction and drama provided the only genres in which she could express her feelings and thoughts about being a mother and about her own mother. In the midst of a carefully maintained silence, the emotional depths of her experience are disclosed solely by the intensity of those infrequent eruptions of maternal happiness or agony. The small number of personal remarks regarding Robert Gregory in *Seventy Years* and in Lady Gregory's other writings intended for publication belies the powerful feelings that could not be articulated by the public figure with whom her identity had become synonymous to a readership. But from the formal autobiography to diaries transcribed by her for publication or posthumous scrutiny, to letters and diary entries intended only for the eyes of close friends or family, and to those fragmented jottings kept private but not destroyed, the inscription of maternal emotion gains force as the projected audience narrows. Additionally, its nature changes from an utterance that sustains patriarchal models of female service to one uttered in defiance of such controls.

Seventy Years, Augusta Gregory's only attempt at a full-length retrospective autobiography, proved a disappointment to her and her friends. According to Yeats, she felt the document to be "formless," and her late diaries expose her flagging interest in the work beyond its potential as a historical record and source of income. Yeats was himself dismissive of both its contemporary interest and literary quality (L. A. Gregory 1978, 2:639–60). Ill and in need of money, she quickly compiled the book in a cut-and-paste fashion from diary entries and scrapbook clippings. Rejected by her publisher, the typescript rested forgotten among the family papers until Colin Smythe edited and brought it forth in 1973 as part of the Coole Edition.

The circumstances under which a work is produced, however, are not the only determinants of its eventual success or lack of success. Numerous constraints resulted in an autobiography that is little more than a collection of historical documents cautiously selected to protect the privacy of their subject. As others have observed, she deflected her private experiences into literature, so that the growth of her authorship is told in the guise of a theater history, while her feelings about sexuality, motherhood, and her struggle with breast cancer surface indirectly in various poems, plays, and stories.[10] Although Lady Gregory worked at *Seventy Years* throughout the late 1920s, it more resembles mid-Victorian women's autobiographies than other life writings of the modernist era, particularly in her often strained attempts to represent family life within an ethic of privacy that disallowed such discussion.

When she poured over her diaries, collecting accounts of her life's events for inclusion in *Seventy Years*, she chose not to select and retype the most intimate reflections on her son's boyhood nor on his death. The chapter concerning her son's death in World War I, "My Grief," consists of the testimonials of others, of all classes, as to how well he played the role of an Anglo-Irish gentleman. As throughout her writings intended or revised for publication, Lady Gregory represents the positions of mother and son as the fulfillment of class and nationalist functions. The "soldier, scholar, horseman" of W. B. Yeats's elegy "In Memory of Major Robert Gregory" is less a private individual than the emblem of a specific ideology more important to the poet and his mother than to Robert Gregory himself, and when Augusta Gregory emphasizes her son's role as a gentleman in "My Grief," she defines the term through her own ideals of social duty. The voices she gathers in the chapter repeatedly point to his graciousness as a beneficent landlord and publicly minded citizen, although Gregory himself found such positions antipathetic to his own interests in art and stage design and his preference for a residence in England or France. As John Kelly observes, Augusta Gregory differs from Yeats in elegizing her son's character rather than his actions and brings to her memorial chapter witnesses to his kindness and mild manner (1987, 235–45). But the remote, unsettled man who never quite found his place or his profession and who allegedly told Bernard Shaw that his half year in the air force—away from his family and his duties—was the happiest period of his thirty-six years fails to appear on the pages of *Seventy Years*. Shaw remarks that he thought it "an amazing thing to say considering his exceptionally fortunate circumstances at home; but evidently he meant it" (L. A. Gregory 1973, 558). Lady Gregory places even

---

10. Lucy McDiarmid (1996) discusses the sublimation of the erotic into poems and *The Gaol Gate*, as well as the transference of anxieties over motherhood and the horror of breast cancer into *The Story Brought by Brigit*; in her 2001 book on Irish women's autobiographies, Taura Napier treats "An Emigrant's Notebook" as autobiography; and James Pethica (1987) interprets Gregory's poems and the 1894 short story "Dies Irae" as explorations of the affair with Wilfred Blunt and fear of losing Robert's love. Pethica also sees traces of tensions about both motherhood and her experiences as a daughter in "A Phantom's Pilgrimage" and "An Emigrant's Notebook" (L. A. Gregory 1996).

Shaw's tactless condolence letter containing this revelation in the context of other comments praising Robert's unselfishness as an officer and the esteem in which soldiers of various ranks held him. The alienation implicit in Shaw's anecdote seems to have escaped her notice, and by situating his letter among other very different recollections she alters its apparent meaning to suit the virtues she wishes to assign to her son.

This insistence that Robert Gregory fill an inherited place within a disinherited and archaic social order colludes with her own self-representation as a matriarch of her nation. In some ways, Augusta Gregory understood and even welcomed the democracy that brought with it a diminished role for her class (1978, 1:610–11). She wrote in 1897, "It is necessary that as democracy gains power, our power should go; and God knows many of our ancestors and forerunners have eaten sour grapes and we must not repine if our teeth are set on edge. I would like to leave a good memory and not 'a monument of champagne bottles' " (1973, 284). But she continued to believe in the ongoing national significance of her husband's family and her son and grandson. Their "good memory," she repeatedly asserts, is one of selfless national service inspired by "the woods and solitudes that have been loved by all of these," an inheritance of character and property without which "the country would be poorer" (1978, 1:283).

She never mentions her granddaughter Anne within such a context, and the omission underscores just how much she saw the family heritage of service as bound up with the passing on of family property. Her granddaughter's genial memoir, Me and Nu, relates with some amusement that Augustus John had been commissioned to paint a portrait of her brother but had found Anne the more interesting subject: "Grandma," Anne remembers, "had insisted on the son of the house being painted and she was paying" (1970, 47). A strange and apparently unflattering portrait resulted from this battle of wills. Much as Lady Gregory constructed her memoir of her son's life and death to fit a predetermined class narrative, she placed the painting exactly where it had been meant to go, despite its oddity. Until Coole was sold, it was prominently displayed in the drawing room.

Anne may have been a mere female grandchild, but as the wife, mother, and grandmother, Lady Gregory saw herself as one who must protect the inheritance for the remaining male heir and, by extension, for the nation. In Seventy Years and other journal entries that she typed or had typed with a view toward publication, she writes often of her efforts to save Coole both for her son and grandson and for Ireland, thus merging the notions of familial and national inheritance while merging her position as a mother with the position of cultural godmother. Some of her contemporaries ridiculed such self-representation, as does Abbey actress Marie nic Shiubhlaigh, who maliciously points out a resemblance in both manner and appearance between Lady Gregory and Queen Victoria (1987, 24). Yet to do so is to underestimate how difficult it was for many women of Augusta Gregory's generation to know just how to be both a mother and a public figure in the eyes of their colleagues and their audience. They carried the burden of reconciling two worlds many people found irreconcilable.

During the most significant years of her career as a playwright and theater manager, the glorification of motherhood that dominated nineteenth-century popular culture deviated toward an open repugnance among contemporary male artists. If the mid-Victorian woman writer composed at peril to her sanctified vocation as a mother, the early-twentieth-century woman's writing was mocked as a form of reproduction as bestial as childbirth. As Elaine Showalter has demonstrated at length in *Sexual Anarchy: Gender and Culture at the Fin-de-Siècle*, at the turn of the century the "celibate male creative generation was valorized, and female powers of creation and reproduction were denigrated" (1990, 78). The derisive mockery in Marie nic Shiubhlaigh's remembrance of Lady Gregory "presiding maternally" over theater suppers and addressing the players "rather as children in need of special advice" (1987, 24) comes out even more sharply in George Moore's verbal caricature of her as a reproductive animal who "delivers herself, and very easily, of her own plays and stories" (1985, 52). As others conflated her writing and her motherhood in ways that diminished both, her own synthesis of nationalist, class, artistic, and maternal identities seeks to maintain the integrity of each. Some may have laughed at her public persona of cultural dowager and literary midwife, but such criticisms were the result of conflicting and generally negative images of mothers, older women, women of the landed classes, and above all a woman who dared to author plays and manage one of the most important and influential theatrical companies of the twentieth century.

In speaking solely from this public persona, Lady Gregory closely patterns her autobiography after the narrative models for female literary autobiography predominant in the mid-nineteenth century. Valerie Sanders explains the dilemma faced by women of Augusta Gregory's generation: what could a women write about when "too much attention to her professional life . . . would make the author look conceited, while too much attention to her private life would violate the sacred notions of decency" (1989, 76)? As if to counteract negative judgments, Lady Gregory places both the story of her emerging authorship and her domestic story within a broader narrative of a life of public service, a role compatible with notions of female service to the nation as a fatherland and to the working classes as children.[11] Borrowing George Eliot's eloquent phrasing, Sanders observes of Victorian women autobiographers, as she might well have observed of Augusta Gregory: "The few who attempted anything approaching a serious analysis of their lives, faced a web of conflicting impulses and rival claims that silenced any real revelation of professional or personal feeling. All the critic can conclude with any certainty is that in the voice of the subtext speaks the roar that lies on the other side of silence" (100).

That roar becomes more audible when Lady Gregory seems less conscious of a public readership, but even when writing entries in a diary, she is rarely as expressive as in her poems and plays. For women of Augusta Gregory's age, diary writing was not necessarily a private act. Both sexes were encouraged to keep diaries as an aid to the development of moral character and a means of recording family history; diaries were read by or to family members (usually, although not exclusively, female), and many diaries were published. In place of the confessional and often titillating diaries popular in the 1700s, diaries in the second half of the nineteenth century draw extensively on models of writing from more public genres such as travel literature, moral and religious tracts, and historical records of public events. Diary writing as practiced by Queen Victoria, whose diaries were widely read and wildly popular, established a narrative persona who was, as Cynthia Huff concludes, "neither distinctly public or private, covert or revealed, but rather both at once, an amalgam of domestic and political interests" (1988, 46).[12]

Much of what Augusta Gregory wrote in her diaries is governed by the same ideological concerns that shape *Seventy Years*. This socially constructed voice was for many years understood as an unmediated representation of Lady Gregory's thoughts and feelings, leading some to assume she lacked maternal emotion. Mary Lou Kohfeldt, for example, contends in her biography that Lady Gregory cared little for her son because she wrote little about him during his infancy and demonstrated "an inability to call him anything but 'Baby' for the first several years of his life" (1985, 55). But the letters of both parents

---

11. See works cited above, as well as Lucy McDiarmid and Maureen Waters's introduction to Gregory's *Selected Writings* (McDiarmid and Waters 1995).

12. Such generalizations invite the enumeration of exceptions, and some works demonstrate an oscillation between modes so drastic as to be of its own psychological and literary interest. Although never intended for publication, the 1791–1795 diaries of Wolfe Tone's friend and fellow revolutionist Thomas Russell provide an example. Their entries move quickly between observations on the growth of potatoes, the nature of revolution, and detailed descriptions of his alcoholic and sexual adventures; interspersed in a single diary entry, for instance, are sketches of unusual coins, a small essay on women's rights, and a drawing of an erect penis (see Russell 1991).

demonstrate that they also referred to him as "Babba" and "Mr. Babba" during his infancy, suggesting that "Baby" was but another affectionate nickname. The paucity of written observations on her baby reveals less about any lack of emotion than about the discursive restraints under which middle-class men and women of Lady Gregory's generation lived.

Unlike *Seventy Years*, however, Lady Gregory's extensive diaries record in detail the games she played with her son, the names of his various pets, his love of specific dogs and pigs, his delight in the woods around Coole, his drawings, and his other interests. These entries provide a striking contrast with her husband's letters, which refer exclusively to Robert's scholastic achievements and Sir William's relief that "Sir H. [Henry Layard] will be pleased with his godson, that he is not a noodle" (L. A. Gregory Papers, box 46). The vocabulary of his mother's descriptions is tender: Robert is a "dear little mannekin" and "my dear little son." After relating how Robert, nine years old and frightened at the prospect of his imminent departure to a boarding school, clung to her for comfort at bedtime, she suddenly breaks off after a double dash, "Oh, my child," and does not write again until the following evening (ibid.). Some of Lady Gregory's thoughts about Robert are included in letters to her former lover and longtime friend, the Land-Leaguer and poet Wilfred Scaven Blunt, and to her friend Lady Layard who, like herself, had married a much older man. Given very specific and sympathetic audiences who were in many ways positioned against her husband ideologically and emotionally, her maternal experience could find language and voice.

But perhaps the strongest testimony that her feelings about Robert were fuller and more complicated than anyone could have imagined speaks out of a scrap of self-reflection she copied in 1925 from a diary entry of seven years before. In May 1918, soon after he was shot down over the Italian front, she writes this most startling sentence: "With all the anguish of Robert's death I have lost my one great fear of losing his affection. Now there is nothing that could hurt me so much to dread" (1978, 1:571). As a confession of a life's experience of intense love wrought with anxiety, it is all we have to indicate the years of worry and longing, the years of self-negation and restraint.

Lady Gregory's most revelatory writing about her son appears in such fragments, and they expose a woman much different from the perennial dignified widow, charitable lady, and director of the Abbey Theater. These bits and pieces of letters and diaries express her anguish at sending him away to school at a young age and demonstrate her sympathetic understanding of his boyish tastes and inclinations. They do so in a style much unlike her published works: elliptical, broken with double dashes and exclamation points, emotive, and often concerned with the need to keep all feelings secret, even from her husband. As Robert readies to leave for school in his ninth year, she writes in her diary:

> [W]hen the bell rang, and gave my last kiss and they got in, my heart failed and though I kept my veil down tears kept rolling down beneath, so that I could not take a last look at my child as the train went off. I had already a racking headache which suppressed sobs made more acute. . . . Home with a heavy heart, missing the bright head at the window and quick hand at the door. I got off dining with the Gearys, but went to Lady Osborn's box at the Opera "Faust" where I sat quietly at the back and listened to the music—but all seemed dull and sad. (L. A. Gregory Papers, box 46)

Or later, at his return three months later:

> To Gort to meet Robert! . . . He has grown, but his little fair face is not changed. We went all round to see his pig Hampden and his garden and cricket ground—and then I made him take a nap—and when he woke . . . they played cricket—*I* being called in to join the game. . . . And so he went to bed sleepy and happy—but no one can know how happy *I* am! (ibid.)

No one could know. This is a language unwritten in the autobiographical genre, conceived until recently as an aesthetically crafted representation of a unified self. Here, self is dispersed among multiple texts and multiple readerships; the maternal self remains the most secret, to be spoken only in diaries or in correspondence to a few selected friends.

Readers of autobiography should never confuse the textual absence of mothers or children with an absence of thought and feeling on the part of the writer. Rather, the absence of a clear statement of maternal consciousness is better understood as an evocative counterpoint to the few moments of its articulation. Textual silence can also indicate an effort to control regret or grief at the absence of maternal care. The reminiscences and letters Augusta Gregory prepared for publication, for example, contain next to nothing about her mother. In contrast with the detailing of Robert's childhood in her private writings, she says very little about her own childhood in *Seventy Years*. Comparisons of the last draft with earlier drafts indicate that Lady Gregory abbreviated the portrait of her mother in what appears to have been an effort to disguise the bitterness with which she wrote the section on her life at Roxborough. But among the material surviving that severe editing is the book's opening scene in which the infant Augusta nearly dies of neglect, having been shunted at birth by a mother interested only in male offspring. In a passage in her diary commemorating her son's fifteenth birthday she also observes that "my first real recollections of myself" did not begin until the age of fifteen (1996, 114). It would appear that as she wrote little about her mother because the memories were too harsh, she also wrote little about herself as a young person because her sense of self did not emerge until she had gained some measure of emotional and intellectual separation.

In an April 11, 1896, diary entry, Lady Gregory attempts a reconciliatory reminiscence by imagining her mother through eyes other than those of a daughter. Reflecting on her mother's recent death, she muses, "It is strange to think of her long life being over—I can hardly say it was a very happy one—An only daughter, an heiress, she married at 17 a man with 3 children. . . . He seems to have treated her, to the end of his life, much as a spoiled child—doing as he liked in gr [sic] things—& giving her a dress or paying her compliments to pacify her" (1996, 111). Continuing in this sympathetic vein, she relates her father's many foolish actions and his demeaning attitude, but the diary entry soon falls away in discussion of her mother's triviality and bigoted religious fanaticism, then trails off completely. She does not write again until May, remarking only that "another interest" kept her from finishing the meditation on her mother begun the prior month. For Lady Gregory, the best response to her ambivalent feelings toward a mother she pitied but could never quite forgive was apparently one of studied neglect. In the case of Enid Starkie, another Anglo-Irish woman of another generation, those feelings come to the forefront of an autobiography pointedly titled *A Lady's Child*.

"Matrophobia": Enid Starkie's *Lady's Child*

The expectations of a later era force less of a discursive gap between the Anglo-Irish woman's domestic sphere and public voice, and Enid Starkie, born some fifty years after Lady Gregory and publishing her autobiography *A Lady's Child* in 1941, dramatizes and analyzes the gulf between her and her mother rather than implying it by elliptical silence. Her approach resembles neither the comical family gossip offered by Violet Powell and Anita Leslie nor the self-effacing record of regional, family, or political history that constitutes most life writing by Anglo-Irish women. Nor does it foreshadow the childhood memoirs of Elizabeth Bowen, which, like Samuel Beckett's, are deeply personal in their evocation of the child's impressionistic consciousness but elide factual information about the familial world surrounding the child. With the possible exception of W. B. Yeats, Hannah Lynch, and Katherine Everett, no other Anglo-Irish autobiographer is quite so willing to "talk about her inside" in relation to her parents. By revealing the inner life of her family, Starkie exposed herself to criticism Yeats, Lynch, and Everett had avoided by various means.

Yeats had already cast his family into public and symbolic roles through his poetry by the time his prose autobiographies appeared; readers were accustomed
to interpreting the biographical figures in his work as players in a comedy or
tragedy of national and even metaphysical proportions. Hannah Lynch moved
to the United States before publishing her 1899 record of a childhood shadowed by a violent, irrational mother whose abuses went unchecked by her passive husband; Katherine Everett, whose 1949 autobiography *Bricks and Flowers*
appeared in the same decade as *A Lady's Child*, mutes the pain of her troubled
upbringing through her tone of world-weary flippancy.

In its indictment of the ideology by which her parents lived, *A Lady's Child*
perhaps most resembles *Father and Son*, the 1907 autobiography of the English
critic Edmund Gosse. Both writers alternately denounce and pity their parents, communicating the anguish of what would appear to outsiders to have
been a placid, privileged childhood, while recognizing that much of their anguish ensued from their parents' incapacity to understand or adapt to the demands of a new period of history. Like Gosse's father, who in his son's eyes
wasted his career attempting to reconcile his biblical literalism with modern
science, Starkie's parents lived by codes of class and gender behavior that could
not survive the changes brought on by the First World War and the Irish revolution. Explaining in the 1939 preface to *A Lady's Child* her purposes for publishing an autobiography, she writes, "I do not know what changes this second
war may bring to Ireland, the country of my birth, but I know that the establishment of the Free State completely metamorphosed the Ireland in which I
was born and in which I spent my childhood. It is that Ireland which I would
like to fix on paper before it has faded from my mind" (1941, 11). Starkie believed, as did Gosse, that the autobiographer should trace the transformation
of history, as well as an individual life.

Just as *Father and Son* powerfully conveys both a specific historical moment and its effect on one boy's psychology, so *A Lady's Child* explores the effects of Anglo-Irish mores on the mental and emotional life of one girl. Few
reviewers understood that her book was both historical and personal. *Life and
Letters of To-Day* declares that "the title of the book . . . is misleading. . . . Her
difficulties were not social, they were psychological, and cry for the help of a
psychoanalyst on every page" (Spalding 1942, 142). Elizabeth Bowen, however, understands that what she deems Starkie's "ruthless but brilliant" autobiography could not be shrugged away as the product of a neurotic
temperament. Commenting in the *Tattler and Bystander*, she writes,

> Absence of spontaneous feeling . . . between parents and children, emotional
> starvation of the children and the consequent warping of their characters, the

queering of friendships formed outside an approved circle and an inhibiting, frigid self-consciousness are shown . . . to beset the upper middle class home. To offset this, nice manners, correct education, the flattery of adoring family servants and pre-views of dinner tables beautifully set for parties do certainly not, for the children, seem to go very far. (1941, 308, 310)

Enid Starkie, Bowen realizes, captures the world of early-twentieth-century Anglo-Ireland while she delineates the effect of that world on the nuclear family and the character of those children who are shaped, and sometimes distorted, by its imprint.

Starkie was able to produce such an unusually penetrating study of a young girl's psyche because of several factors that distinguished her from other Anglo-Irish autobiographers. She was interested in Freudian analysis and considered being analyzed; her voluminous correspondence demonstrates an insatiable craving for self-exploration and rooting out the causes of her failure to secure enduring love and companionship. Her research as a fellow and tutor of French literature at Oxford concerned those late-nineteenth-century writers who sought to replicate the manner and content of the psyche in a more direct way than had been realized before, and her biographical criticism of Baudelaire, Rimbaud, Flaubert, and Gide explored a level of psychosexual complexity rarely before discussed by any academic, let alone a woman. The very subject of her professional life gave her narrative models for the exploration of her own upbringing and psychology.

Most of the Anglo-Irish who hung on to their depleted identity in Ireland or as émigrés in England were not readers of Rimbaud or Proust, whose method of recollection she compares to her own. Predictably, her family was offended by *A Lady's Child*, and the *Dublin Magazine* disapproved of it as "bitter and ill-tempered" (Review of *A Lady's Child* 1942a, 64). A brief, unsigned notice in the *Irish Times* declares that "most Dubliners will dismiss the book as an unpardonable piece of disloyalty" (Review of *A Lady's Child* 1941, 5). More sophisticated readers were riveted. Although it was not advertised in Ireland and booksellers sold it under the counter in Dublin, people went to great lengths to procure a copy. Anglo-Irish writers from Bowen to Joseph Hone and Shane Leslie found it, in Leslie's words, a powerful "revelation of the Irish life that we all lived in" (Richardson 1973, 135). The book was frowned on publicly, but it was devoured privately and quickly went into a second printing.

An anonymous review in the *Listner* acknowledges that "if we judge *A Lady's Child* by the standards of more conventional memoirs, we may well find it a shocking and painful book" (Review of *A Lady's Child* 1942b, 121). But by the early 1940s, many English women's autobiographies had already opened the doors on family life as part of a more exhaustive critique of the politics of their parents' generation. The same reviewer was able to grasp that the motives of such a book could be more than mere egotism or malice. "It becomes quite clear," the reviewer continues, "that Miss Starkie is doing this not to hurt, not to pay off old scores, nor to look clever herself, but to lift a burden at last from her shoulders by putting it, as exactly as possible, into words. The burden was family life" (121–22). In England, women writers of Starkie's age had left a legacy of writings that openly criticizes the patriarchal families from which they came, along with the nationalistic and capitalist ideologies they believed to be replicated and reinforced by the family structure. The writings of the pioneering generation of women with whom Starkie attended Somerville College during and directly following the First World War—Vera Brittain, Winifred Holtby, Rose Macaulay, and others—took sharp aim at the "burden of family life" they had fought to escape and for which they blamed in part the disaster of the war.[13]

As is the case among most of these writing daughters, Enid Starkie identifies her father as the enabler of her literary career. Like other writing daughters of Anglo-Ireland, she regrets the personal unhappiness her father experienced through the decline of his stature and influence in the new nation. Yet Starkie also understands that subservience to this same man limited her mother's intellectual sphere and her ability to value daughters as highly as she did sons. Given her narrow views of gender roles, Starkie's mother could not comprehend a daughter who had little interest in clothes or visiting, refused to attend church, and professed the desire to earn a doctorate. In a pattern repeated in most Anglo-Irish women's autobiographies, the mother devalues her daughters as the result of her allegiance to the patriarchal family; as the emissary of its ideological values, she enforces its restrictions on them.

When Starkie explains what it meant to be "a Lady's child," she describes a set of expectations and regulations that many middle- and upper-class European women decry, whatever their nationality:

> I was a *Lady's Child* and only those who knew Ireland before the days of the Free State will realise the full implications of this statement. . . . We were always being told by our Nanny that some boy or girl we wished to play with was not a *Lady's Child* . . . but I have never been able to discover what were the

---

13. A comparative study of the Somerville novelists is provided in *Dangerous by Degrees: Women at Oxford and the Somerville College Novelists* (Leonardi 1989).

necessary qualifications for this curious, well-defined, and apparently easily recognisable status. I hated being a *Lady's Child* for it seemed to me that the status brought nothing but restrictions and obligations and no corresponding privileges or pleasures. (1941, 21)

Although some women, like Lady Clodagh Anson, Anita Leslie, and Maud Wynne extend the blame to the larger social order for the restrictions that cramped the ambitions of young women, Starkie targets her mother and the nursemaid who was her mother's emissary. It is the feminine sergeants of the father's authority who bear the brunt of her dissent. Like the mothers of Augusta Gregory and many others, Starkie's mother is seen by her daughter as a functionary of the conservative patriarchy and, as such, a source of frustration to a girl with ambitions toward greater education and a career. In part because she has the work of upholding the world that he is freer to doubt, this mother figure appears even more conservative than the father.

May Walsh Starkie displayed her lack of interest in girl children in ways less dramatic than did Augusta Gregory's mother. But her daughter was aware, even in girlhood, that males were the important members of the household. Although it was pleasant for her mother to dress female babies as dolls, any evident regard was saved for her brother and especially for her father, around whom all life revolved: "In my mother's opinion," she reflects, "everything he did was right, everything he said had the weight of divine revelation. . . . She considered it right that the life of a wife, that the life of all women in a household, should revolve round its male head" (36). Starkie interprets her mother's focus upon the father as a sign of her lack of identity and power. Although she fails to mention that her mother was eleven years younger than her father and had been a student in his class at Alexandria College, Dublin, she does take into consideration that May's youth was likely to have reinforced her inherited notions of wifely subordination. "My mother," she writes, "married my father when she was very young, before she had time to develop her own personality and, as long as he was alive, she saw everything through him. She saw herself not as a separate human being, but only as his wife. . . . My father was everything to her, she rarely thought of herself or of her own development, and I believe that none of her children—she eventually had six—meant much to her in comparison with him" (41).

In similar terms, Starkie reviews the life of her younger sister Muriel. Thoughtlessly cooperating with their mother's sense of the necessity of maintaining appearances, Muriel receives new dresses even during the family financial crisis that restricted funds for Enid's Oxford education. Muriel, she writes, became in her adulthood much like their mother "in her selfless, unthinking devotion to her husband and child. . . . Sometimes it saddens me to see how few demands she makes on life for herself, how restricted are her aspirations, how little nowadays she needs an outlet for her emotions or a means of self-expression. . . . She adopted my mother's ideals and later changed those for those of her husband" (285, 286). In the chapter titled "Sisters," Starkie takes pains to distinguish herself from Muriel in every way. Defining oneself in opposition to a mother figure—or a sister much like one's mother—who is a fundamentally powerless representative of conservative masculine power takes the shape of what the American poet Adrienne Rich calls "matrophobia": a "splitting of the self in the desire to become purged once and for all of our mothers' bondage. . . . The mother stands for the victim in ourselves, the unfree woman, the martyr. Our personalities seem dangerously to blur and overlap with our mothers'; and, in a desperate attempt to know where mother ends and daughter begins, we perform radical surgery" (1976, 236).

In an obverse relation to the lower-class narrative in which fathers are neither moral centers nor breadwinners and exercise physical force as their sole form of domestic authority, in these tales from another side of the Irish world it is the mother who has no income to disperse and who acts primarily as the agent of her husband's ideas. Her sphere of control is limited to her daughter's dress and manners; it gains her temporary obedience and trifling respect. And unlike the working-class testimonies that laud the hardworking and frequently brutalized mother's attempts to feed and protect her children, in those autobiographies of Anglo-Irish women who came of age during the First World War, reflections on the mother most frequently take the form of matrophobia, even—and perhaps especially—when the writer acknowledges her mother as the determined product of a patriarchal way of life. Because she views her mother and sisters as the creatures of an outmoded and insufficient way of life, Starkie pities them but never summons forth the admiration and affection that could result from imagining the unspoken struggles they might have endured against attitudes they appeared to have taken on as doctrine. Forgiveness may well depend upon a vision of the wrongdoer struggling, however failingly, against whatever forces drive her to commit acts that require forgiveness.

The reluctance or inability of mothers to rise in defense of themselves or their daughters to challenge what Francis Power Cobbe called in 1894 the "Parental and Marital Authority" of the husband can lead to the pity, scorn, and terror that Rich calls "matrophobia." Constance Malleson, whose autobiography *After Ten Years* appeared in 1931, confesses to a childhood matrophobia on just these grounds. Her first chapter draws a picture of her mother as a lively, beautiful, young Dublin girl married to a dour widower thirty-five years her senior. With a combination of boldness and naïveté, her mother set out to his remote estate in the North with a "boxful of high-heeled shoes and a quantity of bright-coloured clothes" (13). Despite her husband's "fathomless gloom" in which "for days on end he would never utter a word," she wore her cherry-red dresses and faced down impudent servants (15). Although she had no experience or interest in horses or dogs, she taught herself to ride and to handle the dogs. Her sense of imprisonment on the estate found an outlet in her long walks outside the high demesne wall and in the hundreds of letters she wrote and received from friends—often men—scattered all over the world. "Fifteen years of married life could not beat my mother," Malleson recalls with admiration (13). And yet reflecting on the many times she was called in to "make conversation" with her mother at the table, thereby " 'standing by' one's poor martyred mother and, so to speak, 'seeing her through,' " while her father sat at the other end "well back in his chair and never uttered" (19, 16), Malleson admits that "in my heart, I sided with my father: I felt stolidly and stoically unsympathetic towards my mother. She and my sister Clare . . . used to sob and weep together and comfort each other in soft womanish fashion. I despised all that. I respected my father. He was solid and immovable. . . . I discounted the women-folk entirely" (19). Despite her reverence for her mother's show of bravado, she can hardly bear her mother's appetite for pity and the requirements it made on her as a daughter; the sympathy she clearly felt for her mother's plight fails to suppress her repugnance at the demonstration of weakness.

In *Bricks and Flowers*, Katherine Everett comprehends that her mother was a victim as well as a frightening fixture of the parental house. Even with this understanding, she remains critical of what she judges her mother's snobbery and bullying manner. She titles an early chapter "Our Home," but rather than a nostalgic picture of an era, place, or parent, Everett gives a genuine blow-by-blow account of the terrifying atmosphere of her upbringing. With the ironic humor typical of her tone throughout, she proposes that the house itself was the cause of her mother's chronic distemper. The very age of the seventeenth-century house makes it damp and devoid of comfort:

> "It really was horrible," [Mother] said, when describing the place to me years afterwards. "There wasn't a tap or a closet in the house, and I had to make my way out past all those great wet laurels to huts—eight of them, beginning with a giant-sized one down to one for a dwarf or an infant. I wanted, of course, to slip out unseen, but an old man—Patrick Doran was his name, though everyone called him Patsy the Bucket—would be at my side directly I appeared, with an old carriage umbrella as large as a tent, and would insist on coming

with me and choosing which booth I should occupy. 'The middle one, I should say, my lady—that's three up from this end—would just suit your lady-ship, and they are all fine and clean,' he would point out. It was no use my telling him quite stiffly, 'You can go now, Doran', for he would only answer, 'Faith, I wouldn't do that and be leaving yourself to go back in the rain; I'll be waiting here for you.'

"It was all odious, and I made your father see how much I disliked it, and everything else about the place." (1949, 13)

In context, the humor of the scene accentuates rather than diffuses the morti-fication of her mother's recollection, yet the compassion it reveals in the auto-biographer does little to mitigate the irony with which she treats her mother, or her vehement repudiation of her mother's values and position.

Narrative Representation and the Domestic Tyrant

These mother figures, however intimidating in their enforcement of rigidly gendered codes of behavior, are not equal to the fictional tyrants whose an-tecedents Vera Kreilkamp has identified in the works of Maria Edgeworth and Somerville and Ross and who come to fullest expression in the novels of Molly Keane and Jennifer Johnson. Among the many Gothic figurations of Anglo-Irish demise in the Big House novel, in addition to the impotent male and the tortured child, is one Kreilkamp calls the "monstrous woman." In an inversion of the colonial metaphor of masculine subjugator and feminized subject, Kreilkamp explains, the woman appropriates the power of husband and father who "have abdicated any role in governance of family, household, or country and whose neglect of their children works itself out as a passive tolerance of maternal brutalities" (1998, 186). In the novels that, like so many autobiogra-phies, take class decline as a plot parallel to the fortunes of their characters, she explains how "moving into the void created by politically and economically emasculated fathers and husbands, twentieth-century Big House women ex-pend their voracious energies and appetites by decorating their homes, snub-bing their social inferiors, or torturing their children" (185).

Because this motif is so prevalent in Anglo-Irish women's fiction, we have to ask why it generally fails to appear in their autobiographies. A small number of autobiographies resemble their fictional cousins in so representing the fam-ily: Hannah Lynch portrays her glamorous mother as physically abusive and mentally cruel, and her debonair barrister father as benign but completely neglectful of his unprotected children; like a character from Molly Keane, Katherine Everett's mother indulges her snobbery and petty brutalities, while

her elderly husband putters about their declining estate in Kerry randomly demolishing hillsides with dynamite and building ugly concrete slabs without
function. But these examples are exceptions to a more common representation
in which the father is honorable and capable, if disappointed by his diminished
place in the modern nation, and the mother is most frequently a potentially
enervating feminine counterpart the daughter seeks to repudiate. The maternal figure is rarely demonic or portrayed without compassion, as is her counterpart in fiction.

There are several possible reasons for the discrepancy between autobiographical and fictional representations. The wider sampling of experience offered by autobiography demonstrates the inherent problems in drawing from
the evidence of a handful of novelists generalizations concerning the lives of a
large number of people, most of whom were not professional writers. Studies
of Anglo-Irish fiction generally consider a small group of novelists, whereas
the autobiographical record is much larger and its authors more diverse in
background. Historical documents could disclose how many females headed
Anglo-Irish households or controlled financial and domestic decisions, and
life writings such as letters, diaries, and autobiographies reveal whether that
power was perceived as having been wielded tyrannically or with cruelty toward children. From the autobiographical record, it appears that the rampant
ascendancy of the "monstrous woman" is, in fact, a fiction. Yet her presence in
fiction may point toward a different form of truth telling. In his essay "Fictions
and Truths," Tzvetan Todorov draws important distinctions between what he
calls the "truth of reality" and the "truth of unveiling." He explains the former
as the establishment of facts (such as whether an event occurred) and the latter
as "the identity of a phenomenon" (such as the causes or subjective experience
of an event) (1994, 24). In the figure of the female domestic tyrant, the Anglo-
Irish novel might lack the former species of truth yet excel at expressing a prevailing cultural anxiety about the decline of Anglo-Irish masculine power and
the domestic trauma of what Margot Backus names the "autophagous" (or
self-digesting) family that "intergenerationally devours itself" (1999, 108).
Thus, it is entirely possible to assert, as does James Cahalan, that "Somerville
and Ross's women tend to be strong and their men weak," to identify this division of power among their own relatives, and to find within that pattern a sign
of the tensions in Anglo-Irish political and domestic life. However, to argue
that "Somerville and Ross show how the Big Houses were really run by
women" may result from relying for historical evidence on a limited number of
novels and stories (1996, 67).

The influence of generic conventions constitutes a second reason for the
absence of the "monstrous woman" from Anglo-Irish autobiography. The

forms of narrative embedded in the literary autobiography, the Gothic novel, and the country-house novel differ so widely as to determine a widely divergent content. Many autobiographies do draw on Gothic motifs to express the sense of being haunted by ancestral guilt and family secrets. Nearly all make at least some reference to uncertain or illegitimate lines of ancestry and inheritance or to a house that in splendid decay damages its inhabitants.[14] Nevertheless, autobiographers refrain from portraying the figure, so common in the Anglo-Irish novel, of a woman in midlife plagued by sexual repression or sexual voraciousness, drunk with power unchecked by the emasculated males around her, and ruining the lives of the children she controls. This Gothic element may be too alien a generic feature to have been assimilated into the traditions of autobiography available to Anglo-Irish writers. Although the Gothic novel articulates the hitherto unspoken secret and figures the nightmares of family relations, self-censorship generally guides the more overtly referential narrative of autobiography. Despite what Elizabeth Bowen identifies as the "feeling of a descendant towards an ancestor . . . the child's first wish to drag anything awkward up" (1950, 166), one has to live on with one's relatives after the publication of an autobiography. In light of codes of good behavior and family politics, demonizing one's mother in print might be a precarious venture.

As the conventions of family relations affect the forms of life writing, so do the conventions of the literary autobiography. The roots of European literary autobiography in Rousseau's declaration of self-making, tales of travelers and captives who endured astonishing hardships in order to return to tell their stories, and Christian testimony as a narrative of redemption and liberation impel the autobiographical narrator to adopt the position of one who has overcome the foe. The Anglo-Irish autobiographer often speaks from the position of a childhood sufferer who has prevailed to tell the story as an aesthetically satisfying narrative. The Gothic novel's obsession with the ongoing suffering of the victim at the hands of his or her tormentor contrasts too sharply with the generic conventions and motives of the literary autobiography. To tell the story, and to tell the story well, awards the autobiographer a dominance over the childhood tyrant that may subdue the need to expose the tyrant's every wrong. The childhood Goliath can be overcome by, rather than in, the autobiographical text.

A final, but related, explanation for the absence of the "monstrous woman" emerges from what Penny Brown calls in her study of British

14. The Gothic elements of Anglo-Irish fiction are particularly well analyzed in Backus 1999, Kreilkamp 1998, and McCormack 1992a and 1993a.

women's childhood autobiographies an inexplicable "impulse to exculpate parents" (1993, 136). Although writers may treat the mother with the cautious silence of Lady Gregory, the undisguised distaste of Katherine Everett, or the lingering hurt of Enid Starkie, a longing for identification and intimacy with her runs as a subterranean current through their stories. In *A Lady's Child*, Starkie's frustration at the absence of maternal warmth is exacerbated by her continuing desire for it and her lifelong search for surrogates to fill that vacuum. She dedicates her autobiography to a woman friend who gave her courage and confidence, and throughout much of her life she exchanged long, intimate, and self-searching letters with a woman she had met only a few times; according to her biographer, one of her most important romantic relationships was with another woman. Large sections of *A Lady's Child* are devoted to her imaginative and rebellious Aunt Helen; Lizzie, the beloved housekeeper and cook of her childhood; and Miss Pope, her mentor at Oxford whom she describes as "one of the finest and most warm-hearted women I have ever known," a woman who "had all the kindness, the warmth, the integrity, and especially the infinite simplicity of the really great" (1941, 270). Despite their comfort and wisdom, these figures fail to compensate for her mother's lack of tenderness:

> I do not believe that she approved of external manifestations of affection or emotion. As a small child I often longed for the animal warmth of simple maternal love. I longed for some one to take me in her arms, to kiss me and to hug me, to rock me to sleep in her lap. Later, when I began to read French stories, those to which I returned most frequently were those which described close family life and the deep instinctive love of parents for their children. This was the feature in French and Italian home life which was to move me most profoundly when, in later life, I visited these two countries, the expansive emotion of parents for their children and of children for their parents, an emotion that finds expression in both words and action. (45)

Starkie identifies the paucity of spontaneous affection as a cultural trait rather than something that simply occurs or not in particular families; nevertheless, her sense of personal deprivation from a keenly imagined maternal ideal remains pungent. Although her portrait of her mother is negative, it is by no means cynical. Caricaturing the mother as a Gothic grotesque of the kinds encountered, for example, in Molly Keane's *Good Behavior* would require surrendering any faith in the elusive but much longed for "animal warmth of simple maternal love."

The chosen title of her autobiography, *A Lady's Child*, encapsulates

Starkie's personal struggle and her analysis of her culture. To be "a lady's child" was to live in an exclusive, restrictive, and by 1941 completely anachronistic sphere. In her last paragraphs, anticipating the difficult yet fulfilling life she chose to lead as an impoverished student at the Sorbonne, she writes, "In these later days no one would ever have believed that the *lady's child* had ever existed, for she had vanished completely, without even leaving a ghost. I was no longer a lady's child, even as I drove away" (341). The shedding of the worn-out shell of class privilege, to borrow from Yeats's image of the empty seashell to describe the same, is here accomplished by the shedding of an appellation aligning her with her mother.

Very few Anglo-Irish women's autobiographies provide exceptions to the pattern of matrophobia, even if they stop short of presenting the mother as a Gothic villainess. One of the fondest portraits of a mother appears in the late nineteenth century, offered by a woman then more than seventy years of age. Frances Power Cobbe sees her mother in terms more typical of writing by English working-class women. She credits to her mother the education to which her later feminist activism was indebted. As part of the chapter in her autobiography devoted to "Ireland in the Forties," she explains at length the patriarchal family of her time:

> [I]n the Thirties and Forties (at all events in Ireland) there was very little declension generally from the old Roman *Patria Potestas*. Fathers believed themselves to possess almost boundless rights over their children. . . . My brothers and I habitually spoke of our father, as did the servants and tenants, as *"The Master;"* and never was a title more thoroughly deserved. . . . The laws which concerned women at that date were so frightfully unjust that the most kindly disposed men inevitably took their cue from them, and looked on their mothers, wives, and sisters as being with wholly inferior rights; with *no* rights, indeed, which should ever stand against theirs" (1894, 170, 171).

She adds that in her own family, her father forbade her to learn Latin from her brother and disapproved of "study of any serious sort" for girls, insisting that she prepare instead for a "suitable" marriage by studying housekeeping, needlework, and music.

For the sake of the daughter, her mother struggled against the rule of the father, and Cobbe remarks, "Other Irish girls my contemporaries, were much worse off than I, for my dear mother always did her utmost to help my studies and my liberal allowance permitted me to buy books" (171). Cobbe describes her mother with an unequaled degree of expressive emotion and sensory pleasure. She recounts proudly that her mother nursed her and that as a child she had "been often cuddled up close to her on her sofa. . . . All these memories are infinitely sweet to me. Her low, gentle voice, her smile, her soft breast and arms, the atmosphere of dignity which always surrounded her,—the very odour of her clothes and lace, redolent of dried roses" (34).

Cobbe presents an exceptional case. Her language, unlike the vocabulary of more modern women, draws from the conventional rhetoric of maternal piety ubiquitous in the popular verse and devotional writing of the mid-nineteenth century. She was also unusually devoted to women as a class, having shared her life with the feminist Mary Lloyd while engaged in work on behalf of battered wives and for women's suffrage and improved conditions for women in workhouses. If there exists a twentieth-century Anglo-Irish woman who writes about mother in as effusive or even complimentary way, she has yet to be recovered to a current readership. Of modern writers, Elizabeth Bowen is most strongly sympathetic to her mother, although her reflections are more personal than Frances Cobbe's and make no overt reference to the feminist questions raised by any of the autobiographers previously discussed. In the evocative memoirs Bowen wrote concerning her mother, we see in place of the vigilant defender a woman whose powerful presence in her daughter's literary imagination was dependent upon both her absence from her daughter's life and the detachment of both mother and daughter from the father and his world.

Presence in Nonpresence: Elizabeth Bowen's Childhood Autobiographies

Maternal relations were integral rather than antithetical to Elizabeth Bowen's professional ambitions. Bewildered motherless girls on the cusp of adulthood are the central figures of the novels and short stories by which she achieved her distinguished reputation. In her autobiographical writing, references to her mother are brief but poignant. Although she and her mother were surrounded by her father's relatives during their summers in Cork, she chooses to represent Florence Bowen in a sphere apart from the universe of familial relations and the patrilineal history of the family and house related in her 1942 chronicle, *Bowen's Court*.

Much of her later childhood was spent with her mother, but away from Ireland and her father. For her first seven years, summers with her mother in Cork alternated with winters in Dublin, where her father practiced law. When he began to suffer from increasingly debilitating depressions and violent rages, her mother took Elizabeth abroad. After six years in England, Florence Bowen died suddenly of cancer. For the remainder of Elizabeth's adolescence, she boarded at school or stayed as a guest in the homes of relatives, occasionally returning to Bowen's Court to visit her father. In her memoir *Pictures and Conversations* (edited and published posthumously in 1975), mother and daughter share a nomadic existence along a wind- and sun-swept coastal landscape unencumbered by claims of property and family. During their sojourn in England, they drifted among their Anglo-Irish relatives and a series of hotels and rented villas along the English coast. The brief childhood sketches in *Pictures and Conversations* and *Seven Winters* (1942) depict a matrifocal youth in a sensuous prose that eludes obvious narrative emplotment and historical emphasis. Bowen meticulously delineates a child's mind, explaining the imaginative effect of a framed print on the nursery wall or the abrupt recognition that traffic overheard outside the darkened nursery meant that other lives were proceeding independent of her own. Characteristically, she establishes even this inward turn within the framework of a larger culture and history. For instance, the nursery decoration, a picture of young Casabianca standing amid the flames of his father's burning ship, was chosen "when my mother still expected me to be Robert," the never-born male heir. Its function, she says, was "to stimulate courage—for my father and mother, like all Anglo-Irish people, saw courage apart from context, as an end in itself" (1962, 11).[15]

Throughout the autobiographies, Bowen describes her mother as both distinct from the world typified by Bowen's Court and very much of it. As a woman whose "most intense moments of . . . existence all through her life had been solitary" (1962, 28), Florence Bowen was quintessentially of her group even in her very solitude. Although living out what Bowen identifies as the essential attitudes and habits of their culture, her ways of navigating Anglo-Irish social relations served to protect her child against their more damaging as-

15. Bowen does not explore a thematic relationship between her position as the chronicler of her family's demise and the popular poem by Felicia Hemans (1793–1835) illustrated by her nursery picture, but the potential to do so is there. The poem praises a boy—"a creature of heroic blood, / A proud though childlike form"—who accompanies his father, an admiral in Napoléon Bonaparte's imperial navy. During the Battle of the Nile, the Egyptians set fire to the ship, and although the "chieftain lay / Unconscious of his son," the boy continues to call out through the smoke for permission to leave the burning ship. Without an answer from the father, the boy remains to die in the flames. When a voice asks where the child may now be found, the narrator voice answers, "Ask of the winds that far around / With fragments strewed the sea!" (1865, 434). Mary Pakenham recalls imagining herself in childhood as "Casabianca and all the heroes of Jutland rolled into one" (1938, 13), suggesting that the poem was frequently read to children in late-nineteenth- and early-twentieth-century England and Ireland as an example of courage and obedience to the father as a colonial patriarch, even when he is disempowered, and that obedience will result in martyrdom.

pects. Repeatedly, she is depicted as having adapted tradition for her daughter's sake, and the effect was to implant "most important of all as a start in life—the radiant, confident feeling of being loved" (1942, 407).

One of those traditions, as explained by apologists of Anglo-Ireland from Sir Jonah Barrington to Molly Keane, was a concern that children not become "muffish." Bowen recalls that her mother fed her milk rather than tea so that she would not grow "runty"; she was taught to ride "not long after I was able to stand"; and although apparently terrified of horses herself, Florence Bowen controlled her fear sufficiently to drive the phaeton despite her husband's cautious objections (1942, 406–8). At the same time, young girls were subject to strict social restraints, particularly among the urban upper classes. Because her mother was distracted ("vague" is Bowen's term), Bowen was subject to far fewer restraints than other Dublin girls. In *Pictures and Conversations* she recalls, "I was let run wild, to an extent at which other mothers lifted their eyebrows—falling off horses, flopping about in the sea . . . plunging dementedly round and round till I fell smack down on the roller-skating rink, or death-diving on the precipitous Folkestone switchback railway, when money was to be found." To her mother's loose reins, she attributes the development of those inward resources that allowed her to survive the ordeal of a childhood uprooted by her father's inherited dementia: "I was a tough child, strong as a horse—or colt. I had come out of the tensions and mystery of my father's illness, the apprehensive silences or chaotic shoutings (while he was still there with us in the Dublin house) with nothing more disastrous than a stammer" (1975, 12). The stammer she kept until her death, as if her life's sadness could be narrowly channeled into one predictable, and thus endurable, manifestation.

In yet another way, Bowen's memoirs indicate how her mother's motives altered the effects of traditional attitudes toward girls. As Augusta Gregory, Enid Starkie, and many other women lamented, the mores of Anglo-Irish society—like the standards of most European bourgeoisie—discouraged girls from reading or studying of any substantial kind. Bowen's mother kept her from reading and any difficult studies, but her reason differed from the common rationale that female education was unnecessary or would make one unfit for marriage. With "her constant, underlying, watchful anxiety with regard to me, as my father's child," she feared her daughter might, by "overtaxing her brain," stimulate the "uncertain mental heredity"—the "violent mania"—of her father's family (1975, 10–11). It was to protect her against her patrilineal inheritance rather than to subject her to patriarchal rule that Florence Bowen kept her daughter illiterate through most of her childhood.

As Bowen explains the understanding between the two of them, her mother hired a governess to issue reprimands because she could not bear to act as the representative of a system of rules and restrictions. Bowen writes in *Seven Winters:*

> [A]bout her caresses and ways with me I remember a sort of rapture of incredulity. Her only child had been born after nine years of waiting—and even I was able to understand that she did not take me or her motherhood for granted. She was so much desolated that she unnerved me when anything went wrong between her and me. . . . She explained to me candidly that she kept a governess because she did not want to scold me herself. To have had to keep saying "Do this," "Don't do that," and "No," to me would have been, as she saw it, a peril to everything. . . . When she was not with me she thought of me constantly, and planned ways in which we could meet and could be alone. (1962, 28–29)

Although her mother's refusal to enforce rules was the indulgence of a privilege granted by her class and could even be seen as maternal laziness, Bowen interprets it otherwise. As a sign of the "unnerving" intensity of her mother's love, it opposes the customs of a society that would restrict its attention to boys. The dread that "everything" would be imperiled by reprimands also insinuates that their relations were constituted by primal sympathy rather than the conventional authority of parent over child. In its personalization of alliances, her mother's anxiety undermines the cult of genealogical preoccupation and family hierarchies.

Florence Bowen also used her Anglo-Irish relations to allow herself and her daughter to move at will among them, and the network of relatives aided her in muting the effects of their estrangement from home. A beautiful woman traveling alone with a child, she was vulnerable to malicious gossip, and Bowen relates in *Pictures and Conversations* that after overhearing a muffled conversation between adults, she asked her mother the meaning of the word *blackmail.* Consequent assurances that their various cousins would testify to their propriety and "would tell everybody that those were lies" impressed young Elizabeth "as proof of the dominance of my more or less synonymous race and family: the Anglo-Irish—with their manner of instantly striking root into the interstices of any society in which they happened to find themselves, and in their own way proceeding to rule the roost. One could perpetually be vouched for" (1975, 14). The story speaks to the force of kin and the child's satisfying conviction that her people ruled the world as she knew it. But it also inadvertently announces how fully Bowen knew, even in girlhood, that she and her mother were unmoored ships tied together and drifting.

In the bibliographic essay that introduces *Representations of Motherhood*, the editors recapitulate four major categories of maternal representation in feminist psychoanalytic theory: a weak and unhelpful ghost, a terrifying and magical force, a strong figure of identification, and an autonomous person who fosters in her child both differentiation and relationship (Bassin, Honey, and Kaplan 1994, 7–8). With the exception of Francis Power Cobbe, most Anglo-Irish women portray their mothers as either the ghost or the terror. When Augusta Gregory, Enid Starkie, and Constance Malleson attempt to discern the lives their mothers led apart from their interactions with their daughters, the effort to empathize breaks down in the face of their bitterness on behalf of the remembered child. Bowen, however, declines to make overt judgments; in one of the few moments in which she speculates about her mother from an adult narrator's point of view, she disavows any ability to know her mother's mind. Of Florence Bowen's decision to leave her husband and Ireland, she writes, "A heartbreaking decision for her to make: she must have been torn by the rights and wrongs of it. She showed me no signs, however, of what she was going through, and I asked no questions" (1975, 11).

Virginia Woolf also lost her mother at the age of thirteen and, like Elizabeth Bowen, felt compelled in midlife and during the first years of the Second World War to place on paper what meaning could be extracted from an individual life. She too struggles with the problem of how to realize her mother in writing without the layers of feelings and family lore that amassed over the decades since her mother's death. The problem, Woolf ascertains, lies in how to "get any closer to her without drawing upon all those descriptions and anecdotes which after she was dead imposed themselves upon my view of her." Her answer is to move immediately to the shorthand of impression, pared down in an effort to get at the essence: "very quick; very definite; very upright; and behind the active, the sad, the silent" (1985, 83). Likewise, Bowen tries to extract the substance of her mother from the strata of the years. Woolf's method is one of narrative contraction, whereas Bowen's is accumulative. She spends pages in an inventory of recollected details, vividly re-creating textually this woman, her mother: her bronze coiled hair held up with curved tortoise-shell combs, her blue-veined hands, her rings and strand of pearls, her eyes "alternately pensive and quizzical . . . triangular, with arched upper lids . . . of a grey-blue that deepened," her dark eyebrows, the turn of her chin, her complexion like "the downy bloom of a peach," her manner of smiling, and the precise perfume she favored, "Peau d'Espagne" (1962, 30). Except as a subtle and unspoken site of longing, the daughter-writer disappears from center stage.

In order to realize the memory of her mother's presence rather than discuss it, Bowen also enlists a sophisticated maneuvering of perspective. Near the conclusion of this segment of *Seven Winters,* she plummets into the child's experience of seeing her mother far across a lake, then with a cinematic shift in angle looks from the eyes of her mother onto herself, visualizing her child's body from her mother's view. As she removes herself as the center of readerly attention, she slips from subject to object position and becomes instead the center of maternal attention. The transfer of perspective takes place during a scene in which she has been taken for a walk by her governess:

> At one of those minutes I remember my mother standing on the bridge over the lake, looking for us. She sometimes came here on an impulse to join Miss Baird and me. Her hat was perched on the hair piled over her pointed face; I could have known her only by the turn of her head as she looked along the lake for my scarlet coat. I was as easy to see as a pillar box. She started toward us through the strolling and standing people as though through a garden that was her own. . . .
>
> I know now the feeling with which she stood on the bridge, looked along the lake till she came to my scarlet coat, then thought: "That is my child!" (1962, 28, 29)

In these lines is an anxiety of absence like that articulated so powerfully by the anticipation of presence in Augusta Gregory's diary entries: "To Gort to meet Robert! . . . the bright head at the window and quick hand at the door." Yet here it is the daughter, not the mother, who expresses how it feels to flood the consciousness with the sensory image of a child who is not there: who very likely will be there, but at the moment is still an anxious distance away, separated by all the dangers of the world, even if visible across the lake in Stephen's Green or expected to return within a short time. In that moment of transference, she is able to imagine herself as a loved child and to imagine her mother loving her.

In stepping away from the identifiably adult speaker and refraining from analytical commentary, except to say that she now understands her mother's emotions, Bowen allows her reader to feel the imaginative presence of her mother and to see from her eyes. Her achievement stops short of providing a forum for the underrepresented maternal voice, and as Susan Rubin Suleiman complains, "Just as motherhood [in Freudian analysis] is ultimately the child's drama, so is artistic creation. In both cases the mother is the essential but silent Other, the mirror in whom the child searches for his own reflection, the body he seeks to appropriate, the thing he loses or destroys again and again, and seeks to recreate" (1985, 357). But Florence Bowen did not author her own autobiography, and the daughter has no choice but to either refrain from discussing her or produce her as a character in a text. No writer can present her mother without creating her as an embodiment of the writer's present concerns. "For what reality," asks Virginia Woolf, "can remain real of a person who died forty-four years ago at the age of forty-nine, without leaving a book, or a picture, or any piece of work—apart from the three children who now survive and the memory of her that remains in their minds" (1985, 85)? Nor can Lady Gregory describe her son except through her own fears of losing him and her ongoing sense of social obligation. The lack of physical and emotional intimacy that seems to have been part of Anglo-Irish life perhaps only exacerbates the difficulties mothers and children undergo in attempting to know one another through the recollective and creative medium of autobiography.

Writing the unwritten mother is a difficult accomplishment. So often women—like Augusta Gregory, Joan de Vere, Daisy Fingall, Elizabeth Hamilton, or Katherine Everett—practice a studied reticence regarding their lives as mothers, except when, as in the case of Augusta Gregory, motherhood could be discussed in terms of the endowment of property, name, and position. For the autobiographer who speaks from the position of daughter, the mother is most frequently relegated to private discourse or cast off as a repudiated doppelgänger. Bowen's portrayal seems to be possible only as she can imagine her mother without the context of Anglo-Irish social relations that render her the powerless sergeant of patriarchal authority. She is there instead as a sensuous presence, a voice, a tilt of the head, a coil of hair. And by an act of her daughter's own creation, she is there as a consciousness the daughter can, if only for a moment, imagine and enter and from whose eyes see a world that includes herself, "my child," in a scarlet coat.

4

Spiritual Autobiography and the Social Body

*A*nglo-Irish autobiography has adapted to its own occasion the diverse traditions of the family history, topographical poetry, the autobiography of childhood, the psychotherapeutic narrative of family relations, the bildungsroman, the Gothic novel, travel writing, and satire. Because religious identity has been so significant in Ireland, spiritual autobiography also leaves its impress on the life writing of Anglo-Ireland. However, beyond the memoirs of clergymen and their wives, few texts record mystical experiences, use biblical analogies to explain the individual life as an instance of divine grace, or trace a pattern of conversion from a fallen or inadequate state to one closer to Godliness.[1] Nor do Anglo-Irish narratives of deconversion emulate the familiar Irish Catholic terrain of *Portrait of the Artist as a Young Man:* youth driven toward a secular worldview by the unbearable harshness of religious upbringing, riven by the irreconcilable desires of flesh and spirit, terrorized by hell and a sense of one's own sin, and browbeaten by the priests and nuns who serve as teachers and guides to the adult world. In contrast, Augustine Martin observes, "The Church of Ireland scene yields no such emphasis. Though . . . Ernest Boyd could boast truly of the number of 'distinguished heretics, in literature, politics and religion, who have been born into Irish Protestantism,' he could hardly point to a work of literature in which the Anglican *non serviam* achieves

---

1. Pascal 1960, Fleishman 1983, Peterson 1986, and Henderson 1989 provide useful studies of the relationship between religious narratives and of English-language autobiography. Inclusive definitions of the spiritual autobiography as it evolved from Augustine through Rousseau are offered by Bell 1977 and Barbour 2001. Among the descriptive features of the spiritual autobiography are the Pauline motif of religious crisis and illumination, the dichotomy between the past fallen self and the redeemed self, and a narrative perspective that looks back from the present state of enlightenment while often contrasting the reborn soul with the fallen body. Other traits include seeing the life as insignificant in its individuality but of importance as a manifestation of divine will, the use of biblical analogies and metaphors to explain the life, and the hope that the autobiography will act to convert souls.

any sort of memorable resonance" (1970, 120). Similarly, Gerald Dawe and Edna Longley assert that "when it comes to literary expression—to put the case crudely—few Protestants produce neo-Joycean juvenilia about adolescent sexuality at odds with Catholic teaching, and few Catholics are haunted by images of a decaying house or one that shuts them out" (1985, ii).

As with all attempts to draw patterns in broad strokes, these polarities are not without exceptions. Some Protestant autobiographers, like J. B. Yeats or John Synge, depict the struggle between church teaching and a sensuous perception of life as expressed in art, nature, and sexuality. In a few cases, the contradictions of religion and science precipitate deconversion stories similar to those of English writers like Thomas Henry Huxley and Edmund Gosse. For many more Protestant Anglo-Irish, conflicts of a different kind lead to crises of faith, the accounts of which diverge from more familiar patterns of religious life writing. Very rarely do biblical tropes provide the structure of the Anglo-Irish autobiography or serve to merge the individual story with sacred history. Neither do writers invoke biblical figures as a means of explaining their experience. With few exceptions, there is little effort to examine the life as a spiritual discipline, provide a witness to suffering or captivity, or affect the conversion of the reader through autobiographical testimony.[2]

Instead, religion appears as a formative influence allied with class, education, and political ideology. The inseparability of Irish politics and sectarian affiliation turns autobiographical attention away from an individual's apprehension of the divine and toward his or her alliance or misalliance with the church as a social body. Autobiographers frequently explain their departure from Anglicanism as part of a broad reconsideration of political and class allegiance. Because the Church of Ireland stood for Conservative Party politics in the minds of many, the embrace of socialism or Irish nationalism often parallels the repudiation of Anglicanism and the subsequent espousal of secularism, Roman Catholicism, or ecumenicalism. Although numerous Irish Anglicans in the later nineteenth century followed Cardinal Newman into the Roman

---

2. In his study of twentieth-century American spiritual autobiographies, David Leigh defines four traits consistent among their protagonists: a lack of selfhood and the desire to create one, fear that one has no freedom from determining forces, alienation from established churches, and resistance to an identity deriving from hierarchical society (2000, xiv). Looking at deconversion narratives from Augustine to the present, John Barbour creates a taxonomy of experiences comparable to David Leigh's: repudiation of a belief system, moral condemnation of the way of life associated with that system, emotional upheaval, and rejection of the community in which one had previously belonged (1994, 2). Although inner turmoil plays a critical part in the religious crises described by Synge and MacNeice, in most texts the social factors are overwhelmingly predominant.

Catholic Church and, like Aubrey de Vere (1897) and George Tyrrell (1912), emphasize the theological grounds of this change, most explain their deconversion from Anglicanism as part of an overall ideological transformation. The rhetoric of conversion and deconversion thus takes on emphases unusual in English-language autobiography but not surprising in a region where denominational affiliation has been so strongly tied to politics, class, and a sense of cultural identity.

"The Best Definition of an Irish Protestant"

Many Anglo-Irish Protestants saw their religious affiliation as a crucial element of their social affiliation. Although not all Protestants owned large properties in rural areas or held professional positions within the city, most of those families and individuals who did were Protestant, and most of them were Anglican. Excluded by the Test Act of 1704 from most positions of power, by the early nineteenth century Dissenters lived primarily in cities as members of the merchant or laboring classes. Even in the South, they were often further differentiated from their Anglican neighbors by their Scottish, rather than English or Norman, origin.[3] The degree to which they lived apart from other Irish differs according to historical period and local circumstances. Over several centuries, Anglicans, Roman Catholics, and Dissenters formed, dissolved, and reconfigured allegiances and distinctions among themselves that varied tremendously from one region to another and between urban and rural settings. Some Anglicans, like the Synge family south of Dublin or the family of Louis MacNeice in Antrim, lived exclusively within Protestant circles that, in the case of the more evangelically minded Synges, could include Dissenters as well as Anglicans of the same class. Numerous families intermarried between Protestant denominations or included converts within the family circle.

But for the most part, Anglicans perceived Dissenters, especially in Ulster, as a different group altogether. Dissenters appear to have shared that view: arguing in a 1945 essay that Northern nonconformist literature is genuinely regional rather than "strictly colonial" like the writings of the Anglo-Irish to the South, Belfast poet John Hewitt wryly threatens, "Call an Ulster Scot an

3. By the late eighteenth century, few landed rural families remained affiliated with Dissenting sects. Outside of Ulster, Dissenting congregations consisted of members of the working class, merchants, and some urban professionals concentrated primarily in Dublin and Cork. Toby Barnard comments: "The lack of weighty advocates within their own ranks may have doomed the Dissenters to a longer period of legal constraint. Cut off from the society of Ascendancy Ireland, they came to be sneered at rather than feared by the members of the elite" (1995, 35).

Anglo-Irishman and see what happens" (1987, 111).[4] In his analysis of North-ern Protestant autobiography, Barry Sloan suggests that in addition to many other cultural distinctions, the Dissenting mind is particularly formed by its typological reading of personal and current events as reenactments of selected biblical and historical occasions, and by its opposition to an Anglican church perceived as dangerously close to Roman Catholicism. Moreover, it is marked by perplexing contradictions between social authoritarianism and a theology rooted in private conscience, a doctrine of human depravity and a call to disci-plined right action, and the archly conservative position of the last century and a legacy of radicalism (2000, 92–122). Such distinctions in outlook prove even more significant to autobiography than differences in doctrine.

Within the Anglican Church, members might have very different experi-ences given their time, place, and familial practices. The evangelical enthusi-asm recalled by John Butler Yeats differs from Elizabeth Bowen's impressions of genteel formality, and Shane Leslie's comical anecdotes about the eccentric clerics of Monaghan contrast with John Synge's somber account of his youth-ful fears of perdition. Despite a conviction as to the significance of a Protestant upbringing, explanations of what it meant to be a Protestant are often cir-cuitous and contradictory. In a 1909 letter to her father, Lily Yeats repeats a story told to her by the dean of St. Patrick's. She calls it "the best definition of an Irish Protestant I ever heard." "Someone," she writes, "asked of a man was he a Protestant or a Catholic. 'He has no religion, but in every other respect is an out & out Protestant,' was the answer" (W. B. Yeats Papers, ms. 31, p. 112).[5] The circularity of this "best definition"—he is a Protestant because he acts like a Protestant—is less than helpful except as it points to how much certain be-haviors were so generally understood to be "Protestant" that everyone in the conversation could presumably understand what was meant, even if we in the

4. Donald Akenson (1988) argues that postindependence methods of data gathering and the nationalist focus of much modern Irish historical research have blurred the degree to which Protestant denominations kept separate from one another, particularly Anglicans and Dissenting groups. In their preface to *Across a Roaring Hill: The Protestant Imagination in Modern Ireland*, Ger-ald Dawe and Edna Longley provide a substantial discussion of the ways southern Anglicans have perceived Ulster Dissenters as members of an alien society (1985, iii–vi). For a vivid representation of the distinctions among Protestants of various classes, see Louis MacNeice's memories of the "untouchable" Protestant working class who lived near the linen mill in Carrickfergus before the First World War (1965, 49).

5. Lily Yeats to John Butler Yeats, 24 Oct. 1909. I am grateful to R. F. Foster for reproducing in a letter to me the text of William Michael Murphy's transcription of this letter from the Yeats Papers, National Library of Ireland, Dublin. Assistant Keeper of Manuscripts Ciara McDonnell kindly verified the quotation at my request.

twenty-first century must reconstruct that meaning through often inconsistent documentary evidence. Would they have been referring to Protestantism as a theology, a set of political and social views, or some ineffable combination of outlook and manner?[6]

As Lily Yeats suggests by her assertion that the "best definition" can present as its prime example a man who "has no religion," few autobiographers discuss their Anglicanism in terms of its theology, although in a dubious and very public conversion complicated by sibling rivalry and compulsive exhibitionism George Moore claimed to be attracted to the primacy of individual conscience and private revelation available in Anglicanism, unfettered by the strictures of more evangelical faiths (1985, 447–58). Regarding Moore's shock at being asked during his ceremony of induction to affirm his belief in the Resurrection, biographer Adrian Frazier quips, "his notion of a Protestant had been an English Atheist in favor of morality and independent judgment" (2000, 332). When autobiographers raised in the Anglican confession reflect on its theology, they have little to say about independent judgment and a great deal to say about their childhood terror of hell. Those individuals who most vividly remember these facets of their doctrinal upbringing are the ones most affected by the evangelical movements of the nineteenth century that emphasized original sin, adult sanctification, emotionalism, and the rejection of Deist or Tractarian tendencies.

The poet William Allingham captures much of that atmosphere in his autobiographical recollections of his childhood in the early 1830s. The dark, lofty church in Ballyshannon, he writes, imparted a "sense of a solemn stringency of rule and order" where "the smallest infraction, it was felt, might have unimaginable consequences. A child's prayer-book falling from the gallery astounded like an earthquake" (1992, 101). Thoughts of eternal life brought panic rather than comfort: "A terrible thought of Eternity sometimes came, weighing upon me like a nightmare—on and on and on, always beginning and never ending, never ending at all, for ever and ever and ever—till the mind, fatigued, fell into a doze as it were and forgot. I suppose this was connected,

---

6. Parallels between religious affiliation and culture need to be offered with exceeding care, particularly given the tendency among both Catholics and Protestants to see such traits as inheritable and, by extension, matters of "race." In his comparative sociology of nineteenth- and twentieth-century Catholics and Protestants in Ireland, Akenson laments the preoccupation with "semiracial" thinking that influences not only romantic nationalists like W. B. Yeats but also those historical empiricists who attempt to explain apparent divergences in social behavior through theories of cultural determinism and whose predisposed notions of culture hinder the discovery of similarities, as well as fresh analyses of differences, between the groups (1988, 11–14).

though not definitely, with the idea of a state of punishment. The suggestion of eternal happiness took no hold upon my imagination." His visions of the dreadful day of judgment take on a distinctively local setting, with his own church forming the stage for the wrath of God: "Connected with Church and churchyard was a thought, vague, vast, unutterably awful, of that Last Day, with Eternity behind it: yet it was definitely localized too, and it seemed that not only the Rising but the Judging of our particular dead must be in our own Churchyard" (102).

Born in 1824, Allingham felt the impact of the wave of religious feeling that swept over prefamine Ireland in both Catholic and Protestant churches. Historian T. C. F. Stunt remarks that even Dublin was affected by the fervor:

> According to one late nineteenth-century Irish writer, "drawing room meet-
> ings for prayer and study of the scriptures were then [in the 1820s] quite the
> rage with all serious minds," and certainly this was the conclusion of the
> Quaker J.J. Gurney in early 1827 when visiting the home of the lawyer John
> Henry North. After dinner there was a sermon and "forthwith the company
> dropped to their knees. . . . This description will give you some idea of the
> state of society in Dublin. I should imagine that these Bible readings are ex-
> tensively supplanting cards and other such amusements." (1989, 219)

Although some evangelicals were concerned with the conversion of Roman Catholics, the movement's primary effect was to intensify religious feelings among Protestants of many denominations, creating splinter groups like the Plymouth Brethren and, on occasion, bringing Anglicans together with Pres-byterians, Quakers, and Methodists. Its impact continued to be felt through-out the nineteenth century. As a student at Trinity College in the 1850s, J. B. Yeats too felt the effects of a religious fervency with the Anglican Church: "I do not know how it is now-a-days," he writes, "but at that time Churches were so crowded that young men, unable to find a seat, remained the whole service through standing in the aisle" (1971, 72). In the English boarding school to which he was sent as a youth, he recalls, "we slept with our Bibles under our pillows with directions to read them as soon as we awoke in the morning; but hell was the driving force" (6). One of the most influential writers of tracts in the mid-nineteenth century, Bishop John Charles Ryle, identifies in *The Prin-ciples of Evangelical Religion* the doctrine of human sinfulness and corruption as a foremost feature of evangelical Anglicanism. His tracts enjoyed a circulation of more than twelve million readers, and their wide popularity indicates the pervasiveness of this kind of thinking among Anglicans throughout the nineteenth century and into the modern period.[7]

Like Allingham and Yeats, John Synge and Louis MacNeice were sons of families firmly entrenched in the Church of Ireland and felt the impact of Evangelicalism. In his notebooks, Synge recounts a childhood in a household filled with notions of supernatural forces—the Holy Ghost and Satan himself—and describes his ecstatic apprehension of the former and his abysmal horror of the latter. Although Louis MacNeice's father, according to his sister, "disapproved strongly of 'hell-fire religion' " (1965, 42), it permeated the general atmosphere around Antrim, where his father was rector in the Parish of Carrickfergus, and it came directly into their home by means of the servants:

> It was Miss Craig who brought Hell home to me. . . . Miss Craig made it almost the Alpha and Omega, hell-flames embroidered her words like Victorian texts. I realised now that I was always doing wrong. . . . I had done so much wrong I knew I must end in Hell and, what was worse, I could imagine it. Sometimes when Miss Craig had jerked me and thumped me into bed she would look at me grimly and say: "Aye, you're here now but you don't know where you'll be when you wake up." (42)

As MacNeice writes about his early years, his autobiographical sketches and poems recall Synge's in their revelation of a nightmarish inner world of "terrors and depressions" exacerbated by hours spent in a gloomy, dark church and his nurse's fixation on eternal punishment. His sister, Elizabeth, has insisted in her notes to *The Strings Are False* that their childhood was not all that dismal and that "my mother and father liked Carrickfergus and its inhabitants, and were on friendly terms with all kinds of people—Roman Catholics and Protestants, gentry and mill-girls" (49). Accurate or not, MacNeice recalls this world as, in Shaw's words, "gloomy, sour, Sabbath-ridden Ulster-Covenanting" Irish Protestant society (1970, 14). Despite the differences between middle-class Ulster and the social elite of Synge's Wicklow, the atmosphere of his home as MacNeice recalls it bears more resemblance to households like the Synges' than to those homes where religion was a lighter fare and ironic good humor an essential aspect of the way one saw oneself and

7. Ryle's writings continue to be read as inspirational guidance in English-speaking churches most associated with biblical literalism and a militant antiecumenical stance such as Ian Paisely's Free Presbyterian and various Calvinist and Puritan independent churches in Northern Ireland, Scotland, and Australia. See, for example, Ryle's presence on the informational Web site and the extensive links provided by the William Farel Society of the Australian Reformed Network at http://www.users.bigpond.com/farel/.

other fallible members of fallen humanity. Their autobiographies confirm that although the Irish Protestant may not write the traumatic hell and sex-tormented story characteristic of Joyce and other Catholic writers, a pattern of rebellion against hellfire theology emerges across several generations of Anglo-Irish artists, from Allingham and the elder Yeats in the early and later nineteenth century, to Synge and MacNeice at the beginning and middle of the twentieth.[8]

For those autobiographers less affected by the fear of damnation, the greatest impact of their religious upbringing arises from the historical alliance of Anglicanism and unionist politics. In Ulster, the sectarian division exacerbated by the Home Rule crisis, the Easter Rising, and the terrible losses suffered by Irish regiments in World War I fixed with even greater emotion the association between loyalty to Britain and loyalty to one's God. Having grown up in a small Northern town during the First World War, Muriel Breen vividly illustrates how Anglican identity converged with unionist patriotism: "Every Evensong ended with the Rector reading the names of the latest victims from the chancel. When he finished the organ clashed out with great chords and shivers ran down one's back. . . . Mr. Jones, the organist, gave his best and was good. 'He had to fortify himself for the weekly ordeal,' people said" (1993, 122). The Sunday evening following the devastation of the Ulster Division found a group of curates gathered for their weekly recreation at the Breen home where they all sang first the customary popular songs—although omitting Irish ones that "were not encouraged at the time"—and eventually turned to hymns and then, weeping, to the British national anthem. "Everyone joined in," she recounts. "I'll never forget the fervour of it" (124). Popular English tunes, Anglican hymns, patriotic British songs, and the presence of young clergymen in a household of as yet unmarried daughters surge into a tide of feeling still overpowering to the elderly woman who tells the tale.

Most autobiographers also correlate Anglicanism with class privilege and an exaggerated sense of class differentiation. Contrasting his childhood in Monaghan with the modern era in his 1916 autobiography *The End of a Chapter*, Shane Leslie observes:

In Ireland the Anglican bishops amounted to Cromwellians in lawn sleeves. To-day they are the leaders of a stranded crusade and the trustees of a dises-

---

8. In her study of unbelief among Britons of the past two centuries, Susan Budd notes that most freethinkers from the era of Thomas Paine through the First World War reported that excessive emphasis on hell drove them out of the Anglican Church and away from Christianity (1977, 116–18).

> tablished church. . . . Though the native cathedrals and old revenues had been made theirs, the duel had proven unequal. The Catholic Church thrived on poverty and persecution, and became more than ever the church of the people. . . . [T]he Catholic Church in Ireland became so identified with popular rights and opposed to feudalism that I remember an old Catholic peer exclaiming: "We have held the faith in spite of the priests!" (97–98)

For many centuries, mandatory tithing required a laboring class to support the livings of Anglican clerics drawn almost exclusively from the middle classes and above. Even after disestablishment, the oppressive bond remained through the Church of Ireland's position as the owner of lands on which persons of other faiths farmed and raised livestock. Class snobbery often took a sectarian turn, sometimes asserting Anglican superiority over Dissenters, who were more frequently urban and of the lower middle class or working class, and at other times grouping all Protestants together in contrast with Catholics. William Allingham, who believed his Protestantism condemned him to be a man without a country, remembers how he once argued with his nurse for "the superiority of Protestantism because 'the Catholics, you see, are poor people,' to which Kitty replied, 'It may be different in the next world' " (1992, 103). Poor they were, but they had a sense of nationality and, according to Kitty, a heavenly destination.

The relationship between Anglicanism and class identity was not so troubling for Elizabeth Bowen; it offered to her mind a vital sense of historical continuity and social cohesion. Bowen never rejected the Church of Ireland. Rather, she embraced it, defended it, and balked at proposed reforms to the service. She attended church frequently and in 1960 wrote a nativity play to be performed in St. Mary's Protestant Cathedral in Limerick; to her great pleasure, it was also presented ten years later as part of a rare ecumenical celebration in the Protestant cathedral in Derry. Belonging to the Church of Ireland was in her view an integral part of being Irish, a reification of class, family inheritance, and of a whole way of being that informed her lifework as a writer. In her autobiographies, novels, travel writing, journalism, social essays, and even her ghost stories, the features she associates with her religious experience appear again and again as fundamental to her life and thought.

In *Seven Winters*, she devotes a full chapter to the evocation of the Dublin Sunday mornings of her childhood and reflects how the

> clear sombreness, sane proportions, polished woodwork and brasswork, and aisles upon which confident feet rang, had authority—here one could feel a

Presence were it only the presence of an idea. It emphasized what was at once august and rational in man's relations with God. . . . There was an honourable frankness in the tone in which we rolled out the General Confession—indeed, sin was most felt by me, in St. Stephen's, as the divagation from the social idea. (1962, 48)

Bowen emphasizes the importance of "the social idea": a sense of belonging to a community, here defined as Protestant Ireland and, more narrowly, as Anglican Ireland. Bearing the authority of a "Presence," it has the substance of the incontestable. Associated with this powerful concept is the code of emotional reserve that has proved so consequential in the autobiographical rendering of mothers and daughters and will be in the next chapter particularly important to the analysis of comedy as an Anglo-Irish autobiographical form. In the context of religion, this attitude takes the form of the "august and rational" relation with God that prompts Bowen as a girl to scorn the Psalms as a "chanted airing of troubles" that "outraged all the manners I had been taught" and to assume of the frequent mass bells of city Catholics that "this predisposition to frequent prayer bespoke . . . some incontinence of the soul" (49, 50).

Bowen's other writings indicate how her reverence for the ritual and expressive restraint of Anglican practice is but one facet of an adamant belief in formality as a means of maintaining both individuality and human community in the face of latent personal or social chaos. Among the many books she reviewed during the late 1930s as part of her effort to raise money to sustain Bowen's Court, two ephemeral works on etiquette and fashion became the vehicles by which she again articulates this idea. In both reviews, she declares that formalized social behavior provides a meeting point of individual consciousness and social organization. "We are so romantic, so Protestant," she acknowledges, "that we each believe our own personal taste, or fancy, to be unique, independent, perhaps divinely implanted. Whereas fashion appears coercive, *voulu*." Furthermore, she argues that "Protestant" individuality as expressed in dress allows for a compromise between the self and the received world of the community beyond the self: "Fashion expresses us more truly . . . than we can, by individual effort, express ourselves. As individuals, we hardly exist at all; as unique beings we are very little effective. Any force that we exercise is a mass force. It is the general part of us—foggy and unrealized—that is powerful, that precipitates events" (1950, 114).

Just as ritual allows the believer to enter into engagement with the divine through historically sanctioned practices, manners—like fashion—produce through ritualized behavior the same kind of necessary compromise between self and other: "an exercise of the imagination on other people's behalf" (200). Gently mocking the dining habits of the ancient Romans in her travel memoir, *A Time in Rome*, she proposes that their manners, no matter how odd, were commendable if for no other reason than that they were communally held and sanctioned by practice: "Were they not the better for two things," she asks, "devotion to ceremonial, faith in tradition? Once one breaks with either, endless unease begins" (1960, 103). For Bowen, personality, social cohesion, and a relationship with the divine presence all depend upon the kind of ritual formality in which she grew up as an Irish Anglican of the early twentieth century.

More than any Irish autobiographer besides the iconoclastic George Bernard Shaw, she attributes to her Protestantism the very structures of her emotional, political, and imaginative life. Her biographer, Victoria Glendinning, recognizes this relationship between Bowen's fiction and her belief in what Glendinning calls "a world elsewhere." She comments: "[Bowen] found atheism 'claustrophobic.' This was part of her feeling of the thinness of the barrier between the living and the dead. . . . If one were to see a ghost, she said, it would not be in the grim dark but on a hot summer's afternoon" (1977, 236). To an acquaintance who told her that he did not believe in God but did believe in ghosts, she answered "severely, 'I believe in God *and* ghosts' " (236–37). She brought this sense of the other world to the life narratives in which she defined her personal, national, and aesthetic history. "To talk of 'entering' the past is nonsense, but one can be entered by it," she asserts in *A Time in Rome*. "All happenings, whatever their place in time must have *as* happenings, something in common—whatever went on, goes on, in one form or another. . . . What has accumulated in this place acts on everyone, day and night, like an extra climate" (1960, 11–12). Her autobiographies, particularly the family chronicle, *Bowen's Court*, are populated with that which can no longer be seen; ancestors, parents, and, finally, the house itself form that "extra climate" in which an individual life takes place.

Elizabeth Bowen's sense of what it meant to be an Anglican is visible in nearly every aspect of her work. But even among those autobiographers who ridicule, repudiate, or simply ignore their Protestant upbringing, the Protestant childhood provides language, ideas, and images around which the emergent intellect creates an inner world. In their discussions of religious experience, some write with the same disparaging attitude toward emotionalism and performative view of language that shape the peculiar Anglo-Irish hybrid of comic autobiography. Instead of an inward struggle with God, they accentuate the style and strangeness of religious forms. Under his father's tutelage, the Bible served as a model for the young George Bernard Shaw to follow while performing belletristic exercises. If it was, according to his father, "the damndest parcel of lies ever written," it was also "a literary and historical masterpiece" (1970, 36). Shaw also recalls the effect of church services on his boyhood imagination: "[I]n my childhood I exercised my literary genius by composing my own prayers. I cannot recall the words of the final form I adopted; but I remember that it was in three movements, like a sonata, and in the best Church of Ireland style. . . . I did not care whether my prayers were answered or not: they were a literary performance for the entertainment and propitiation of the Almighty" (1970, 30).

Mary Pakenham and her siblings engaged in similar performances as they pretended to conduct church services in the tower of Pakenham Hall:

> The service was taken out of an astronomy book appropriately called "Peeps at the Heavens" or else from Peter Parley's "Tales of Animals," an unappetizing-looking Victorian natural history book. . . . The Litany, unlike the C. of E. Litany, was the most popular item in the service, the responses rendered in threatening tone being either "Sun, Moon and Stars" or, even more direful, "The Fox."
>
> "The Fox has a face which bespeaks great cunning. (*The Fox.*) He is everywhere the same voracious animal (*The Fox.*) Should all other food fail him he can subsist on rats, mice, serpents, lizards, toads and moles and even roots and insects (*The Fox.*) Foxes near the sea coast will devour crabs, shrimps and shell fish (*The Fox.*)" (1938, 21)

The passage goes on at great length, demonstrating how fully the imagination of the children adapted the Litany's ritualistic rhythms and organizational structure to incongruous purposes. The biblical language that fascinated Shaw in his boyhood and the church ritual that formed the basis of the Pakenhams' childhood theatricals nourish the child's intellectual growth, but in the same way that Shakespeare or Dickens might. As recounted in these autobiographies and others, religious language constitutes part of a performative theory of self-presentation. Relishing it as a form of linguistic embellishment and artifice, even to the point of absurdity, these writers adapt the most solemn discourse of their experience to express a comically reductive attitude toward one of the most principal facets of Anglo-Irish identity.

John Millington Synge and the Power of "Wildness"

Even before John Synge recognized where his own fertile ground lay as a writer, he experienced severe alienation from the social, political, and religious world of his family. Synge's ancestors and living relatives, including his elder brother Samuel, were professional clergymen well established in Wicklow since the seventeenth century; his family, and particularly his mother, espoused the salvationist piety of evangelical Protestantism, mixed socially with their Brethren neighbors, and harbored grave reservations about imaginative literature. His early deconversion was followed by his discovery of a literary vocation and a fascination with nationalist ideology and the folk culture of the rural Catholic poor. All of these new interests were inconsistent with what he perceived as the cautious propriety and unremitting dullness of the religious life of his class. In his study of childhood autobiographies, Richard Coe suggests that it is precisely that sense of pious tedium that leads toward the rejection of faith in European Protestant autobiography more generally:

> The primary reaction is not one of spiritual torture, self-doubt, and anguish, but rather a sense of dazed disbelief, followed by anger, in the crudity, stupidity, and plain ineptitude of standard religious instruction. The betrayal, in a sense, was social rather than spiritual; and the rebellion, not so much against God as against the inane reasoning of adults. It is the implacable judgment of the exceptional mind leveled against complacent mediocrity. . . . The resulting atheism is, at bottom, a refusal to perpetuate human, rather than to condone divine, stupidity. (1984, 46–47)

Although many alternatives to Protestantism have been available—from outright atheism to the Order of the Golden Dawn—most Irish Anglicans, at least in the South of Ireland, imagine their own world in diametric opposition to that of the Roman Catholic. One could be a colorless Protestant or a so-called peasant, endowed, it was said, with strong emotions, a lively folk imagination, a plethora of songs and stories—and a Catholic identity. Mary Pakenham's facetious comments on the traits associated with Protestants and Catholics expose the kind of classifications that made many Anglo-Irish writers believe that their artistic development depended upon a rejection of their upbringing: "I was born knowing the difference between the Protestant Church and The Church of Rome," she writes. "There wasn't a time when I was not aware that Protestants were respectable but dull, while Catholics were dirty but amusing" (1938, 49). Catholicism, according to John Butler Yeats, was "a fraud—but . . . a beautiful fraud," and he judged Protestantism "broad but stupid" (Murphy 1978, 137). "Given the Protestant efficiency," he wrote in a letter to John Quinn, "the Catholic Irishman would leap to far higher altitudes than the Protestant will ever attain—because of his imagination and traditions" (249–50). The typecasting is conventional in its pitting of the pedestrian but efficient Protestant against the lively but undisciplined

Catholic, and the language echoes distinctions between "Saxon" and "Celt" that were widespread throughout the nineteenth century and popularized in Matthew Arnold's influential 1866 essay, "On the Study of Celtic Literature." As in Arnold's essay, the dichotomy disparages the Protestant (or "Saxon") virtues as much as the Catholic (or "Celtic") vices and does so in such a way as to portray the Irish Protestant writer as bereft of sufficiently vital imagination.

John Millington Synge seems to have understood early that he could not live with the religious, political, and social views of his evangelically oriented Protestant family. The unrevised sketches Alan Price has edited into the "Autobiography" rely upon a fundamental pattern of Christian spiritual autobiography: the writer constructs the plot of his or her life around a crisis moment and depicts on either side of it two distinct selves, one who existed before the moment of crisis and the new man or woman who is born afterward. In Synge's case, these figures are the spiritually restless and hell-tormented youth and, after the transition, the apostle of what he called a "passionate" state of being ungoverned by dogma or convention, a young man whose apostasy would cut him off from the inner circle of his family, the devout woman he sought to marry, and the type of life he was expected to live. "I laid a chasm," he writes, "between my present and my past and between myself and my kindred and friends. Till I was twenty-three I never met or at least knew a man or woman who shared my opinions" (1982, 11).

As John Stuart Mill depicts in *Autobiography* the life-changing moment of his encounter with Wordsworth, Synge attributes to his reading of a passage in Darwin the emotional upheaval that shattered belief in the family's values and the system of upbringing to which he had been subjected, causing him to conclude that his family had kept him from a crucial part of life, if not the most crucial part. Unlike Mill, Synge does not criticize his family so explicitly, but he locates the origin of his religious crisis in a book that undercut the beliefs that governed their lives: that they were a particular people, chosen and saved by a God who formed them in his own image and with whom they could experience an intimate relation unmediated by priests and unavailable to the majority of their countrymen. Both Mill and Synge collapse what must have been a protracted course of doubt into a literary moment, and in doing so both employ the structure of the conversion narrative that, like Saul's transformation into Paul, involves a sudden seeing. As Mill is thrown from the world of logic into the dangerous, but fulfilling, world of emotion, Synge is taken from the road to piety by the blinding light of science. Gaining a new vision, each embarks on a new path with a new mission.

The new path led to an intensified way of living in which profound responses to the mysterious, and even supernatural, element in nature overcome allegiance to Christian doctrine, and unreserved emotions—desire, anger, jealousy, joy—overrule verbal and behavioral constraints. As part of this shift, Synge immersed himself in the culture of the rural poor who, he believed, incorporated within their Catholicism a pantheistic "paganism" illustrating Irish culture at its most imaginatively compelling and distinctive. In a revelatory juxtaposition, he writes that "soon after I had relinquished the Kingdom of God I began to take a real interest in the kingdom of Ireland. My politics went round from a vigorous and unreasoning loyalty to a temperate Nationalism. Everything Irish became sacred . . . and had a charm that was neither quite human nor divine, rather perhaps as if I had fallen in love with a goddess" (1982, 13). Cultural nationalism becomes here a vehicle for a contrast between the impulses he believed to be innate within himself and the Christianity he had learned as a boy, those "monotheistic doctrines" that "seem foreign to the real genius of childhood" (7).

Synge identifies Darwinian theory as the source of his rejection of biblical literalism, but Darwin appears to have enhanced tendencies already present in Synge's mind. At sixteen, he recalls, he began long walks in the Dublin mountains where the strong sensations experienced since childhood continued to take place:

> To wander as I did for years through the dawn of night with every nerve stiff and strained with expectation gives one a singular acquaintance with the essences of the world. The obscure noises of the owls and rabbits, the heavy scent of the hemlock and the flowers of the elder, the silent flight of the moths I was in search of gave me a passionate and receptive mood like that of early man. . . . The forces which rid me of theological mysticism reinforced my innate feeling for the profound mysteries of life. (9–10)

Far from becoming a skeptic, he acquired a new frame of reference for his mysticism in the experience of the natural world. Yet from the "heavy" scent of hemlock to the dusky moths, his perception of nature resembles the "Ode to a Nightingale," saturated as it is with the Keatsian confluence of sexuality and death that Synge calls "passion." Although it may seem far away from an evangelical prayer meeting in a middle-class Dublin home, his dramatic and poetic obsessions with ungoverned emotion, extremity of language, and powerful, sexualized images of fecundity and decay speak to an aesthetic rooted in a vision of sublime horror not only folkloric but evangelical. In another autobiographical fragment, he makes even more explicit his association between beauty and damnation. Walking out of St. Patrick's Cathedral into the surrounding slums, "Sunday after Sunday, strained almost to torture by the music," he finds something appalling and fascinating in the "extraordinarily passionate quarrels" of "wild children." He reflects on the synthesis of his "transcendent admiration" for the "white harmonies of the Passion according to St. Matthew" on one hand, and his "relish of delightful sympathy with the wildness of evil" on the other: "The man who feels most exquisitely the joy of contact with what is perfect in art and nature is the man who from the width and power of his thought hides the greatest number of Satanic or barbarous sympathies. His opposite is the narrow churchman or reformer who knows no ecstasy and is shocked chiefly by the material discomforts of earth or Hell" (6). Even if his language is jejune, the idea nevertheless speaks to the way his later plays, poems, and prose draw from—rather than cast aside—his evangelical upbringing. It takes a "narrow churchman" to imagine that the creed and aesthetic of passionate living Synge adopted are the products of "Satanic or barbarous sympathies."

In an essay on Ulster poets John Hewitt and W. R. Rogers, John Wilson Foster remarks, "We tend to assume . . . that whereas the Catholic Irish writer weathers an artistically fruitful crisis of faith before apostasy, his Protestant counterpart simply walks away from his religion and finds other matters of literary concern. Yet even without a crisis of faith . . . no one completely escapes a religious upbringing" (1985, 140). Foster maintains that these two nonconformist poets articulate "in the refracted ways of literature" a culture and aesthetic of nonconformism that endure even when its doctrines have been "ignored or disavowed" (140). "A religious upbringing," he continues, "establishes habits of mind which clothe the secular and, openly or secretively, the creative life" (141). Although Synge made a decisive break with the theology his family professed and turned his eye toward the world of impoverished rural Catholics, an evangelical tendency toward highly emotional, even ecstatic, apprehension of supernatural terror underlies his imaginative life even after he ceased to believe in his mother's god.[9]

Synge's development follows the Augustan narrative in what David Leigh calls its horseshoe design: the autobiographical narrator undergoes a long spiritual voyage, but returns after much struggle to his or her beginnings. In his book on structural design in the modern spiritual autobiography, Leigh offers as an epigraph the words of Albert Camus: "A man's work is nothing but a

---

9. Vivian Mercier maintains that Synge's departure from Christianity was entirely intellectual and that "he remained to the end of his short life essentially puritanical in both morals and manners" (1982, 62). I am suggesting that he also retained an attitude toward nature and human behavior that would consider as profane and dangerous that which he calls "wildness," despite its attractiveness to him.

slow task to rediscover, through the detour of art, those two or three great and simple images in whose presence his heart first opened" (2000, 1). Synge's journey took him a long way from the drawing rooms of his family's world, yet his path seems perpetually guided by those "great and simple images" that affected him in childhood. The primary image is unmistakable, and the sensation it produces reappears in his writings in many different contexts: one evening while collecting insects in the Wicklow mountains, a specter of visionary terror, "two immense luminous eyes" and "a black sinister forehead," leaves him "fascinated." "For a moment the eyes seemed to consume my personality, then the whole valley became filled with a pageant of movement and colour. . . . I did not know where or when I was existing." The image, he explains, revealed "the fearful and genuine hypnotic influence such things possess upon the prepared personality" (1982, 10). Continuing to seek "excitement near to pain," he speculates that all art arises from "prolonged unsatisfied desire" (13, 14).

Synge portrays himself in his poems, letters, and prose as filled with "unsatisfied desire," a wanderer unlikely to find peace. Yet if he did not find peace, his writings suggest that he, like his forebears in the spiritual autobiography, returned to his beginnings. His friend W. B. Yeats preferred to see Synge's journey as having found its fulfillment when,

> . . . long travelling, he had come
> Towards nightfall upon certain set apart
> In a most desolate stony place,
> Towards nightfall upon a race
> Passionate and simple like his heart.
> (1983, 133)

Perhaps as Yeats suggests, Synge's path led to a place both geographical and literary that, in resembling his own heart, provided a sense of having come home. But the evidence of his essays, poems, and plays suggests that the path also circled back home toward a potent sense of suffering, an aesthetic of beauty found in bodily distortion, death, illicit desire, and chaotic social organization: in short, the hellfire of his childhood.

Conversions to the Secular: George Bernard Shaw, J. B. Yeats, and Louis MacNeice

The evangelical fervor that captured the household of Synge's mother also drove John Butler Yeats and Louis MacNeice away from the churches in which their fathers were clergymen. Shaw's experience was different, and his revulsion was directed less against the doctrine of original sin and biblical literalism than the social and political attitudes he saw reflected in the church. All three men, however, tell stories that, as they deviate from more common patterns of deconversion and secularization narratives, incorporate the concern with political ideology and class that characterizes the Anglo-Irish autobiography. In his study of modern spiritual autobiographies, John Barbour defines a structural difference between deconversion and secularization stories:

> As a literary narrative, a version of deconversion represents a series of events arranged as a plot and a decision that the writer tries to justify. Secularization is a gradual fading away of beliefs, as religion simply ceases to inform a person's life. . . . In this century, secularization is probably the more common way that people lose their faith, but, in contrast to deconversion, it does not usually motivate or decisively shape the writing of autobiography. A version of deconversion involves the narration of the significant events that call a faith into question, an analysis of choices, and usually a rather dramatic reversal. (1994, 2–3)

The kind of crisis moment and subsequent anguish John Synge relates as his experience of deconversion fails to occur in the stories of any of these three writers, but neither does their faith "simply cease to inform" their lives. Instead, their reactions against their upbringing propel them into an insistent, lifelong reiteration of a selfhood independent of religious beliefs or affiliation.[10]

In the assortment of life writings that Stanley Weintraub has collated into *Shaw: An Autobiography*, Shaw repeatedly condemns the Church of Ireland as a source of "intolerable bondage"; "vulgarity, savagery, and bad blood" (1970, 31); and a vehicle for the expression of class contempt:

> I believe Ireland, as far as the Protestant gentry is concerned, to be the most irreligious country in the world. . . . I was never confirmed; and I believe my parents never were either. Of the seriousness with which English families

---

10. C. Day Lewis presents his "secularization" in accordance with Barbour's paradigm. Like Synge, Yeats, and MacNeice, he grew up in a clerical household, and he titles one of his chapters on early childhood "The Curate's Child." Because of his father's profession, religious practices were part of his everyday life, but he describes himself as an agnostic from childhood and says little more about the subject. Perhaps his isolation as the only child of a widowed Anglo-Irishman assigned to an English parish limited the importance of his religious affiliation to his community identity and therefore rendered it a less controversial issue in his experience and autobiographical self-construction than it might have been had he grown up primarily in Ireland. See his autobiography, *The Buried Day* (1960).

took this rite I had no conception; for Irish Protestantism was not then a religion: it was a side in political faction, a class prejudice, a conviction that Roman Catholics are socially inferior persons who will go to Hell when they die and leave Heaven in the exclusive possession of Protestant ladies and gentlemen. (14)

These sentiments first appeared in a version of the essay titled "In the Days of My Youth" published in 1898; the reappearance of the idea in 1939 (*Shaw Gives Himself Away*) and then again in 1949 (*Sixteen Self Sketches*) attests to how critical it was to his conception of his own political and artistic evolution, perhaps in part because so much of his literary life was devoted to the development of an alternate theology he only half-facetiously called "a gospel of Shawiantity" (1965, 551).

In keeping with Shaw's emphasis on practical ethics, the moment of crisis—to the degree that there is one—occurs when he decides to give up prayer as well as church attendance. "I suddenly asked myself," he writes in the preface to *Immaturity* (1930),

> why I went on repeating my prayer every night when, as I put it, I did not believe in it. Being thus brought to book by my intellectual conscience I felt obliged in common honesty to refrain from superstitious practices; and that night, for the first time since I could speak, I did not say my prayers. I missed them so much that I asked myself another question. Why am I so uncomfortable about it? Can this be conscience? But next night the discomfort wore off so much that I hardly noticed it; and the night after I had forgotten all about my prayers as completely as if I had been born a heathen. It is worth adding that this sacrifice of the grace of God, as I had been taught it, to intellectual integrity synchronised with that dawning of moral passion in me. . . . Up to that time I had not experienced the slightest remorse in telling lies whenever they seemed likely to help me out of a difficulty; rather did I revel in the exercise of dramatic invention involved. (1967, 35)

The crisis itself carries no thematic or structural importance in his lifelong vituperation against what he saw as the hypocrisy, class snobbery, colonialist insolence, and general tedium and irrelevancy of Irish Protestantism as he understood it. According to his own recounting, he became a "boy atheist" at a very young age and relied on an independently achieved sense of honor to guide him. He offers neither a series of events that led to his deconversion nor a particular moment in which it transpired. Any guilt over his decision quickly dwindles. However, as an autobiographer, Shaw uses the anecdote to portray a turning point from which he became a devout follower of the "moral passion" of honesty. Ever the ironist, Shaw finds himself born again as he shakes off the vestiges of piety.

In the autobiography of J. B. Yeats, the experience of deconversion is similarly downplayed. Like Synge and one of his own exemplars, John Stuart Mill, Yeats associates his repudiation of his father's system with his response to a book: in this case, *Butler's Analogy*, which not only failed to direct him away from Deism as his father intended but also led him to the radical and sudden conclusion that "revealed religion was myth and fable" (1972, 71).[11] Although his reliance on what he sarcastically terms "school ethics" disappears along with the family hope for his church career, the book that "had shattered all my orthodoxy" seems to have produced little emotional upheaval. Despite an organizational principle based on oppositional categories, his autobiography does not posit two distinct selves situated before and after the deconversion, nor does its relatively plotless narrative depend on the moment as a pivotal point in the story of its author's maturation. He presents the anecdote instead as "yet another memory which comes to me from Trinity College," remembered "pleasantly" (71–73).

J. B. Yeats was a painter and only a very reluctant writer. Although many people urged him to write his memoirs, he could hardly bring himself to do it. In a letter to his daughter Lily he worried, "I have many doubts. The whole thing looks dubious. I would not know how to set about it" (Murphy 1978, 386). Only the persistent nagging of his children and his friend John Quinn pressed him to produce three notebooks of memoirs that W. B. Yeats then edited and published posthumously in 1923 as *Early Memories: Some Chapters of Autobiography*. In his study of its antinomial structure, George Bornstein concludes that *Early Memories* "suggests how much the two Yeatses came to share—not only myriad ideas . . . or perceptions . . . but also a common allegiance to the principle of personality in their special sense of the word" (1979, 210). Because no manuscript copy exists and the structural sophistication uncovered by Bornstein's analysis indicates a more accomplished editor than the elder Yeats would have then made, biographer William Murphy believes that "the book was largely shaped by WBY's editorial hand" (1978, 637). However, J. B. Yeats wrote to his elder son in 1918 that he had discovered a principle of organization in the contrast of the refined civilization represented by the Yeats

11. The story also echoes Benjamin Franklin's account of a book intended to sway him from Deism but that instead further confirmed his doubts about church doctrine. I have no evidence that J. B. Yeats was familiar with Franklin, although the wide circulation of the *Autobiography* renders it likely; no matter whether Yeats was following a literary model of a specifically rationalist deconversion, in each case a book serves to affirm the inner leading of the skeptical mind.

family and the primitive civilization represented by his wife's family, the Pollexfens. Elsewhere, he expresses a similar tendency to think in terms of oppositions often resulting in paradoxical resolutions.[12] It is thus likely that the fundamental structure of *Early Memories* represents the intentions of its writer, despite the extensive editorial work of his son.

The question is important because the oppositional structure of *Early Memories* is integral to its narrative of deconversion. Without the crisis as an organizational device or even a consistent chronological sequencing, Yeats as autobiographer depends upon his oppositional pairs, almost all of which bear some relation to a recurrent contrast between the pleasures of free thought and the inhibitions of Evangelicalism. The civilized manner he ascribes to the Yeatses in his letter to W. B. Yeats persists despite the detrimental influence of what he calls "Puritanism." Whether he is describing its preoccupation with conversion, its moral severity, or the worshipful fervor of its faithful, Yeats contends that Evangelicalism adulterated what he believed to be the gentlemanly values of tolerance and intellectual exploration epitomized by his father as a clergyman and member of his class. His father, obliged to have "regarded the Catholic Church as the Enemy," was at heart more at odds with the strict Presbyterianism of his neighbors in Northern Ireland (1971, 39). "I have always distrusted puritanism," Yeats asserts, and "in that respect I am a genuine Irish Protestant and believe with Christ that the law was made for man and not man for the law" (15). He objects to what he describes as a social and aesthetic prudery, suppression of individuality, and disregard for beauty. The joy and "self-loyalty" he believes necessary to artistic achievement conflict with doctrines of original sin and the necessity for self-abnegation. In the text, his friend and brother-in-law, George Pollexfen, epitomizes the man whose imagination has been limited by his evangelical religion. Only when he could dash along on a "wild and splendid race-horse" would Pollexfen's morose Puritanism be "shattered, torn away, a mere rag of antediluvianism. Then he loved all men, he loved humanity, he even loved himself" (18). In a passage from his notebooks (retained but abbreviated in *Early Memories*), Yeats contrasts his reverence for the beauty of the natural world with the meaninglessness of his obligatory church attendance. Having lost his faith but not the family obligation to attend services, he recalls, "I would stand all two hours at the door, half

---

12. A 1920 letter to John Quinn reveals in another context the extraordinary degree to which father and son echoed one another's ideas and use of contraries to express them. The elder Yeats reiterates the paradoxes of W. B. Yeats's 1903 poem "Adam's Curse" as he distinguishes between the opposing categories of sketch and portrait, then argues that at its highest level the portrait becomes a sketch (Murphy 1978, 515–16).

within and half without, so that while listening to the clergyman I could at the same time comfort my eyes and my spirit by looking out towards the sea and sky. . . . Though my mind was negative towards 'the great truths,' it was by no means negative towards matters which to my present judgment are fraught with a finer illumination" (Murphy 1978, 32).

He also complains that "puritan doctrine" serves the financial interests he associates with England and Ulster: "Commerce is war," he writes, "each man watching to take the bread out of his neighbour's mouth, and puritanism with the doctrine of the inherent badness of human nature is well calculated to hearten the fighters" (1971, 92). He receives some solace from his idea that conversions merely reinforce preexistent class and cultural traits, rather than produce them. The Wesleyan influence, he claims, made the middle classes of England even more commercial than they had been before, but "when Wesleyism affected the Irish leisured class, gentlemen before, they remained gentlemen, only with more refinement of heart and a more subtle sympathy. The wild men, described by Charles Lever, who cared for nothing except romance and courage and personal glory, now walked in the footsteps of their Lord and Master" (48).

His assessment of the relationship between theology and class perhaps explains why *Early Memories* returns repeatedly to questions of religion, rather than displaying the gradual indifference to religion that John Barbour observes in modern secularization narratives. As Yeats describes his aversion to the Northern Dissenters, he makes few distinctions between questions of theology and matters of class. "Though I hate puritanism," he writes, "I don't think I would like it to be entirely removed from the world, unless it be the Belfast variety, which like the east wind is good for neither man nor beast. There was a phrase sometimes on my father's lips, forced from him by sudden annoyance: 'Nothing can exceed the vulgar assumption of a Belfast man,' " that is, the merchants and small farmers of Ulster. Contrasting Pollexfen with the Ulsterman, he continues, "The root of my old friend's puritanism was self-immolation, the other sort is the glorification of self-assertion" (15–16). From his perspective, the "vulgarity" of Puritanism most affects the already vulgar commercial classes, but the theological ties that bind his father the gentleman to the "Belfast man" remain an irritant. Despite the years that separate the young man's experience from the elderly painter who recollected it shortly before his death at eighty-two, much of the memoir discloses his unswerving antagonism toward Evangelicalism as a theology, a way of life, and a manner of being he associates with the commercial classes. Because religion in Ireland has been so much more than a private conviction, Yeats cannot simply leave it behind.

Louis MacNeice abandoned the world of Protestant Ireland as well as his father's church, but in his poetry, radio talks, and autobiographical prose he never ceased to address his upbringing and the issues it engendered. His response is fuller and more complex than most, in part because his career was long and prolific, but even more so because his probing led him beyond the sectarian experiences of his childhood to larger questions of spirituality. As liberal Anglicans from the West of Ireland, his parents felt out of place in the gritty mill town in County Antrim where his father was rector and, eventually, bishop. Despite his desire to shift his imaginative base away from that world, in his late poem "Carrick Revisited," he affirms its abiding presence within him:

> Torn before birth from where my fathers dwelt,
> Schooled from the age of ten to a foreign voice,
> Yet neither western Ireland nor southern England
> Cancels this interlude; what chance misspelt
> May never now be righted by my choice.
>
> Whatever then my inherited or acquired
> Affinities, such remains of my childhood's frame
> Like a belated rock in the red Antrim clay
> That cannot at this era change its pitch or name—
> And the pre-natal mountain is far away.
>
> (1967, 225)

What in that past life would the speaker choose to right? The "wrong" is entrenched in the very landscape of Ulster—the "melancholy lough / Against the lurid sky over the stained water" (1967, 17)—that stood apart from the expansive skies and wide hills he held as an ideal, the dreamland of the Connemara countryside from which his parents came. Again like Synge, he found that his imagination bent toward " 'The West of Ireland,' a phrase which still stirs me, if not like a trumpet, like a fiddle half heard through a cattle fair." "For many years," he continues, "I lived on a nostalgia for somewhere I had never been" (1965, 216, 217).

Nostalgic fantasy leads him west, but memory leads back toward his mother's devastating depression and the horror of his brother's mental affliction, the gray grim skies of Antrim, the theological and political quarrels between the community and his more broad-minded and nationalist father, and a dour approach to life that permeated everything:

guilt, hell fire, Good Friday, the doctor's cough, hurried lamps in the night, melancholia, mongolism, violent sectarian voices. All this sadness and conflict and attrition and frustration were set in this one acre near the smoky town. . . . At times everything outside seemed clammy and everything inside stuffy . . . so that from a very early age I began to long for something differ- ent, to construct various dream worlds which I took it were on the map. (216)

While a university student in England, MacNeice mocked with Oxford friends the religion that nevertheless, he acknowledges, allowed "my father . . . to come into breakfast on Easter Day beaming as though he had just received a legacy" (233). But it was less the idea of God from which he distanced himself than the "mumbo jumbo" of July twelfth, "my father and Home Rule and the bony elbows of Miss Craig and the black file of mill-girls and the wickedness of Carson and the dull dank days between sodden haycocks and foghorns" (78). His principal aversion is to those "sodden haycocks and foghorns," a dreari- ness associated with evangelical theology, Northern landscapes, family trauma, and social isolation that were his experience of life in Protestant Northern Ireland.

In his analysis, the Anglicans of Ulster—being neither Catholics nor Dis- senters—experienced a constitutive loneliness for which relics of historical prestige could not compensate. He writes in his 1937 poem "Carrickfergus":

> The Norman walled this town against the country
> To stop his ears to the yelping of his slave.
> And built a church in the form of a cross but denoting
> The list of Christ on the cross in the angle of the nave.
>
> I was the rector's son, born to the anglican order,
> Banned forever from the candles of the Irish poor;
> The Chichesters knelt in marble at the end of a transept
> With ruffs about their necks, their portion sure.
>
> (1967, 69)

As a context for his childhood melancholia, MacNeice sketches the inte- rior of his father's church: the conflict implicit in its architecture between a theology of humility and its origins in conquest, its self-perpetuated isolation from the communion of the poor, and the cold formality of the marble statues commemorating their "portion" both heavenly and material. This conflict drew him, again like Synge, toward the one Catholic he knew, the good- natured cook whose "gay warm voice" and fairy stories were "our bulwark for so long against puritan repression" (1965, 41, 56). From his perspective, his world stood counter to expressions of gentleness, humor, and appreciation of natural and human beauty.

In sorting through the details of his life during a tumultuous period prior to his marriage, he wrote to a good friend that by the age of fourteen "I had already escaped from the 'fear of God' & the missionary atmosphere & general unwholesomeness" (Stallworthy 1995, 139). Yet never in any of his poems, letters, or autobiographical prose pieces does he identify a sequence of events or a single occasion during which his faith altered. Unlike Synge or J. B. Yeats, he did not encounter a book that changed his views, nor does he, like Shaw, describe an incident that finalized his rejection of religion in his own mind or revealed it to others. Neither can Jon Stallworthy, in his comprehensive biography of the poet, uncover such a story.

Perhaps no such story exists because, as his poems intimate, MacNeice may have retained his sense of the possibility of a divine presence, even if he lost his certainty of it how might be known. In the title poem of his 1941 collection, *Plant and Phantom*, MacNeice explores humanity's frustrated but ongoing search for a metaphysical reality. "Man," he writes,

> . . . felt with his hands in empty
> Air for the Word and did not
> Find it but felt the aura,
> Dew on the skin, could not forget it.
> Ever since has fumbled, intrigued,
> Clambered behind and beyond, and learnt
> Words of blessing and cursing, hoping
> To find in the end the Word Itself.
>
> (1967, 160)

The "air" in this poem is "empty," and the human subject feels no assurance that "the Word Itself" is recoverable; nevertheless, he has in the most tangible, physical way "felt" the aura of the Word like dew on his skin. MacNeice's rejection of Christian literalism and moral prescriptions, like his rejection of the Puritanism of his early childhood surroundings, does not appear to encompass a complete rejection of the spiritual domain.[13] Nor does it include a complete rejection of his father. In the gracious reconciliatory gesture of his late poem "The Truisms," the protagonist is led by an unknown guide to visit his child-

---

13. Among the abiding effects of MacNeice's religious upbringing on his lifework, Barry Sloan notes his sense of the existence of an infinite world beyond the temporal yet revealed by it, the inescapability of time and mortality, the authority of individual conscience, and the primacy of the word (2000, 172–202). MacNeice, Sloan argues, "always accepted the importance of fundamental religious questions concerning the nature of reality and the source of ultimate value in a temporal world" (201).

hood home as if in a dream, and to bless it. A little coffin holding the beliefs of his father transforms itself into a bird, and a tree emerges from the grave of his father (1967, 507). For the most part, however, MacNeice's writing remains haunted by the spiritual gloom of his childhood. The sadness of those years, like Synge's terrors, Shaw's indignant boredom, and Yeats's irritation, endures into his secular adulthood and imbues the literary achievements of his maturity.

Transformations and Adaptations

No Anglo-Irish autobiographer baldly states, "I became a nationalist or a Socialist and was obligated then to become a Roman Catholic." Many of those individuals involved in the Irish Revival worked to create a sense of tradition that could be Protestant yet very distinctly Irish and integral to the nation, and Elizabeth Bowen saw her Anglicanism as fundamental to her sense of a place in Irish history. Even before disestablishment, the Anglican Church in Ireland had its own character, formed in part by the desire to distinguish itself from Roman Catholicism by rebuking High Church tendencies in clergy or parishioners. Disestablishment brought fundamental administrative changes and ended what historian Donald Akenson calls undue English political influences and episcopal absenteeism.[14] Subsequent debate over the revision of the Book of Common Prayer also proved a testing ground for the independence of the Irish church. The conservatism of some members was even labeled "Ecclesiastical Fenianism" by an editorialist in the *Irish Ecclesiastical Gazette* (Daly 1970, 36). Church historian Gabriel Daly explains the views of Archbishop Plunket during the revision debate:

> His watchword was "patriotism," by which he meant a consciousness of the specifically Irish nature of the problems his church was facing. . . . He protested strongly against what he regarded as an exaggerated Irish concern about English opinion. "We are not, as some would represent us, 'the English Church in Ireland.' . . . Let the word Anglicanism as describing our faith and practice, be banished from our vocabulary." . . . Plunket saw the English connection as a real danger to the Church of Ireland. (36)

Some autobiographers, however, equate Anglicanism so thoroughly with England that, as their ideologies moved toward Irish nationalism, they shifted their allegiances toward either Roman Catholicism or an adamantly ecumenical stance. Stephen Gwynn notes that his aunt "took the Nationalist side, and,

14. For a summary of the effects of disestablishment, see Akenson 1971, 322–33.

later on in her life, sympathy with the people made her join the Roman Church" (1926, 14). Shane Leslie explains religious affiliation in Monaghan before the First World War as if cleric and king were one and the same: "We were not much troubled by sects," he recalls. "Everyone believed in William of Orange or the Pope. Anybody else was probably an atheist and not likely to come to any good. . . . New sects were hardly needed" (1938, 31). When he became a nationalist—and consequently withdrew his allegiance from William of Orange—the former John Leslie changed his name to "Shane" and, like Gwynn's aunt Charlotte, his religion to Roman Catholicism.

Leslie never explains the reasons for his conversion in any of his three au- tobiographies, although an unpublished letter to his friend Elsie Hope in the summer of 1908 confirms the seriousness with which he made his decision. He explains, "I took thirteen weary months to come to my decision. It is extraor- dinary what strange arguments and counter arguments will struggle in one's mind if one leaves it open to a question of this kind. However the end came and I believe I could not have chosen otherwise. . . . I have got to study here and abroad for four years and then I hope to enter the Dominican order" (1908, n.p.). How very different in tone are the remarks of his descendants who, in the family history that makes up a major part of the Castle Leslie Hotel Web site, treat his conversion to nationalism and Catholicism as if it were principally a way to pique his parents and, later, his fashionable wife: "He was also one of the few Anglo-Irish to side with the Irish cause, even compiling a Latin-Irish dictionary just in case some Ancient Roman should visit the Gaeltacht. All of this was slightly too much for his staid Protestant parents. Just as his obsession for inviting droves of elderly clerics to Castle Leslie proved too much for our poor Mother when she was trying to hold amusing house parties. He would then order us children to entertain them, which proved too much for us" (Banon and Leslie 2002, n.p.).

With their comic approach to autobiography, the Leslies discuss few mat- ters of religion or politics with sobriety, at least in public. Throughout his au- tobiographies, Sir Shane frequently addresses religion as a topic, but never with the serious tone of his letter to Elsie Hope or his publications in Catholic journals. Instead, he offers derisive and witty anecdotes about the eccentric clerics of his childhood and the outrageous forms of sectarian bigotries that would be laughable were they not so lethal. "Ireland is distracted between two divided nations and two unforgiving religions," Leslie reflects in *Long Shadows*, completed only a few years before his death in 1971. "The Son of God Himself could not act as Speaker to a united Irish Parliament without having to revise the Sermon on the Mount" (1966, 137).

Like Shane Leslie, the liberal activist and longtime Labour Party MP

Frank Pakenham altered his politics and his religion during the first half of the twentieth century, but his autobiographical approach to the subject is radically different from Leslie's. *Born to Believe* is a true spiritual autobiography, and although it begins with the detailed survey of family history and properties typical of the Anglo-Irish autobiography, the text quickly moves inward and traces the interconnected development of the four passions of Pakenham's life: Christianity; his wife, Elizabeth; socialism; and worldwide efforts toward national independence and human rights. In the early 1930s, Pakenham became an active Socialist and supporter of the "full Irish Nationalist claim." Until that period, his nationalism had been emotional, "on an imaginative, almost poetic plane. Yeats's poems and autobiographies jostled for pride of place with Roger Casement's speech from the dock" (1953, 72, 73). But his study of anticolonial nationalism around the world led him to argue for normalized relations between England and Ireland and to "ponder for the first time over the deeper meanings of international principles and values" (76). And, at the same time, he felt his path leading toward Roman Catholicism, although he was fearful of making such a momentous leap and anxious about the reaction of his wife (a Socialist herself and a nominal Unitarian who found the Church of England superstitious). Consequently, he held off from the profession of his beliefs until the prospect of being killed in war forced his decision; as a soldier on leave, he was received into the Catholic Church in 1940.

He declares in his autobiography that he will "make no attempt to estimate . . . how much my Catholicism owes initially and subsequently to Ireland" (72), but his Christianity forms the foundation of his political views rather than deriving from them: "The Socialist doctrine of equality," Pakenham writes, "seemed to me . . . the logical extension of Christianity to politics" (93). He depicts his conversion as in many ways inexplicable; he acknowledges an inability to explain why he sought a Catholic priest to answer his spiritual quandaries, but reflects that he found his way to the Jesuit residence as might a "homing pigeon." More analytically, he defines what he calls the "special blend of certainty and humility" in Roman Catholicism as having attracted his democratic instincts (97). In keeping with his ethic of tolerance, Pakenham refrains from disparaging Anglicanism or other forms of belief but makes clear that a radical Catholic socialism perhaps more English than Irish in character spoke firmly to his political consciousness, while his political views were in turn shaped by his belief in a Christian mandate to pursue social justice.

The inner life fashioned in the Anglo-Irish spiritual autobiography invariably merges with a communal identity or the desire to form a different one. The desire for greater community drives many of these narratives, whether taking the form of the imaginative interaction with "the social idea" Elizabeth

Bowen found in Anglican service, an escape from the terrible loneliness of a childhood vision of abandonment in hell, an effort to join in a socialist reformation of society, or a transfer of allegiance to what Shane Leslie calls "the church of the people." With the 2000 census reporting that only 2.5 percent of the population of the Republic of Ireland claim an affiliation with the Church of Ireland (in contrast to the 91.6 percent who identify themselves as Roman Catholic), Anglicans as a religious minority now struggle to assert themselves as part of the national life.

A communal identity at best offers more than an occasion for pensive nostalgia. In both the autobiographical essays of novelist William Trevor, it is all the decaying church buildings of his Cork childhood appear to offer. The three small towns of his youth, Trevor remarks, might "be three towns anywhere in Ireland: big Catholic church, old Protestant graves, a cinema struggling on" (1993, 1). The formerly glorious St. Mary's Parish Church ("the most impressive parish church in Ireland") is now rented as a movie backdrop; the movie's directors, as Trevor and the local clergyman observe, know so little of Irish Anglican practices that they have placed massive candles around the empty coffin they are filming (4–5). With its crumbling building and enervated atmosphere, the scene evokes a mood like that of Philip Larkin's much anthologized 1954 poem, "Church Going." In the poem, the narrator—a tourist on a bicycle—wanders by a deserted Anglican Church in the English countryside. Noting the "tense, musty, unignorable silence" of "a shape less recognisable each week, / A purpose more obscure," he drops an "Irish sixpence" in the coin box and reflects, "the place was not worth stopping for." However, he grudgingly awards it his respect as having once been the place where the primary rituals of life were enacted, a place "proper to grow wise in, / If only that so many dead lie round" (1989, 97, 98).

The consciousness of decline has shaped the plot of almost every Anglo-Irish autobiography, yet some writers have been able to resist that particular narrative without necessarily writing themselves out of the Church of Ireland. Having been appointed a select vestryman at the Church of St. Anne's at the turn of the century, Stephen Gwynn's declaration as a nationalist MP resulted in his being "quietly and unobtrusively . . . dropped. The posts were plainly held to be incompatible" (1926, 270). But Gwynn continued to believe that an ecumenical outlook would prove a way to reconcile what had been—and would be again under De Valera's government—"incompatible" identities. At the turn of the present century, the Church of Ireland as an institution energetically champions ecumenism; a recent work by Timothy Kinahan, rector of Gilnahirk in East Belfast, goes so far as to argue the case for ecumenical Christianity on biblical as well as practical grounds (1995). The Church of Ireland regularly promotes and hosts interfaith gatherings, offers itself as a mediator between warring parties, and—as difficult as it might have been to imagine only decades ago—the 2001 Christmas homily in the *Ecclesiastical Gazette* counsels readers to meditate on the figure of Virgin Mary as a source of spiritual guidance. The hunger for community that drove various writers out of or into their Irish Protestant identity appears to require the embrace of a much wider community than ever before.

5

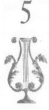

Comic Autobiography and the Satiric Tradition

At the Web site of what has now become the Castle Leslie Hotel in Monaghan, Ulton Banon and Desmond Leslie demonstrate the junction of travel writing, family history, and class mythos that produces the singular phenomenon of the Anglo-Irish comic autobiography. Fourteen sections describe in lively detail the interiors of particular rooms and the history of the family members associated with each room. As part of the general account of the house and family, they write:

> Charles II Powell Leslie . . . was a keen amateur architect designing the present farm buildings and the fairy tale gate lodge which looks down the lake to the castle. His widow Helen ran the estate during the time of the famine. . . . She had a famine wall built around the estate to provide work (this was not to keep the Leslie's in as some people have suggested) and set up soup kitchens to provide food for the starving. She continued to run the estate most capably until her son Charles Powell Leslie III came of age. Charles Powell Leslie III simply loved big house parties and wanted to entertain on the Grand scale. His taste in architecture ran from "Free Range Gothic" "Early Taj Mahal" "Late Rothschild" "Bahnhof Baroque" and "Jacobean Bloody." Some of his plans included a cut price copy of the French Chateau de Chambord at least six times larger than the present house and a nine storied gothic tower in the middle of the lake reachable only by Venetian gondolas. Although Charles Powell Leslie III never married he achieved a number of quite successful erections among them the Grain Merchant Store in Glaslough village and the entrance lodges at the main gates to the Castle. Sadly for Charles but fortunately for Leslie family finances he choked on a fish bone before he could realise any of his major architectural fantasies. (2002, n.p.)

Here are the wild, extravagant ancestors of a declined family, their story peppered with ludicrous elements of sex and death and meshed with the story of the house as if it were a member of the family. Other pages of the Web site

126

present the Castle's numerous ghosts, its outlandish toilets, and the ruminations of the family dogs. The self-ridiculing humor draws from more than three centuries of caricature originating in England and adapted in the early eighteenth century by the Anglo-Irish as a language of self-description.

Written with the bemused, derisive wit that characterizes the autobiographies of Desmond Leslie's sister, Anita, the Web site exists to amuse its creators and attract customers, in all probability prosperous local ones, in that the hotel caters weddings and business conferences, while sponsoring a local gourmet club and classical musical recitals. Offering moderate prices, elegant dinners, and Cuban cigars, Castle Leslie appears to be marketed less at the American tourist and more at young urban professionals from the region who fancifully identify themselves with the owners. The Leslies act as the conservators of good taste, made interesting by their eccentric edge, and their guests—people drawn by gourmet vegetarian dining, good wine, chamber music, and outrageous chamber pots—presumably see themselves in the same way. As Banon and Leslie describe the estate improvements and famine-era charity so common in Anglo-Irish family histories, they pay homage to what I have earlier called "the genealogical mandate" while also lampooning it. The inheritors of Castle Leslie participate in one of the most distinctive gestures of Anglo-Irish self-portraiture: a mockery of tradition that is itself traditional.

Like Desmond Leslie and Ulton Banon, G. B. Shaw expresses an attitude that both defines a primary trait of Anglo-Irish life writing and, at the same time, works to counteract the relentless saga of familial and cultural decline in and against which individuals came to write their lives. Relating the story of his family's foibles and failures, Shaw quips, "If you cannot get rid of the family skeleton, you may as well make it dance" (1970, 40). Anglo-Ireland dressed its demise in a tragic buskin, but its autobiographers also take a surprisingly comic outlook toward the historical and familial anxieties treated so solemnly by writers like Elizabeth Bowen, T. R. Henn, Sybil Lubbock, and W. B. Yeats. The sardonic humor that pervades many Anglo-Irish autobiographies centers on shared preoccupations with childhood, the social indicators of language and manners, family history, inherited property, religious difference, and even the narrative of extinction itself. In satirizing the very tropes that are regularly summoned to fortify Anglo-Irish assertions of superiority, the comic autobiographer examines them as sites of critical inquiry as well as emblems of a lost way of life.

Generic Relations and Historical Influences

Comedy has been integral to Anglo-Irish life writing since the eighteenth century to a degree unknown in other English-language autobiography. In the familiar traditions of English and American life writing, comedy and autobiography seem to be incompatible genres. Offering tales of the triumph or defeat of individuals in accordance with their own power to develop or with the clear intervention of higher powers, English and American autobiographers rarely articulate the acceptance of life's limitations and the follies of human character endemic to comedy. Even political memoirs or tales of hunting and fishing adventures tend to valorize human volition or skill, and whether that skill reveals itself in the salmon stream, on the battlefield, or in the diplomatic mission, such autobiographical writings base themselves on a theory of human development as much as do narratives of conversion, autobiographical bildungsromans, or the picaresque adventures of sailors, thespians, prostitutes, and thieves.

The comic autobiography, instead, engages a vision Susanne Langer has defined in *Feeling and Form* as one both

> religious and ribald, knowing and defiant, social and freakishly individual. The illusion of life which the comic poet creates is of the oncoming future fraught with dangers and opportunities, that is, with physical or social events occurring by chance and building up the coincidences with which individuals cope according to their lights. This ineluctable future—ineluctable because its countless factors are beyond human knowledge and control—is Fortune. (1953, 331)

The outlook that Langer calls "the essence of comedy" expresses a fundamental skepticism about human possibilities and a concurrent sense that the fortunes of any individual are dependent on a confluence of wit, coincidence, and a thousand other factors beyond the protagonist's control. It is grossly at odds with the patterns of providential intervention and inward development established by biblical models in so much English-language life writing. Because the comic outlook is generally alien to autobiography, there must be particular reasons Anglo-Irish life writing so often proceeds according to its rhythms.

The motives for depicting the self in such an unusual way derive from a confluence of factors: the unmistakable incongruities of the Anglo-Irish position in Ireland, the development of a behavioral code that encouraged a strange wedding of emotional reserve and vehement speech, a religious tradition that inclined autobiography toward less earnest and confessional directions than did Low Church Evangelicalism, and the literary traditions of travel writing and political caricature based in an unusual colonial condition.

The first of these four factors, the simultaneous instability and inflexibility of the Anglo-Irish position, compelled in more perceptive observers recognition of its potentially comic paradoxes. Family prominence could be fleeting, given intermarriage, frequent changes between religious affiliations, and the ups and downs of private income. Yet the rules governing a family's specific social position could be so unbending, as Shaw recalls of his own Dublin petit bourgeois family, as to restrict an individual with maddening precision and predictability. Added to such complications is the question of where one stands within Ireland more generally. Stephen Gwynn, J. C. Beckett, and Monk Gibbon—all of whom had full lives and successful careers in modern Ireland—attest to their bewilderment and regret at being distinguished from the majority population by a hyphenated descriptor. As if in answer, George Moore jokes that a man cannot be considered Irish if his family has lived in Ireland only four hundred years: a hyperbolic witticism, but reflective of an attitude taken seriously enough to provoke frequent recitals of long lineage in defense of one's claims to an Irish identity.[1] The autobiographical narrator of Moore's *Hail and Farewell* (1911–1914) also satirizes the ability of his class to cope with the future. To his brother's admission that "every class has its ups and downs, and there is no doubt that ours in going though a crisis," he retorts, "We have outlived our day, that is all; and in thirty years we shall be, as I have said, as extinct as the Dodo" (1985, 636). Using the satiric techniques of reduction, he dismisses his own society by equating its collapse with the demise of a whimsically named bird that could not adapt to suddenly altered conditions.[2]

1. Only Moore sees the humor in either the accusation or its defense, but the computation of years resident in Ireland as a claim to legitimate belonging is ubiquitous in Anglo-Irish autobiography. Raymond Brooke begins his 1961 autobiography, *The Brimming River:* "The first of my forebears to arrive in Ireland was Sir Basil Brooke, Knight, who came as a Settler in the reign of Queen Elizabeth the First. As that was nearly four hundred years ago and since my family has lived in Ireland from that time onwards, I think I may claim to be Irish—though I know there are many who would not admit the claim in one of English descent" (1961, 11). Frustrated by having been dubbed an "Anglo-Irishman *par excellence*" and consequently "spiritually hyphenated without knowing it," Stephen Gwynn maintains that "if anybody in Ireland should have been considered as Irish, it was my mother's people" who descend from "the old Gaelic dynasties." His father's family, he reminds the reader, came to Ireland from Wales "about ten generations" past (1926, 11, 13).

2. The dodo, whose name is thought to derive from the Dutch *dodoor* (sluggard) or the Portuguese *doudo* ("foolish"), died out because they had few defenses and did not hide from the sailors who slaughtered them or the newly introduced predators who disturbed their habitats and hunted them. Nothing in the context of Moore's simile suggests that he is imputing blame to those individuals who are taking power from the landlords, as one could blame the sailors who cruelly and

In the third volume of *Hail and Farewell*, Moore depicts the quandary of his brother Maurice as typical of the best of his class. Earnest, reformist, and energetic, Maurice, in Moore's eyes, is nevertheless doomed by the impossibility of his irrelevant position. Through leveling analogies, the narrator rebuffs his brother's aspirations to restore Moore Hall to its former grandeur by reminding him that his modern improvements are anachronistic in a house that is itself an anachronism:

> On our way to the bathroom he explained how the drip might be mitigated. Here, he said, is the bathroom, and I answered: 'Tis well; but the great eighteenth century knew not bathrooms, and we talked of the footpans and the bidets that once formed part of the furniture of every bedroom, and the disrepute into which bathing had fallen since Roman times, all through the Middle Ages, until Anglo-Indians reintroduced the habit of the thorough washing of the body into Europe. (618)

An eighteenth-century life, Moore here implies, cannot be brought into the twentieth century except when its uncomfortable realities are disregarded, whether outdoor privies or a near-feudal system of brutally enforced privilege: two elements that through the leveling techniques of satire enter into an unlikely coupling. The modern bath, he suggests, is the souvenir of the English occupation of India, and his comparison insinuates more parallels between the Anglo-Indian and the Anglo-Irish than those writers who felt they needed to argue for their Irish identities would prefer to admit.

The stance taken by the narrator of *Hail and Farewell* requires little empathy and less pity. It draws upon a behavioral code of "coolness" that emerges as a second possible source of the unusual tendency toward comedy in Anglo-Irish autobiography. This quality appears frequently as a flattering epithet in the comic autobiography, as in George Birmingham's book *An Irishman Looks at His World* (1919) where he repeats the term numerous times in conjunction with "sanity," "skepticism," and "aloofness" as the highest compliments he could pay. Shane Leslie recalls the book of family caricatures in which his father and grandfather sketched cartoons demolishing with "wild humour" the dignity of the family, their neighbors, and their servants (1938, 24–25). Those autobiographers whose tone inclines toward mordant wit also abjure any evocation of sympathetic emotion for the childhood self. The novelist and physician Henry de Vere Stacpoole abhors the revelation of emotions in

---

unnecessarily killed masses of dodos. Instead, he draws this loose parallel to invoke biological determinism as a way of understanding national and individual character.

autobiography, calling "self-revelations" "bits of cat's meat on a slab for the fe-
lines that are fond of such stuff to devour" (1942, 15), while Samuel Hussey declares, "I have none of those infantile recollections which are such an insult on
the general attention when put in print" (1904, 17). George Moore turns an
equally cold eye on childhood: as depicted in *Confessions of a Young Man* (1888)
and *Hail and Farewell*, young "Master George" is no sensitive youth longing
for art but an ignorant barbarian who maims cats, torments his younger
brother, and waves pig bladders at his nursemaids. Elizabeth Bowen's autobiographies are rarely comic, and she delineates the "infantile recollections" of
childhood consciousness with attentive precision; her novels and short stories
resonate with the suffering of isolated motherless girls. Yet even Elizabeth
Bowen insists that as an adolescent, she too was temperamentally insensitive.
Placed in a boarding school after the death of her mother and the incapacitat-
ing mental illness of her father, she reflects that as "a toughish, thick child, I
did not in fact suffer in any way" (1950, 192). Apparently, an ethic of stoic reserve rendered admissions of emotional vulnerability unthinkable in either life
or life writing, although they could be deflected into fiction.

In the first volume of *Sixteen Self Sketches* (1949), George Bernard Shaw
excises any sign of pathos in the story of his babyhood. He draws his anecdotes
from George Carter Shaw's affectionate letters to his wife written while she
was away visiting her relatives in Galway, "leaving me and Yuppy [Shaw's sis-
ter] in charge of our father." This tender, lighthearted correspondence relates
the hilarious antics of an audacious toddler inexplicably nicknamed "Bob" and
seems to represent the happiest of families (1970, 5–8). Only in other essays,
published both before and after *Sixteen Self Sketches*, does Shaw reveal that his
father was an incorrigible drunkard whose inability to handle money at last
broke up their family. Even when he addresses the subject in the preface to *Im-
maturity* (1930), it is less as a personal story than as one aspect of a larger analysis of the inflexible class and gender roles that drove his parents into
perpetually dissatisfied lives.[3]

Violet Powell analyzes the ethic of "coolness" as it damaged her mother's
life and her own in the first chapter of *Within the Family Circle*. The opening
section describes the devastating effects of her mother's chronic and crippling

---

3. Readers must take great care in using Stanley Weintraub's edition (1970) of Shaw's autobiographical writings. Weintraub has selected units as small as single paragraphs from Shaw's non-
fiction prose and, without any notation in the text itself, strung these excerpts together into a
narrative divided (by Weintraub) into separate chapters with descriptive titles. Only an examination of the appendix in conjunction with a primary bibliography allows the reader to discover
when each portion was written and for what context.

arthritis, as well as the loneliness of her widowhood. Apologizing for what she fears could be taken as a lack of respect for her mother's privacy, Powell explains how much her mother hated self-revelation or complaints:

> My mother's courage in a life of constant and often excruciating pain was undefeated, but her horror of self-indulgence made her life even harder than her infirmities dictated. . . . A passionate desire for privacy, and a phenomenal reticence about bodily functions, kept her growing family at arm's length, a distance that sometimes became so far stretched that the methods of an Oriental court had to be resorted to when an interview became essential. (1976, 4–5)

This passage presents the only moment when Violet Powell discusses directly the matter of her mother's illness and consequent separation from her children. The remainder of *Within the Family Circle* continues with the witty, flippant caricatures of her earlier autobiography, wherein she narrates the misadventures of the children and the various domestics who cared for them. In its nostalgic humor, *Five Out of Six* (1960) effectively represses the reasons Violet and her five brothers and sisters were brought up by paid caretakers. Likewise, the numerous chapters on childhood in the autobiographies of her siblings Frank and Mary Pakenham are entirely silent on the subject of their father's premature death and their mother's illness and absence; their narratives of childhood concentrate instead, especially in Mary's case, on comic deflations of childhood self-importance.

Such a stringent view toward emotional expression works in tandem with literary models that discourage the writing of one's life as a narrative of inner development. Private libraries and public reading rooms of nineteenth-century and early-twentieth-century Ireland tended to offer the episodic fiction of a century before; instead of Eliot or Dickens, readers devoured narratives of pirates, sea captains, and rogues, as well as novels by Defoe, Fielding, Swift, and even Voltaire, reinforcing a tendency toward picaresque narrative structure and a comic approach to experience.[4] In Anglo-Irish autobiographies, a structural pattern based on change or development of character is far less common than one in which a relatively static protagonist copes with the oddities of his or her environment and a general decline in status. This difference helps to explain why the apparently antithetical genres of autobiogra-

---

4. For detailed studies of the contents of private libraries, public reading rooms, and Irish bookseller inventories in the nineteenth century, see the collection of essays in Cunningham and Kennedy's *Experience of Reading: Irish Historical Perspectives* (1999).

phy and satiric comedy might conjoin. Notoriously parasitic, satire can invade other genres—like poetry, drama, the novel, and even autobiography—so as to make clear generic classifications nearly impossible. Only George Moore's *Confessions of a Young Man* and *Hail and Farewell* brandish the sustained irony and multiple satiric devices that allow them to inhabit equally the genres of autobiography and comedy, but other Anglo-Irish autobiographies offer a surprising number of satiric moments, while they draw from the episodic narrative structure and reductive approach to the self intrinsic to comedy.

The paucity of commentary on the relations of comedy and autobiography testifies to the singularity of this fusion of genres. In one of the few examinations of autobiography as comedy, James Olney argues that its humor derives from the contrast between the past self and the narrating persona. More naive or ignorant than the recollective narrator, the past self suffers as the object of ironic distance and comic disparagement (1984, 197).[5] This repudiative self-recollection forms part of the mockery of youth evident in the writings of W. B. Yeats, Mary Pakenham, and Violet Powell as well as providing the foundational organization of George Moore's *Hail and Farewell*, although Moore also casts his recollecting persona as a naïf whose understanding catches up with his author's only at the book's conclusion. But in most of the texts here under consideration, the source of comedy does not lie in the ironic distancing of present speaker from past self that Olney identifies. Anglo-Irish comic autobiography rarely speaks from the standpoint of a wiser self examining the follies of youth. In most cases, the autobiographical persona presents him- or herself as either a skeptic or a fool from childhood into maturity; the story follows the narrator's various attempts to cope with the surrounding world, rather than centering on a transformative moment of awakening and development.

In comic tours de force like Moore's *Confessions of a Young Man* and *Hail and Farewell*, the idea of transformation is itself subject to parodic reduction. Moore's persona is so frequently thrown from his horse on the path to Damascus by one revelation or another, so perpetually awakened to various siren solicitations of art and desire, so subject to multiple re-creations "in the womb of a new nationality" (1972, 129) that Moore successfully demolishes the trope of transformational development with the comic techniques of exaggeration and

5. In addition to Olney's article on Yeats's autobiographies as comedy, see Hazard Adams's study of the same subject (1965); R. Victoria Arana's study of autobiographical comedy in Gosse (1977); Eugene August's similar approach to the autobiographies of Charles Darwin (1989); and chapters 4 and 5 of my own *George Moore and the Autogenous Self* (1994). To my knowledge, these five studies constitute all that has been published on the topic.

excessive repetition. Repeatedly, he dismisses the idea of human development; in the preface to the 1904 revision of *Confessions of a Young Man*, sixteen years after its initial publication, he declares, "No one has changed less than I" (38). Moore rewrote his self-portrait in this and at least five other autobiographies, but he remained committed to the theory that although the portrait might change, its subject had never done so. To regard the self as an essentially static figure in the midst of an unstable world turns the focus away from internal development and toward a series of events in which, to invoke again Susanne Langer's terms, individuals cope according to their lights with an ineluctable future.

All of these propensities are evident even in a more conventional autobiography than Moore's. Mary Pakenham's *Brought Up and Brought Out* (1938) proceeds chronologically from birth to adulthood, and its humor is genial, if deflating. Her mockery of the childhood self exposes the discrepancy between a child's sense of reality and the adult narrator's; its comedy thus derives from the ironic distancing discussed by James Olney. But as is characteristic of Anglo-Irish comic autobiography, her irony derives primarily from cultural misunderstandings. An incompliant Irish reality persistently frustrates young Mary's confidence that Ireland will deliver itself neatly to the expectations of a party of well-fed children traveling from the South of England to "Ahlan." On the way to an annual summer stay in her father's family home in Munster, Pakenham and her siblings begin their journey to Euston station in a "four-wheeler," "rumbling through the dark streets, laughing and shouting and banging on the windows and screaming 'There's a pub' every time we saw gaslights and frosted glass" (10). The children wield a synecdoche of expectation that the amused reader knows to be absurd: Ireland cannot be reduced to a pub, and frosted glass does not always indicate a pub.

Similar disenchantments transpire when the children fail to distinguish between a tall story and mundane reality. Pakenham relates with chagrin the story of a bog and gravel pit near Pakenham Hall rumored to have been the site of a battle and a place one might find human skulls. Mary and her siblings launch a search for "four each to fit on to the knobs of our bedposts," and years later "after we were all grown up," one of the group claims to have discovered in the same spot a remarkable source of prehistoric bones: "Our crowning find was a complete body, so complete in fact that even we, poor at Zoology as we were, could not fail to recognize the little hooves, the skimpy tail, the long furry ears. It appears that what we had discovered was the local Kensal Green for donkeys" (26–27). Adulthood brings no wisdom: as children and again when older, they maintain exotic visions of Ireland that are summarily collapsed, exposing Mary and her siblings as the butt of the joke they unwittingly play on themselves, and that Mary Pakenham plays on all in retelling the stories of their folly.

The chronological arrangement and retrospective structure of *Brought Up and Brought Out* place the child in the conventional position of being more naive than the adult narrator, although barely so. As a travel narrative, Somerville and Ross's *Through Connemara in a Governess Cart* (1893) derives none of its humor at the expense of an earlier self, although its comedy also arises from clashes of culture and the extreme distances between idealized norms of behavior and what one actually finds in a diverse world. These norms, however, are not easily identifiable as either "Anglo" or "Irish." Escaping the dirt and rain of a June holiday in London, the "Irish cousins" decide to "explore the glories of [their] native country" (3). An acquaintance who traveled through Connemara some thirty years before has warned them what to expect: his request for a dinner other than whiskey and bread brought baffled looks, a horrifying "death screech in the kitchen," and a chicken "served up on a kitchen plate, brown and shrivelled as a 'She' in her last moments, and boiled with a little hot water as its only sauce" (43). The cousins find conditions much improved through the mediations of the many English tourists who now pass through the mountains. Yet these English tourists, with their pink Oxford blazers, faces with "the colour and glossy texture of Aspinall's Royal Mail red enamel" (45), and endless talk of fishing, seem as outlandish as the rural poor.

Armed with a jar of Bovril, a spirit lamp, and a folding rubber bathtub, the cousins prove adequate to the challenge, but their naïveté is as much a source of humor as the behavior of the people they meet, both native Irish and traveling English. Unable to decide what to do when they encounter a ferocious bulldog at the same time as a group of cattle "with the most villainous expression of countenance, and horns like Malay Krisses" (51–52), they stone the cattle, fire a cumbersome pistol that at first refuses to be dislodged from one cousin's mackintosh, and eventually have to pay off a rough man who materializes from nowhere and accuses them of taking out the dog in order to run off his cows. Whether the journey moves through time, as in Pakenham's autobiography, or across space, as in *Through Connemara in a Governess Cart*, the depiction of the self is reductive, and its comedy evolves from scenes of cultural misapprehension rather than a retrospectively ironic view of a past self.

The boundaries often blur between autobiography and travel writing of the kind Somerville and Ross produced. Particularly in the depiction of the self as a predominantly static character whose resources are challenged by the demands of a changing environment, both genres of writing tend to exaggerate those characteristics that distinguish the writer from the population he or she encounters. Given this affinity between genres, I would propose as a fourth

(and final) reason for the development of the comic autobiography the popularity of travel writing and the political satires with which it merged in the seventeenth and eighteenth centuries. The impulse to see one's self, family, and
social group in comic and frequently openly satiric ways may have been shaped
by the combative rhetoric of political satire and the conventions of travel literature set in Ireland, but aimed at an audience of English readers and urbane
Anglo-Irish. Political satirists, travel writers, and autobiographers display local
language, dress, politics, and social customs for the amusement of the readers,
who may or may not be of the same group as the author but who share more
with him or her than they share with the exotic native.[6]

Many Anglo-Irish autobiographies from the eighteenth century to the
more recent past attempt to divert their readers with the language, dress, and
habits of the Irish poor, even if such moments are at odds with the general
tenor of their work. Samuel Carter Hall, who lived intermittently in Kerry and
West Cork, where his English father was garrisoned and eventually managed a
copper-mining venture, writes without sentimentality of conditions among
child laborers, farmworkers, press gangs, and the mentally ill, while recording
with passionate outrage the discrimination against Jews and Catholics he wit-
nessed in early-nineteenth-century England and Ireland. Nevertheless, even a
serious observer like Hall entertains his English readers with examples of the
"pointed, forcible, and generally highly poetic" witticisms uttered by Irish
beggars both to one another and to the tourists from whom they might hope a
donation was forthcoming (1883, 530). In keeping with his sympathetic approach, Hall includes a number of jokes concerning religious differences in
which Catholics take the last word and triumph over Protestants in the after-
life.[7] Grouping these stories under a subheading, "Irish Wit," Hall draws on

6. Seamus Deane explains the eighteenth-century controversy surrounding the ethics of depiction in the travel literature of the time, much of it directly involving English depictions of the
Irish. Swift, he argues, participates in this debate in *A Modest Proposal* and other works. Swift's nar-
rators have been so fully trained to see the native as an exotic figure that they are doomed to con-
found fantasy and reality even after returning to their homelands (1986b, 17–19).

7. For example: "Not long ago this incident took place in Kingston, where the 'pro-
Cathedral' was in process of erection. A man was busily making mortar; a gentleman passed by and
addressed him: 'What are you building there?' 'A church, yer honor.' 'Oh, a church; of what denomination?' 'Of no denomination at all, yer honor; it's a holy Roman Catholic Church.' 'I'm very
sorry to hear it.' *'Yes, sir, that's what the devil says,'* said Paddy as he resumed his work" (Hall 1883,
532). Although "gentleman" could describe a Catholic of means, it here immediately designates an
intolerant Protestant, whereas the designation "man" indicates "workman" and the phrase "yer
honor" signals that the speaker is a workman who is most likely Catholic. Even before the religious theme of the joke is introduced, church affiliation is implied through class indicators and
speech.

the picturesque characterizations that made his wife's *Sketches of Irish Characters* (1829–1831) and *Stories of the Irish Peasantry* (1840) enormously popular works. Autobiographies like Hall's that draw from the motifs of travel writing are often organized as books of travel essays, with chapter titles denoting specific places, groups of people, or typical events rather than periods of the writer's life.

The autobiography of William Orpen, for example, rattles out one humorous anecdote after another, from the outlandish sayings of everyone from Biddy O'Toole the Dublin beggar to Field Marshall Sir Henry Wilson with his "unsurpassed sense of humour" and proclivity for "word contests" (1925, 29). *Stories of Old Ireland and Myself* tells us little about the inner life of the painter; although he entered the Dublin School of Art at eleven and "at once became on old man, one of the world's workers," he never admits the reader into what must have been an extraordinary experience for a young boy (21). The generic features of travel essays and memoirs overlap with the features of autobiography, and even when book titles point more toward a personal subject matter— as in *After Ten Years: A Personal Record, The Child in the Crystal*, or *The Film of Memory*—writers devote whole chapters to the strange ways of the Irish poor, suggesting again how much life writing takes shape from the preestablished patterns of expectation.

Comic representations sometimes amount to no more than the predictable caricatures of an underclass drawn by persons whose norms have been vindicated by their political and economic sovereignty. However, some of the most mordant portraiture is reserved for families and social acquaintances of the writers themselves, whose most eccentric traits are both ridiculed and celebrated. From the memoirs of Sir Jonah Barrington to the Web pages that advertise the Leslie family's hotel in Monaghan, the peculiarities of the author's own family and class take center stage. On one hand, the comedy of self-description highlights traits thought to distinguish the Anglo-Irish from their neighbors. As contrasting stereotypes, they are "cool" rather than hotheaded, "skeptical" rather than superstitious, "sardonic" rather than melancholy, "quizzical" and excessively abstract but not brutal or sentimental. On the other hand, some terms of self-description duplicate, and may be derived from, those characteristics ascribed to the majority population.

From the late 1600s through the early nineteenth century, the Irish elite— privileged by class, ethnicity, religious affiliation, or some combination of the three—underwent many changes in their sense of who they were. From his extensive examination of unpublished Protestant autobiographies of the late seventeenth and eighteenth centuries, Toby Barnard draws several causes for the increasing detachment of the "English in Ireland" from the mother country.

The fashion for amateur antiquarianism, Barnard maintains, resulted in genealogical researches often exposing family origins other than English, whereas opportunities for travel and education on the Continent led to the experience of being identified as Irish rather than English. Travel also resulted in exposure to different religions and a sense of fellowship with an international Protestant community rather than one associated exclusively with England (1998, 216–23). Around the same time, the Anglo-Irish governing class began to see themselves as the true Irish nation in what historian Patrick McNally calls an "elitist and confessional patriotism" founded on economic privilege and access to political governance (1999, 40).

Barnard observes that "English critics may have stigmatised the troublesome English in Ireland as Irish before the latter so described themselves," and as result, the Anglo-Irish often felt, as the Anglican clergyman Samuel Madden wrote in 1738, "envied as Englishmen in Ireland, and maligned as Irish in England" (Barnard 1998, 212–13). David Hayton argues that as early as the mid-1600s, English commentators began to represent the "English in Ireland" as a very distinct group and discuss them in the same terms by which they had previously characterized the Gaelic Irish. This was a particularly important shift in attitude. Near the turn of the eighteenth century, English travel writers, essayists, and composers of jest books like *Bog Witticisms* (1680) began to apply to the Anglo-Irish, especially to the "smaller gentry," descriptors very similar to the ones they attributed to the Irish lower class. From late 1600s on, the Anglo-Irish commentators and novelists then borrowed from the grotesque imagery of picaresque travel writing and political satire to portray themselves as well as the majority population who surrounded them and at times intermarried with them. According to Hayton:

[T]he Irish gentleman, a down-at-heel army officer much given to bragging, duelling and chasing widows, was becoming a familiar literary figure. . . . [O]ften the satire was designed to include the Protestant gentry within its scope. . . . English Country Party polemics over the question of the resumption of the Irish forfeited estates in 1699–1703, which were directed specifically against the complaining "poor Protestant purchasers" in Ireland, those Anglo-Irish squires who had bought or leased lands from the original grantees and who were now to be dispossessed, made great play with the conventions of anti-Irish humour, labelling their opponents as "some Irish folks," and attributing to them "typically" Irish bulls and blunders. (1987, 148)

It is possible to locate, then, the beginnings of a self-identification very different from their English Protestant cousins' and strangely like what were in some cases their Catholic Irish ones. These terms of self-representation continue to appear even in the early to mid-nineteenth century when parliamentary reform and increasing political and economic strength among Catholics made a "British" identity more inviting to the Protestant upper classes than a continued struggle to assert themselves as a separate group constituting the true Irish nation.[8] Into this emergent sense of a contrastive identity, comedy enters as Anglo-Irish autobiographers and commentators draw upon the same figures of barbarous folkways, domestic disorder, and fiscal irresponsibility that they, like so many English commentators, had previously employed against the people they dominated.[9] By doing so, they accomplish both self-congratulatory and self-critical purposes, at times simultaneously.

Identity and Speech

Language distinctions form one of the most frequent targets of satire. Like the " 'typically' Irish bulls and blunders" reported by an English observer at the turn of the early eighteenth century, Anglo-Irish speech was recognized as different from English speech and accordingly stigmatized. Ireland hosts a wide variety of regional and class-based speech forms, and all have been subject to both pejorative and flattering commentary by the outsider and the native. Idiom, syntax, and pronunciation are diverse, socially and economically significant, and erratically measured against protean sets of norms. Because those classes in power have spoken a different language or dialect than those with less power, the varieties of speech in Ireland have long been politically charged. Rather than suppress their speech differences, Anglo-Irish writers frequently highlight their own peculiarities, as well as their neighbors', with bemused pride in their own linguistic eccentricities. The autobiographical voice may be the product of a writer's efforts to represent the self, but when

8. In his autobiography, Valentine, Lord Cloncurry, blames the postunion phenomenon of sending boys to England for a decline in nationalism among the Anglo-Irish. Referring to his own youth in the 1780s he writes, "It was the fashion of that day to educate boys in the community in the midst of which their duties and interests as men required them to live. We were not then sent to learn absenteeism and contempt, too often hatred, for our country, in the schools and colleges of England" (1849, 7).

9. The types of comic figures identified in such studies as Nilson's *Humor in Irish Literature* (1996), Mercier's *Irish Comic Tradition* (1962), and Waters's *Comic Irishman* (1984) parallel the eccentric relatives and ancestors drawn in Anglo-Irish autobiography, particularly, as in Waters's taxonomy, the clown (whose humorous traits are based on cultural differences), the rogue (who lives by wits), the stage Irishman (who is recognizable by his blundering English and extremist politics), and the hero (who is gifted, imaginative, but unconventional).

language is the focus of satire, or even of attention, the voice of one's own family and class is denaturalized. The rhetoric of sincerity typical of autobiographical discourse gives way to a more self-consciously performative speech.

The attitude of the Anglo-Irish toward their own language traits and the traits of the more Gaelic-inflected world surrounding them is complicated. It is not uniformly laudatory, condescending, or critical. In her study of Maria Edgeworth as a comic writer, Eilean Ni Chuilleanain claims Edgeworth pioneered a new approach to the diversities of Irish speech that went well beyond the attitudes of derision in prior generations of commentators. As Ni Chuilleanain explains, in the *Essay on Irish Bulls*, published first in 1802, Edgeworth and her father argue for a tolerant outlook that countered many prevailing notions about "Hibernian English." They maintain that historical conditions rather than innate differences among people produce variations in language use, that the speaker of nonstandard forms can produce a sophisticated discourse strategically incomprehensible to standard speakers, and that laughter at eccentricities of language can arise from sympathy and admiration as much as derision (1996, 26–29).

This attitude is visible in a story like Edgeworth's "Limerick Gloves" (1804), a comedy of language dissonance that nevertheless acts as a parable of mutual tolerance while positing her own class as the mediator of difference. In the story, Mr. Brian O'Neill, an Irish glover, almost loses his suit of an English woman after he tells her that he "expects" her to wear the gloves he has given her. He means merely that he hopes she will wear them; she thinks he is presumptuously calling for her obedience. Both react defensively against what they assume to be the repugnant traits of the other's national character. In a passage that could serve equally well in the *Essay on Irish Bulls*, the narrator explains that the young woman is insufficiently acquainted with English as spoken in Ireland and that the young man is insufficiently acquainted with English as spoken in England. With greater understanding and patience, she concludes, "nothing could be more for their mutual advantage than to live in union" (1989, 51).

Edgeworth gives her narrator a similar Olympian disinterestedness in *Castle Rackrent*, where she provides notes and glosses "for the information of the *ignorant* English reader" (1965, ix). In essay, short story, and novel, she distances herself from all parties: the "ignorant" English to whom she writes; the middle-class manufacturer, Mr. O'Neil, whose "Irish bulls" she defends; and the "half-sirs and squireens," the former O'Shaughlins, who assumably abandoned both surname and faith in order to retain their properties and become the Rackrents of her novel. With whom, then, did the Edgeworths belong? And how might they represent their own speech, given that speech formed such a significant factor in one's identity? The family inhabited Ireland since the 1500s and since the 1670s occupied the land that later became Edgeworthstown; sent to England as a child, Richard Lovell Edgeworth remembers being ridiculed for his Irish idioms and accent and nicknamed "Little Irish," while at home he was taunted for the speech habits learned at school in Warwick (1969, 48). In the *Essay on Irish Bulls*, he and Maria are content to define themselves as neither Irish nor English, even to assert in the conclusion that "as we were neither born nor bred in Ireland . . . we profess to be attached to the country, only for it's [*sic*] merits" (Edgeworth and Edgeworth 1979, 313). Their language, accordingly, strives to occupy a neutral zone as a normative voice.

With attitudes similar to Maria and Richard Lovell Edgeworth's, many autobiographers view the varieties of Irish speech as the product of specific historical conditions and admire their sophisticated rhetorical properties. When, for example, Samuel Hussey remembers his father's generation, it is their speech that most stands out. Hussey recalls with pride his father's stories of a colleague at the Irish Bar, "a confraternity where humour was almost as rampant as creditors," who silenced his pompous detractors by absurdities he convinced them to believe, puns, insults, attacks on his opponent's legitimacy, and sly insinuations about the intelligence of the judges before whom he tried his cases (1904, 11–13). Unlike the Edgeworths, Hussey and other more modern autobiographers go to great lengths to claim their place in Ireland; as a gesture of belonging, they emphasize the very oddness that sets their own speech apart from English norms, particularly when it combines incongruous figures or flaunts propriety and proportion. The letters of Somerville and Ross also indicate most clearly how much language mattered. The long, colorful narratives the two spun into their hundreds of letters to one another reveal how they saw use of English as an indicator of where one stood along a hierarchy of class differentiation and as a key to character, intelligence, and the degree of respect to which one was due. Their correspondence reveals that both women regularly and gleefully noted the verbal affectations of their own class, as well as recording the exotic speech of the lower class.

As the cousins practice the art of mimicry, Somerville enjoys ridiculing in a letter to Violet Martin "your own dear Ja-ack De Burg" who

> developed a new and extraordinary trick in connection with his stutter. When he cant get hold of a word he scrabbles his fingers up and down his nose. They canter from his forehead to the end of his nose, as one makes a spider to alarm children—and sometimes in moments of great difficulty take a little mad gallop round his eye. No words can express my anguish of suppressed laughter, while he was trying to tell me that he knew "La-adies didn't care to dance with

ma-aw-aw-ried men" while his fingers caracoled over his entire face in the
agony. (Somerville and Ross 1989, 14)

Their amusement is typical of a humor tradition that, even before Swift, made
the physical body the most common locus of satirical reference. In a culture
that valued quick wit and emphatic speech, the satire is social as well as personal. Somerville's immediate family, according to Gifford Lewis, eschewed
the exaggerated Anglo-Irish pronunciation that transforms "park" into "pork"
and "Paris" into "Paw-ris"; in drawing a verbal caricature of De Burg's droll
gestures and his pronunciation of the word *married*, Edith Somerville mimics
a distinctively Anglo-Irish way of speaking (Somerville and Ross 1989, 11). By
lampooning the affectations of a class with which she nevertheless strongly
identifies and whose oddities she finds for the most part benign and interesting, Somerville implicitly raises the question of when eccentricity becomes the
irredeemably ridiculous.

The letters of Somerville and Ross abound in similar notations and parodies of Anglo-Irish malapropisms, strained figures of speech, and vowel mis-
pronunciations. Somerville reports that the mother of autobiographer Lionel
Fleming (*Head or Harp*) has remarked to her as author of *The Real Charlotte*,
"Well Edith, all that you wrote is *pairfectly* true" (235). Presumably, this constitutes a humorous pronunciation because it resembles Gaelic-inflected English in a member of a well-established Anglo-Irish landholding family. A local
young man asks Somerville if she is familiar with a composer he thinks might
be named " 'Ross-in-I' '*Who*' I said—'Ross-in I' then I knew, *Rossini*! It
sounded liked a service—Farrant in D" (15). The story resembles George
Moore's anecdote about the Mayo landlord who thought Wagner a cattle
dealer, a tale of which he was so fond he repeated it in both *Parnell and His Island* and *Hail and Farewell*. George De Stacpoole also liked it so much he pla-
giarized it in *Irish and Other Memories* (1922, 16). In truth, the story may have
circulated as authorless folklore long before anyone put it in print. In these instances, the cousins, like Moore and De Stacpoole, travesty those members of
their own class who fail to live up to standards of cosmopolitanism and familiarity with European high culture.

Moore's anecdote is but a fragment of an extended, and, I believe, profound critique of the relationship between art and life.[10] But in many cases,
satires of self, family, and class display less exalted motives and a less corrective
relationship with the intended reader. Much of the humor found in Anglo-

10. For a fuller analysis of Moore's comic autobiographies, see Grubgeld 1994 (chaps. 2, 4,
5).

Irish autobiography refers to the self, to events and people long past, or—like the letters of Somerville and Ross—passes from one satirist to another rather than to the subjects of their caricatures. To catalog the affectations of one's own group is not necessarily to wish those affectations gone. Among the many probable motives for satirizing one's own people—if we put aside the desire to change the behavior satirized—is the wish to protect the group against stronger criticism by controlling the terms of the critique. Similarly, such conservative satire reinforces the writer's sense of intimate relations with a group he or she knows well enough to quote or parody with precision.

Satire, however, need not fit—and perhaps at best cannot fit—neatly into a set of motives deemed either transgressive or celebratory. Like many other contemporary theorists of satire, Dustin Griffin challenges the "notion that clear moral standards are at the center of satire":

> What we behold in satire is not a neatly articulated homiletic discourse but the drama of an inflamed sensibility, or a cool and detached mind playfully exploring a moral topic. The reader's interest is not in rediscovering that greed is a bad thing or that deceit is to be avoided but in working through . . . the implications of a given moral position (how far do you have to go in the public defense of virtue?), the contradictions between one virtue (justice) and another (forgiveness), or the odd similarities between a vice (brazenness) and a virtue (steadfastness against censure). (1994, 37–38)[11]

When, for instance, Shane Leslie remembers the curate who referred to Enoch (the "man who walked with God") as "this most eminent pedestrian" (1938, 55), his story serves a dual purpose. It pays tribute to a verbal flourish whose literalness decontextualizes a common term like *pedestrian* by applying it to a biblical figure and displays the curate's own delight in inflated expressions that call attention to themselves even at the expense of theological sobriety. But the story also opens a moral inquiry, even if it advances no theory about it. Imagining Enoch as a man strolling the town square brings him closer to the lives of the congregation; in this case, verbal pretension, like other pretensions, may be a vice but is also remarkably like a virtue. Leslie tells of another clergyman, known locally as "Skip-the-Litany-Pratt," who, observing

11. Sparked by Bakhtin's revolutionary rereading of satire in *Problems of Dostoevsky's Poetics* (1984) and other works, contemporary theory of satire has reconsidered prior emphasis on the persuasive rhetoric and clear moral positioning of the satirist by drawing attention instead to its inclusive or entropic nature (see Connery and Combe 1995 and Seidel 1979) and to its parasitic ability to overtake other genres and orientation toward inquiry rather than persuasion (Griffin 1994, 38–52). See also Hutcheon 1985 and Palmeri 1990.

during a funeral service a terrier hunting a rat among the gravestones, shouted out to everyone's horror, "The Devil if he hasn't got him at last!" (32). In one quick anecdote, Leslie posits against respect for death the contrary virtue of devotion to the vitality of life that the Reverend Pratt's ill-timed acclamation upholds.

Similar instances of satiric incongruity and inquiry arise in the compilation of familial expressions Edith Somerville and Violet Martin called the "Buddh Dictionary." According to Somerville, the strange and whimsical words collected therein reflect the ascendancy of imagination over the limitations of the English language; additionally, these words succeed at the simultaneous articulation and repression of emotions and failings that would be otherwise outside the realm of expression. She declares them to be "the froth on the surface of some hundreds of years of the conversation of a clan of violent, inventive, Anglo-Irish people, who generation after generation, found themselves faced with situations in which the English language failed to provide sufficient intensity, and they either snatched at alternatives from other tongues or invented them" (Somerville and Ross 1989, 297).

A familial autobiography in the form of a dictionary complete with indications of parts of speech, pronunciation, and word derivations, the "Buddh Dictionary" catalogs the neologisms of their large circle of relatives. Most of the neologisms serve specific social functions. There are code words for caustic epithets: a "blug" would indicate a "low fellow," and a "chip" "one who is erroneously supposed to be the sole prop of morality and order." Dismaying social situations might call for other code words, including an "overflow meeting" ("the human dregs of any social event") and the expression "nooden-afore," which constitutes a "greeting addressed to the contrivances of ingenious poverty, e.g. an article of food or apparel which, having seen its first youth, still presents itself at table or on the person with an artificial assumption of novelty." Disagreeable or explosive feelings could be disguised by references to feeling in a "dwam" (a "heavy and half-conscious state resembling a coma") or exclaiming "squozzums," if one were "suddenly seized with an insane desire to squash or break some soft or inflated object, such as a young kitten, an air balloon, or a baby." Other situations requiring euphemisms might allow one, after perhaps drinking an excessive amount of tea, to take leave to the "tweesortir" in order to "decant" (298–302).

Under their hands, language is codified, removed from its original context to be genially critiqued, and exposed as an unnatural and opaque medium. Although not quite parodies, these family code words and the pronunciations, words, and phrases they reproduced in their voluminous correspondence, travel writing, memoirs, and fiction function much as parodies do. Living amid a discourse of euphemism and elision, Somerville and Ross create their own. They expose the imitable, inorganic quality of socially formed language and provide what Linda Hutcheon in her study of parody calls a "critical revision" of the original, an "imitation with critical ironic distance" (1985, 15, 37). As Hutcheon points out, critical distance "can be normative and conservative, or it can be provocative and revolutionary. Its potentially conservative impulse can be seen in both extremes of the range of ethos, reverence and mockery. . . . In Bakhtin's terminology, parody can be centripetal—that is, a homogenizing, hierarchizing influence. But it can also be a centrifugal, de-normatizing one" (76). Without a deep reformative motive, their mimicry of others is arguably "centripetal": the kind of laughter that the Edgeworths praise in *Essay on Irish Bulls* as arising from "good humoured raillery, not . . . insulting satire" (1979, 309). The "Buddh" words acknowledge socially unruly emotions, people, and bodily functions, and they query the social mores that control these disruptions without necessarily rejecting either the mores or the disruptions. Virtue, for instance, requires charity, but how much self-sacrifice is required with an "overflow meeting"? It is a virtue to put on a good face, but if one presents "nooden-afore," resourcefulness may have become inhospitableness. It is also a virtue to control oneself, but the urge to shout "squozzums" suggests that too much self-control can lead to outbreaks of bad behavior.

Despite the interrogation each term invites, these expressions also work to harness potential disruptions by containing them within a private code. Somerville and Ross raise questions about a way of speaking and a way of seeing the world that compensate for the failure of English "to provide sufficient intensity," but at the same time they pay allegiance to their language and the world it represents.[12] Proudly recording their own Anglo-Irish "bulls," they use language to inscribe their family traditions as cultural traditions and, in doing so, highlight what most differentiates them from their neighbors in Ireland and in England.

George Moore's comic autobiography proves to be more of the "centrifugal, de-normatizing" variety, particularly in its treatment of language. All of his autobiographies recount the birth of the author, but Moore was reborn so many times that each of his life writings returns to the question of how the physical body and material circumstances affect what for him was the life-creating power of artistic language. In *Confessions of a Young Man*, the boy overhears out of "the awful brogue" and the rough, prosaic world of western

---

12. Revisionist readings of the fiction of Somerville and Ross have analyzed those aspects of their work that critique Anglo-Irish life, particularly in its restrictions on women. See especially Kreilkamp 1998 and Cahalan 1999.

Ireland the chance mention of a novel his parents are reading: "Lady Audley! What a beautiful name . . . such thoughts flash through the boy's mind, his imagination is stirred and quickened. . . . The coach lumbers along, it arrives at its destination, and Lady Audley is forgotten in the delight of tearing down fruit trees and killing a cat" (1972, 50). The callous Mayo youth is not yet converted to the gospel of art, but the seed is planted, and the "crystal name" of Shelley completes his conversion. Hearing the word *France*, the adolescent Moore receives a sudden revelation that any hope of an artistic future—and thus, for him, a life worth living—requires that he be reborn as a Frenchman. Later, he discovers that he must "wash himself clean" of French, relearn English style, and start again.

The mock-heroic terms in which Moore tells the story of himself as an absurd youth do nothing to diminish the seriousness of his quest. Voices come, he responds, and the birth of the artist takes place. Moore is frankly amazed that he is the one so chosen, and he allows his own fatuous self-representation to draw laughter, not the quest itself. Although *Confessions of a Young Man* unequivocally maintains that Ireland can never be the birthplace of art and that the callings of art can come only in French or in literary English, nevertheless Moore faces the paradox that the artist in his case is an ignorant, awkward youth from the West of Nowhere. Rather than a polemic on the origins of art, *Confessions* is an inquiry that ponders the mysterious relationship between language and reality symbolized by the oxymoron of George Augustus Moore, the cosmopolitan writer from Ballintubber.

The same issues propel his comic masterpiece *Hail and Farewell*. As he sets out once more on a mock-heroic quest, this time to create the holy book of Irish literature, he is repeatedly thwarted by a recognition that language, even artistic language, arises from a material world. In the three volumes of *Hail and Farewell*, Moore's insight into the embodied nature of language leads him to imagine speech in wildly concrete terms: Douglas Hyde's talk is a "torrent of dark, muddied stuff . . . much like the porter which used to come up from Carnacun to be drunk by the peasants on midsummer nights when a bonfire was lighted" (1985, 139), and he complains that Ireland's problems lie in its incapacity to invent a word as buttery as *sauce béarnaise*. In contrast, the language of his contemporaries seems removed from lived reality, despite their attempts to ground their speech more fully in an Irish identity, either through learning to speak Gaelic or by using the motifs of Irish folklore and mythology in their own work. But according to Moore, Hyde sounds like "an imitation native Irish speaker; in other words, like a stage Irishman," and Yeats offers "an Irish parody of the poetry that I had seen all my life strutting its rhythmic way in the alleys of the Luxemboourg Gardens, preening its rhymes by the fountains."

Yeats attempts a joke, "but it got lost in the folds of his style and he looked at Hyde and Martyn disconsolate." By insisting on the materiality of language and its origin in the human body, Moore lambastes both the ahistorical essentialism of the Revivalist quest for a language to express the whole of the nation and what he believed to be a Catholic resistance to the expression of the body.

Part of Moore's complaint lay against the presumptuous claims to speak for the nation—or worse, "Banva," the soul of the nation—rather than for oneself. Cognizant of how many different "nations" Ireland contained within its borders, Moore was acutely appreciative of the distance between his own privileged upbringing as the son of a major Catholic landholder and the lives of the tenants who came twice a year from "the hovels round the bogs" to pay their rents, muttering in Irish and holding in their hands tall hats out of which "came rolls of bank-notes, so dirty that my father grumbled, telling the tenant that he must bring cleaner notes" (481). *Hail and Farewell* presents itself as the story of its narrator's failure to write the holy book of Ireland, but its author succeeds in demonstrating how the multiplicity of Ireland's voices dooms an artist's attempt to speak for the whole nation. In this sense, *Hail and Farewell* employs its critique of language to demolish the use of the past as a claim to authenticity in Ireland. His compatriots, however, saw their lineage, as well as their facility with learned language, as awarding them a greater authenticity than the majority population. Yeats's famous genealogy of "the true Irish people" from his late work *On the Boiler* confidently lists a canon of Protestant intellectuals beginning with "Berkeley, Swift, Burke, and Grattan" and ending with his own circle (1962, 442). Yeats is by no means alone in his anachronistic turn toward the eighteenth century as a point of reference for the hegemonic national genealogy he fashions. Many other claims to belonging through the evocation of inherited property (much of which was acquired and built upon during the eighteenth century) depend similarly on the idea of an eighteenth-century world invented, in part, by its descendants. Precisely because genealogy held such significance, the ancestors were ripe for mockery.

Abusing the Ancestors

Writing in the mid-1930s, Oliver St. John Gogarty ridicules the effort to imagine an upper-class elite as the essence of the whole nation. The first of his autobiographies, *As I Was Going Down Sackville Street*, begins with the grotesque incarnation of such an effort: "Quaintly he came raiking out of Molesworth Street into Kildare Street, an odd figure moidered by memories, and driven mad by dreams which had overflowed into life, making him turn himself into a merry mockery of all he had once held dear," attended by "his memories of summer evenings on the smooth pitch; the whip, his runs in winter with the staghounds of the Ward." "All gone now," the narrator remarks, "alive only in memory and regret those peaceful, prosperous days when life was fair and easy and men's thoughts were the thoughts of sportsmen" (1994, 1, 2). Discovering that this archaically costumed relic has adopted the name "James Boyle Tisdell Burke Stewart Fitzsimons Farrell," the narrator and his friend engage in the following dialogue:

> "He may mean that he represents in his person an amalgam of the ingredient races that go to make up the nation."
> "He means that he is Ireland? Poor devil!"
> "Its countless Jameses, the Norman, Elizabethan, Cromwellian conquerors, merchants and mediocrities—all the incomers, in short, that make the Irish mosaic."
> "That he is a walking amalgam?"
> "Or that the Irish Farrell has to bear on his back all the rest of them—Normans, Elizabethans, etc. Or that he is leading them in triumph—settlers, planters, merchants and mediocrities, as well as the Shamuses of the people. So he is a nation in himself." (7–8)

James Boyle Tisdell Burke Stewart Fitzsimons Farrell was not a nation in himself, despite his best efforts. Gogarty mocks the imperiousness here concretized by costume and name, his choice of targets deriving from Anglo-Irish concerns with family name and eighteenth-century satiric analogies between clothing and ideology. In utilizing an extravagant figure based apparently on an actual person (a review in the *Times Literary Supplement* calls him "a well-known public figure of the time"), Gogarty, like George Moore, derides the anachronistic presumptions of a class (O'Connor 1963, 275). The character type would not have been part of Gogarty's own family, who had belonged for several generations to the urban Catholic professional class, but the long list of patronyms resplendent in the name points toward another subject of comic representation in Anglo-Irish autobiography: the family history.

In prior centuries, the family history paid solemn homage to ancestry, as do in their own ways such modern versions as Elizabeth Bowen's *Bowen's Court*, T. R. Henn's *Five Arches*, Alannah Heather's *Errislannan*, or Joan de Vere's story of her adoptive family home, *The Abiding Enchantment of Curagh Chase*. As their titles indicate, these books are also loving memoirs of houses lost to the changing economy of a more egalitarian society. They admit little or no comedy on their elegiac pages, but even in those autobiographies that do, the house itself generally remains exempt from the reductive satire to which its inhabitants are subjected. A few exceptions arise: the Leslie family, for instance, organizes much of their comic family history around Castle Leslie and the homes of their friends and acquaintances. Yet the family is un-usual in that they have been able to maintain ownership of their house, make renovations and repairs, and adapt its functions to the conditions of contem-porary life with considerable zest. Novelists like Molly Keane also train a sar-donic eye on the dilapidation of the so-called Big House, and a tourist Web site such as John Colclough's "Country House Tours and Friendly Homes of Ire-land" takes up its mushroomed ceilings and ravaged turrets as points of inter-est. But for the most part, the family house stays relatively safe from comic derision. Perhaps because many invested such strong emotion in the family house—even imbuing it, as do Augusta Gregory and Elizabeth Bowen, with feelings and sight—autobiographers seem unwilling to treat their own family homes with the satiric reductionism with which they have, from the eigh-teenth century on, regaled their often eccentric ancestors.

Explanations for the ancestral satire are both historical and literary. Soci-eties depending upon patrilineage are apt to include its disorders among their nightmares. Accordingly, the ignoble ancestor and the fallen house haunt the pages of the Anglo-Irish Gothic novel. The comic treatment of such nightmares may be accounted for by cognitive theories of humor that explain laughter as, in part, a nervous reaction to the perception of two incompatible scripts, one of which is sanctioned and one of which is illicit. The dream of orderly primogeni-ture that prompts pages of carefully charted descent sits uneasily with a cir-cuitous trail of transfers of property from cousin to cousin-twice-removed, relatives contesting one another's rights in court, families losing or gaining lands according to religious conversions, and the dreaded triumph of illegitimate off-spring or, as in *Castle Rackrent*, the shrewd entrepreneur from the lower classes.

The anxieties of ancestry prove an easy target for the satirist. Violet Pow-ell, whose family's estate in Meath had been under their control since the sev-enteenth century and whose childhood games "were watched from the walls by the miniature portraits of my grandfather, a general, and his six brothers" (1976, 50), remarks that those family members who emphasized grand lines of descent were particularly oblivious to the illegitimacy and bigamy that those lines revealed. Understanding this fact, she can laugh at the family members who fail to. Born into a very different kind of family, one with more pretensions than money to uphold them, George Bernard Shaw relates in the preface to *Im-maturity* how the "contempt for . . . family snobbery" turned to bemused pity when he read the family pedigree, as published in 1877 by a distant relative:

[M]ly gratification was unbounded when I read the first sentence of the first chapter, which ran: "It is the general tradition . . . that the Shaws are descended of McDuff, Earl of Fife." . . . [T]here they were, baronet and all, duly traced to the third son of that immortalized yet unborn Thane of Fife who, being invulnerable to normally accouched swordsmen, laid on and slew Macbeth. It was as good a thing as being descended from Shakespear, whom I had been unconsciously resolved to reincarnate from my cradle. (1970, 13–14)

Although Shaw mistakenly attributes Macbeth's invulnerability to McDuff, his point is clear: family heritage is a matter of performance rather than innate significance, and as ephemeral as an ancestor drawn by Shakespeare. Whether attestations of membership in a distinguished line were in accord or strikingly incommensurable with the family bank account, both Violet Powell and G. B. Shaw refuse to take them seriously, except, as in Shaw's case, when he discusses the ways concurrent social pretensions ruined the family by forcing them to seek professions in fields for which they had no talent. Yet even in his serious discussions of the issue, he portrays his family members as caught in a machination so absurd as to be funny at the same time that it is their undoing.

Ancestral satire may have also derived from the same kinds of eighteenth-century narratives that act as models for the comic autobiography more generally. The motifs of the picaresque novel and scandalous memoir find their way into the tales of prodigious fertility, sexual profligacy, alcoholic dissipation, compulsive gambling, and the assorted bizarre behaviors that fill the eighteenth- and early-nineteenth-century memoirs of writers like Sir Jonah Barrington (1967) and Thomas "Buck" Whaley (1906), or that are secreted in the diaries of Wolfe Tone's friend Thomas Russell (1991). Barrington himself draws comparisons between his autobiography and the novel, proposing that his penchant for drinking, gambling, and womanizing resembles the world of *Gil Blas* or a novel by Fielding (42, 46). Whaley's memoirs were not published until 1906, and Russell's appear only in a recent scholarly edition intended for historians, but Whaley's notorious escapades made him a figure of folklore long before then, whereas Barrington's *Personal Sketches* enjoyed immense popularity and went through numerous editions issued in England, Ireland, Scotland, and the United States.

For readers of the modern period, works like *Buck Whaley's Memoirs* and the *Personal Sketches* reside comfortably in the past. By the middle of the nineteenth century, exposure of the ribald or freakish aspects of oneself or one's relatives was generally restricted to the ancestors. This newfound reticence may be related to autobiography's movement toward the domestic concerns of the Victorian novel and away from the wild adventures of travel narrative or the scandalous memoir. It may also derive from efforts to conform to English middle-class notions of respectability. George Moore possessed a stronger desire to appear bohemian than bourgeoisie, and his exposures of exceedingly private matters in himself and other living persons are an exception to this general rule. Moore, however, steadfastly asserts that he was building comic caricatures from the raw materials of life rather than revealing its facts, which for him had little inherent interest except as material for reflection and representation.[13] Anita Leslie, who also flaunted middle-class propriety with the exuberance of the truly wealthy, established a career on intimate biographies of her cousins, the Churchills. But she only hints at her grandfather's numerous adulteries and her mother's need for male admirers. As the Castle Leslie Web site attests, the young descendants weave the absurdities and vices of their family into an immensely engaging backdrop for their own stylish enterprise, but for the most part, their victims are at least a generation removed.

A third explanation for ancestral comedy may lie in the generic correspondences between many Anglo-Irish family histories and local histories. To the degree that local histories often accentuate the unusual and colorful anecdote, the curious tales of one's family further strengthen assertions to belonging in a specific place and community. As W. B. Yeats writes when introducing the stories of his own wild cousins and mad uncles, "All the well-known families had their grotesque or tragic or romantic legends, and I often said to myself how terrible it would be to go away and die where nobody would know my story" (1965, 10). Within local histories, stories of eccentric human behavior abound. Throughout *Reminiscences of an Irish Land Agent*, for instance, Samuel Hussey quotes from Charles Smith's 1756 *Antient and Present State of County Kerry*, a work that relates the story of the Hussey family and numerous other Kerry natives, including one local who lived to be 112 and buried four wives before marrying at the age of 85 a girl of 14 who bore him several children. Smith, as quoted by Hussey, writes of the old man,

> He drank for many of the last years of his life great quantities of rum and brandy, which he called *the naked truth*. . . . No man ever saw him spit. His custom was to walk eight or ten miles in a winter's morning over mountains with greyhounds and finders, and he seldom failed to bring home a brace of

---

13. The frequency with which Moore asserts this doctrine gives credence to his sincerity. In a letter to John Eglinton, for instance, he compares himself to Max Beerbohm and professes bafflement over the offense others take at his humorous representations (1942, 17). He encourages his brother to fictionalize the death of their father for the sake of a good story (1988, 275), and avows in another letter that his portraits are "mere whimsicality" and "cannot be described as personal animosity" (248).

hares. He was an innocent man, and inherited the social virtues of the antient Milesians. He was of a florid complexion, looked amazingly well for a person of his age and manners of life, for his use of spiritous liquors was prodigious. (1904, 18–19)

Adopting a perspective on Irish history as eccentric and picturesque (when it was not barbaric), Hussey easily moves to his own family story of a great-aunt who, departing for a ball with dresses trimmed in velvet taken from "an ancient pair of nether garments belonging to my great-grandfather," is dispatched by an enthusiastic relative shouting, "Success to the Breeches! Success to the Breeches!" (8).

Similarly, as part of the history of Rebelsfield, the estate in Meath where Mary Hamilton's family lived since receiving it from Cromwell, Hamilton discusses the sedate portraits along the dining room wall and of two who "did not figure on the walls," Pete and Tom McTara:

Of Pete it was said that, when drunk, he would scream for his hunting cap and gallop round the room astride a chair with a tea-cosy on his head yelling: "Yoiks, yoicks, yoicks!" He was the last of his family, it was recorded, to be crammed into their ancestral vault, where owing to lack of space he was obliged to take his eternal rest in a vertical position, with the soles of his feet splayed upwards towards heaven, and the crown of his head burrowing towards hell. Tom, having lost seven children from some dread scourge and not wishing to lose sight of them, is supposed to have embalmed the bodies and dragged them round the United States with him in glass-topped coffins. (1948, 30–31)

Inebriation, prodigious childbearing, exposure of the unspeakable undergarment: nothing is sacred in these versions of the family history, not even death.

The laughter of eccentricity may, finally, arise as a therapeutic response to the sadness or incoherence implicit in the narrative of extinction. The ancestral comedy can be particularly macabre, as when Shane Leslie recalls in *The Film of Memory* his futile attempts to find the remains of an ancestor who had died in 1722:

Irish graveyards are terrible heaps of confusion. I could not find the Non-Juror, but at the time I happened to be seen carrying the bones of an extinct Irish elk which had been found in the Donagh Bog. It was immediately remarked that I had been successful in finding the remains of my ancestor: "but weren't them auld Leslies thick in the hip?"

In Irish graveyards the families are buried in each other's arms so that each can present the thickest rank on the Day of Judgment. The old sexton assured me that he often cut grandparents in half to admit their grand-children and had thrown up the skulls of people he had know in his child-hood. The grave-digging scene in *Hamlet* could be often matched in Ireland. (1938, 18)

In the Leslie graveyard, the pride of families, as in *Hamlet*, is debased to heaps of bone. This reductionism enacts what Frank Palmeri calls the "the material-izing, leveling energy of narrative satire" that "contributes to satiric subver-sion by contesting authoritative distinctions between high and low among bodily functions, social groups, literary genres, and rhetorical operations" (1990, 10). Although not an extended reductionist allegory like *A Tale of a Tub* or *Tristam Shandy*, Leslie's memoir consistently ends its anecdotes with deflat-ing double entendres and anticlimaxes that link sex, class pretensions, death, and the memory of childhood to a physical gesture or function.[14] Family unity becomes in his anecdote the literal cause of all the graveyard chaos.

Shaw, too, describes with macabre wit the grotesque scenes perpetuated by a funeral tradition based on family pride: in his case, the pride of "our soci-ety of the Downstart . . . descended through younger sons from the plutoc-racy, for whom a university education is beyond his father's income, leaving him by family tradition a gentleman without a gentleman's means or educa-tion, and so only a penniless snob" (1970, 3). Describing his large extended family's equally extended funeral processions from one end of Dublin to the other, Shaw remembers how the coaches would dash through the roads (be-cause "the sorest bereavement does not cause men to forget wholly that time is money") only to slow to an agonizing crawl "along to the great iron gates where a demoniacal black pony was waiting with a sort of primitive gun-carriage and a pall to convey our burden up the avenue . . . looking as if he might be expected at every step to snort fire, spread a pair of gigantic bat's wings, and vanish, coffin and all, in thunder and brimstone." Typical of Shaw, his analysis is more social than personal: "Boyhood takes its fun where it finds

14. Leslie finishes a description of his childhood prowess with horses with an anticlimactic allusion to the fact that he was kept from tumbling off by the subtle positioning of the coachman's arm at his back. Illustrative of his relish for sexual punning, Leslie completes the story of his an-cestor the " 'fighting Bishop' John Leslie of the Isles" who built the parish church, rode "from Chester to London (180 miles) in twenty-four hours to salute King Charles the Second," and "married after seventy and proved the powerful father of many children" with the remark: "He was made of stiff stuff" (1938, 17).

it, without looking beneath the surface; and, since society chose to dispose of its dead with a grotesque pageant out of which farcical incidents sprang naturally and inevitably at every turn, it is not to be wondered at that funerals made me laugh when I was a boy nearly as much as they disgust me now that I am older" (17). Citing Philip Thompson's idea of the grotesque as "the unresolved clash of incompatibles in work and response," the editors of *Victorian Culture and the Idea of the Grotesque* suggest that "it is characteristic of cultural moments when inconsistency is experienced without a faith in the dynamic of transformation itself, when irresolution and duality are the content of the experience" (Trodd, Barlow, and Amigoni 1999, 2). The force of this inconsistency in Ireland was all the more great because differences in social behavior aligned with an economic, political, and social authority that was itself unstable. The sense of instability perhaps intensifies a proclivity toward macabre humor targeting so frequently states of insanity or inebriation, sexual behavior, and death.

In his book on narrative satire from Rabelais to Sterne, Michael Seidel proposes that anxiety regarding inheritance, and therefore death, is fundamental to eighteenth-century British satire, as especially evident in works like *Tristram Shandy* and Pope's "Martinus Scriblerus." Representing satire as "a literary system of discontinuities or subversions," Seidel argues more generally that even in much earlier incarnations, "satire's actions depict the falling off or exhaustion of line": for example, the story Aristophanes tells of Zeus's scheme to alter human reproduction so as to shore up his own power, the debasement of "anyone who has heirs of his own stock" at the end of the Satyricon, or the contamination of God's dispensation in the *Inferno* (1979, 46–59). Satire, Seidel maintains, "confuses the moral and spatial notions of direction by divorcing descent from continuity. To be satirically conceived is to be rendered monstrous— too singular, too materially degenerate to carry on" (263). In the Anglo-Irish comic autobiography, the anxieties of inheritance and a cultural emphasis on family history exacerbate the tendency toward entropy Seidel finds already endemic in the genre and import it into the terrain of autobiography.

Life as "Literary Capital"

By the late twentieth century, the eccentric Anglo-Irishman and his (or her) fallen house had become literary clichés and the parlance of coffee-table books. George Moore speaks more frankly than most authors in calling his life experience "my literary capital" (1972, 102), but even by his time casting the Anglo-Irish life as a comic fiction had become a familiar gesture, although with varied degrees of satire or sentiment. By the early twenty-first century, these gestures have become stock features of the tourist industry as well. The "Country House Tours and Friendly Homes of Ireland" Web site, for example, assures potential visitors that the type travestied in Gogarty's "James Boyle Tisdell Burke Stewart Fitzsimons Farrell" still survives and that "the country is still peopled with characters out of the novels of Maria Edgeworth, Somerville and Ross and Molly Keane" (Colclough 2002, n.p.).[15] Long before tourist Web sites were imaginable, when the so-called peasantry were of more interest to tourists than the owners of the lands they worked, Samuel Hussey declares that he had tales to tell of the "Kerry landlords, a race who would have furnished Lever with a worthy theme" (1904, 151); Sybil Lubbock writes that her world was like a page from Somerville and Ross (Lubbock and Desart 1936, 191); Shane Leslie remarks that his neighbor Lord Rossmore "had stepped straight out of a novel by Charles Lever" (1938, 49); and many other Anglo-Irish autobiographies from the late-Victorian period onward offer innumerable comparisons between contemporary figures and those "hard-riding country gentlemen" of the eighteenth-century memoirs of Sir Jonah Barrington.

If we take such depictions as representative history, then Desmond Leslie would be a typical Anglo-Irishman: the author of *Flying Saucers Have Landed* and a prominent figure on the UFO and spiritualist circuits; a tempestuous crank who hit a BBC drama critic on national television for criticizing his girlfriend's latest production; and a spitfire pilot in the Second World War who, according to the hotel Web site, "destroyed a number of aircraft, most of which was piloting at the time" and enjoyed buzzing houses as a practical joke (Banon and Leslie 2002). Desmond Leslie's life is, of course, by no means typical and bears little relation to the quiet world of contemporary novelist William Trevor, brought up the son of a bank clerk in a variety of small towns in County Cork, or Muriel Breen's equally simple upbringing in a middle-class coastal town near Belfast in the years before World War I. Yet a Desmond Leslie, the exception, has become in the popular mind the rule, perhaps because of how forcefully W. B. Yeats valorized a notion of the Anglo-Irish as reckless and imaginative iconoclasts marooned in a mundane world.

15. On the "Country House Tours and Friendly Homes of Ireland" Web site, John Mc-Colough's stories of dilapidated "gentry" emphasize a degree of eccentricity that crosses the border into insanity: "There was Adolphus Cooke of Cookesborough, Co. Westmeath who redesigned his windows to match his balloon backed dining chairs and, concerned that he might be reincarnated as a fox (for his father, whom he had buried in a beehive, had been reincarnated as a dog) caused massively deep foxholes to be built on his estate. The last Earl of Aldborough devoted his life to constructing the largest balloon in the world. It was destroyed in a fire before it ever flew and the Earl abandoned Stratford House near Baltinglass to spend his remaining years selling patent medicines in Alicante" (Colclough 2002, n.p.).

Although the life of Desmond Leslie is more the enactment of a literary type than truly representative of Anglo-Irish experience, it holds in common with the less glamorous a sense of life as performative. Particularly in those writers given to comic representations, life is fodder for perpetual conversational and literary production. Mary Pakenham's "Important Notice" preceding *Brought Up and Brought Out* warns the reader, "My brothers and sisters have not read this book but they wish to say that they are prepared to deny everything in it. Speaking of myself I cannot vouch for the accuracy of any of its statements" (1938, n.p.). In similar terms, Oliver St. John Gogarty announces at the beginning of his memoir, *As I Was Going Down Sackville Street* that "the names in this book are real, the characters fictitious" (1994, n.p.). All dismiss the urgency of fact and uphold the right of satiric autobiography to distort its subject matter in pursuit of an idiosyncratic quality of truth.

George Bernard Shaw believes that his propensity to see experience as an absurd comic drama was the natural outcome of his upbringing. A lethal mixture of alcohol, class pretension, and evangelical piety produced in him, he claims, a boy more likely to make "trifles of tragedies" than "tragedies of trifles" (1970, 40). "As compared with similar English families," he notes, "we had a power of derisive dramatization that made the bones of the Shavian skeletons rattle more loudly; and I possessed this power in an abnormal degree, and frequently entertained my friends with stories of my uncles. . . . [T]he family, far from being a school of reverence for me, was rather a mine from which I could dig highly amusing material without the trouble of inventing a single incident" (42). According to Shaw, the threads of life experience and literature became entangled early in his development. Just as Hussey and Leslie found characters worthy of Charles Lever among their neighbors, Shaw attributes his tragicomic perspective to the early influence of Lever's fiction. In his vision of Anglo-Ireland, Shaw argues, we discover the first attempt to take the figure of the madman seriously: Lever never allows his madman to gain "our affections like Don Quixote and Pickwick. . . . But we dare not laugh at him, because, somehow, we recognize ourselves. . . . His author is not throwing a stone at a creature of another and inferior order, but making a confession, with the effect that the stone hits each of us full in the conscience and causes our self-esteem to smart very sorely" (62–63).

Shaw explains his outlook as the product of a literature that is itself in a symbiotic relationship with a class whose members often express a desire to live up to its representations. As a dealer in "the tragi-comic irony of the conflict between real life and the romantic imagination" (61), Shaw is indebted to Lever for showing him at an early age how closely the madman resembled himself, living as he did amid irreconcilable sets of expectations as to the nature of reality. Those expectations produced a painful recognition of the discrepancy between his family's income and the life of privilege associated with his ancestors and religious affiliation. In his "snob tragedy" Shaw is unable to socialize with young people of his own class because he has no money but feels equally incapable of attending a friendlier experimental school "for the children of persons of modest means engaged in retail instead of wholesale trade, Catholic and Protestant." If he had done so, he would have become "a boy with whom no Protestant young gentleman would speak or play" (53). Young Protestant gentleman did not seem to speak with him whether he conformed with sectarian bigotry or not, yet he feels required to conform. Shaw further catalogs the irrational distinctions of his world: gentlemen could preside in wholesale establishments, but not retail; a gentleman could pound on a door or ring the bell many times, whereas an ordinary soul could knock only once (excepting the postman, who might ring twice); as a young man without a university degree he was addressed as "Shaw," although degreed apprentices at a lower rank of employment were addressed as "Mister." All such experience Shaw invests as his literary capital into tragicomedy of social and economic class conflict.

A self-described shabby genteel, urban Irish Protestant, and the son of a stagestruck mother and an alcoholic pensioner with a penchant for failed business, Shaw could not have experienced a world more different from the inherited leisure and privilege of the Pakenham family, or the horse-besotted, arrogantly rough-and-ready world of Edith Somerville and Violet Martin. Yet like their life writing, his too proceeds by ironic reduction. The recollected childhood self learns early of a certain theatricality required in ordinary living that transforms mere experience into opportunities for performance and narrative.

Born into more prosperous and stable circumstances, Mary Pakenham, like Shaw, makes trifles from tragedies and ludicrous tragedies of trifles. Her clever and insightful autobiography discloses the self-dramatizing impulse of childhood with merciless acuity, while concurrently deflating the seriousness of the adult reality the child cannot grasp. She recalls even as a child her flair for the self-conscious dramatization that rendered everything artificial, even the threat of German torpedoes during the First World War. A pudgy, self-important, red-faced child, young Mary assumes she can rescue all who might go overboard during an attack on the *Irish Mail*. Shamefacedly, she and her younger siblings, "The Babies," must confess to an English child that they harbored no gunmen in their house during the troubles; worse, her mother confiscates "on hygienic grounds" the "dirty tweed fishing hat punctured with what we took to be bullets holes" left by some "masked desperadoes" who steal bicycles, "the house-keeper's brooch and some very old summer hats of Pansy's" (1938, 57). Never invoking the hush of mystical wonder over her youth, *Brought Up and Brought Out* highlights childhood's absurdities and incongruities, and, like the autobiographies of siblings Violet Powell and Frank Pakenham, suppresses the sorrow of their father's death and their mother's illness and consequent remoteness from their daily lives.

The evidence of these late-nineteenth- and twentieth-century autobiographies confirms that the "sardonic detachment" that has become a catchword in most accounts of what R. F. Foster designates "the Ascendancy Mind" accurately describes the way a group of people represented their thoughts and actions (1988, 167). Moreover, it establishes that for more than one hundred years the Anglo-Irish self-consciously endowed themselves with cultural descriptors drawn from the narratives of Sir Jonah Barrington, Maria Edgeworth, and the numerous political satirists and travel writers of the eighteenth century, a period when readers across much of Western Europe expected farcical and satiric approaches even in the serious essay. Comedy, like the other variations on forms of narrative discussed throughout this study, allows writers to acknowledge the interest and value of their world, while querying its foundations and its claims to a future. With comedy's chilling recognition of dissonance and disappointment, it permits the writer to erect a monument to a family past, while at the same time conceding that, as Hugh cautions Maire in the closing scene of Brian Friel's *Translations*, "always" "is not a word I'd start with."

Few in the industrialized West can now write an autobiography as a testimony to the permanence of family, custom, or place. Most can refer to only dimly remembered local cultures from which their ancestors derived, and the absence from contemporary life writing of ancestral properties and extensive family history speaks of exile, displacement, and the loss of language, religion, and traditional arts and family structures. Yet we seek origins, perhaps as an antidote to a homogenous identity produced by mass culture and to feel ourselves more than the sum of a present moment—to give ourselves significance as the outcome of our ancestors' struggles: "the experience of writing this book has been cumulative," Elizabeth Bowen reflects in *Bowen's Court*, "the experience of living more than my own life" (1942, 458). Seamus Deane has rightly understood Anglo-Irish obsessions with diminished families, crumbling houses, and the lost "security and peace" of the past to be more than "historical fantasies." "They are," he observes, "part of the countering energy of the self in the face of circumstances that threaten to dismiss it" (1991, 381). At its very best, the life story emerges at a point of vividly imagined social responsibility in which the life one lives is more than the private sphere of the moment or the ghostly emanations of the past, but the shared life of a world in which one must make, however precarious, a future.

WORKS CITED

INDEX

Works Cited

Adams, Hazard. 1965. "Some Yeatsian Versions of Comedy." In *In Excited Reverie: A Centenary Tribute to William Butler Yeats, 1865–1939*, edited by A. Norman Jeffares and K. G. W. Cross, 152–70. New York: Macmillan.

Akenson, Donald Harman. 1971. *The Church of Ireland: Ecclesiastical Reform and Revolution, 1800–1885*. New Haven: Yale Univ. Press.

———. 1988. *Small Differences: Irish Catholics and Irish Protestants, 1815–1922, an International Perspective*. Montreal: McGill-Queen's Univ. Press.

Allingham, William. 1992. "Church Diversions." In *Irish Childhoods*, edited by A. Norman Jeffares and Anthony Kahm, 101–5. Dublin: Gill and Macmillan.

Anson, Lady Clodagh. 1932. *Victorian Days*. London: Richards.

———. 1937. *Another Book*. London: n.p.

Arana, R. Victoria. 1977. "Sir Edmund Gosse's *Father and Son:* Autobiography as Comedy." *Genre* 10, no. 1: 63–76.

Auden, W. H. 1971. *A Certain World: A Commonplace Book*. London: Faber and Faber.

August, Eugene R. 1989. "Darwin's Comedy: The *Autobiography* as Comic Narrative." *Victorian Newsletter* 75: 15–19.

Backus, Margot Gayle. 1999. *The Gothic Family Romance: Heterosexuality, Child Sacrifice, and the Anglo-Irish Colonial Order*. Durham: Duke Univ. Press.

Bakhtin, Mikhail. 1984. *Problems of Dostoevsky's Poetics*. Translated by Caryl Emerson. Minneapolis: Univ. of Minnesota Press.

Banon, Ulton, and Desmond Leslie. 2002. http://www.castle-leslie.ie/history/index.html.

Barbour, John D. 1994. *Versions of Deconversion: Autobiography and the Loss of Faith*. Charlottesville: Univ. Press of Virginia.

———. 2001. "Spiritual Autobiography." In *Encyclopedia of Life Writing: Autobiographical and Biographical Forms*, edited by Margaretta Jolly, 2:835–37. London: Fitzroy Dearborn.

Barnard, Toby. 1995. "Identities, Ethnicity, and Tradition among Irish Dissenters, c. 1650–1750." In *The Irish Dissenting Tradition*, edited by Kevin Herlihy, 29–48. Dublin: Four Courts.

———. 1998. "Protestantism, Ethnicity, and Irish Identities, 1660–1760." In *Protes-

tantism and National Identity: Britain and Ireland, c. 1650–1850, edited by Tony Clayton and Ian McBride, 206–35. Cambridge: Cambridge Univ. Press.

Barret, Gerard. 1992–1993. "Disrobing in the Vestry: Autobiographical Writing in the Thirties." *Irish Review* 13: 22–30.

Barrington, Sir Jonah. 1967. *The Ireland of Sir Jonah Barrington: Selections from His Personal Sketches.* Edited by Hugh B. Staples. Seattle: Univ. of Washington Press.

Bassin, Donna, Margaret Honey, and Meryle Mahrer Kaplan. 1994. *Representations of Motherhood.* New Haven: Yale Univ. Press.

Behan, Brendan. 1962. *The Hostage.* 1958. Reprint. London: Methuen.

Bell, Robert. 1977. "Metamorphoses of Spiritual Autobiography." *English Literary History* 44: 108–26.

Benstock, Shari. 1988. "Authorizing the Autobiographical." In *The Private Self: Theory and Practice of Women's Autobiographical Writings,* edited by Shari Benstock, 10–33. Chapel Hill: Univ. of North Carolina Press.

Birmingham, George A. 1919. *An Irishman Looks at His World.* London: Hodder and Stoughton.

Bornstein, George. 1979. "The Antinomial Structure of John Butler Yeats's *Early Memories: Some Chapters of Autobiography.*" In *Approaches to Victorian Autobiography,* edited by George P. Landow, 200–211. Athens: Ohio Univ. Press.

Bowen, Elizabeth. 1941. Review of *A Lady's Child,* by Enid Starkie. *Tatler and Bystander* (26 Nov.): 308–10.

———. 1942. *Bowen's Court.* New York: Alfred A. Knopf.

———. 1950. *Collected Impressions.* New York: Alfred A. Knopf.

———. 1960. *A Time in Rome.* New York: Alfred A. Knopf.

———. 1962. *Seven Winters and Afterthoughts.* 1942. Reprint. New York: Alfred A. Knopf.

———. 1964. *Bowen's Court.* Rev. ed. New York: Alfred A. Knopf.

———. 1975. *Pictures and Conversations.* New York: Alfred A. Knopf.

———. 1983. *The Last September.* 1929. Reprint. New York: Penguin.

———. 1986. *The Death of the Heart.* 1938. Reprint. New York: Penguin.

Bowen, Kurt. 1983. *Protestants in a Catholic State: Ireland's Privileged Minority.* Montreal: McGill-Queen's Univ. Press.

Breen, Muriel. 1993. *Liquorice All-Sorts: A Girl Growing Up.* Dublin: Moytura Press.

Brodzki, Bella. 1988. "Mothers, Displacement, and Language in the Autobiographies of Nathalie Sarraute and Christa Wolf." In *Life/Lines: Theorizing Women's Autobiographies,* edited by Bella Brodzki and Celeste Schenck, 243–59. Ithaca: Cornell Univ. Press.

Brooke, Raymond F. 1961. *The Brimming River.* Dublin: Allen Figgis.

Broughton, T. L. 1991. "Women's Autobiography: The Self at Stake?" In *Autobiography and Questions of Gender,* edited by Shirley Neuman, 76–94. London: Frank Cass.

Brown, Penny. 1993. *The Captured World: The Child and Childhood in 19th Century Women's Writing.* New York: St. Martin's.

Brown, Terence. 1985a. *Ireland: A Social and Cultural History*. Ithaca: Cornell Univ. Press.

———. 1985b. "Poets and Patrimony: Richard Murphy and James Simmons." In *Across a Roaring Hill: The Protestant Imagination in Modern Ireland*, edited by Gerald Dawe and Edna Longley, 182–95. Belfast: Blackstaff.

Bruner, Jerome. 1987. "Life as Narrative." *Social Research* 54, no. 1: 11–32.

Buchanan, George. 1959. *Green Seacoast*. London: Gaberbocchus.

Budd, Susan. 1977. *Varieties of Unbelief: Atheists and Agnostics in English Society, 1850–1960*. London: Heinemann.

Burke, Sir Bernard. 1859. *Vicissitudes of Families and Other Essays*. London: Longman, Green, Longman, and Roberts.

Bush, Julia. 2001. "Ladylike Lives? Upper-Class Women's Autobiographies and the Politics of Late Victorian and Edwardian Britain." *Literature and History* 10, no. 2: 42–61.

Butler, Harriet Jessie, and Harold Edgeworth Butler, eds. 1927. *The Black Book of Edgeworthstown and Other Edgeworth Memories, 1585–1817*. London: Faber and Gwyer.

Butler, Hubert. 1996. *Independent Spirit: Essays*. New York: Farrar, Straus, and Giroux.

Cahalan, James M. 1996. " 'Humor with a Gender': Somerville and Ross and *The Irish R. M.*" In *The Comic Tradition in Irish Women Writers*, edited by Theresa O'Connor, 58–72. Gainesville: Univ. Press of Florida.

———. 1999. *Double Visions: Women and Men in Modern and Contemporary Irish Fiction*. Syracuse: Syracuse Univ. Press.

Canby, Henry Seidel. 1925. Review of *My Tower in Desmond*, by S. R. Lysaght. *Saturday Review of Literature* (17 Oct.): 210.

Cloncurry, Lord Valentine. 1849. *Personal Recollections of the Life and Times with Extracts from the Correspondence*. Dublin: James McGlashan.

Cloney, Thomas. 1832. *A Personal Narrative of Those Transactions in the Co. Wexford, in which the Author Was Engaged During the Awful Period of 1798*. Dublin: J. McMullen.

Cobbe, Francis Power. 1894. *Life of Francis Power Cobbe*. London: Richard Bentley and Son.

Coe, Richard. 1982. "Childhood in the Shadows: The Myth of the Unhappy Child in Jewish, Irish, and French-Canadian Autobiography." *Comparison* 13: 3–67.

———. 1984. *When the Grass Was Taller: Autobiography and the Experience of Childhood*. New Haven: Yale Univ. Press.

Colclough, John Michael. 2002. http://www.tourismresources.ie/articles/index.htm#house.

Connery, Brian A., and Kirk Combe. 1995. "Theorizing Satire: A Retrospective and Critical Introduction." In *Theorizing Satire: Essays in Literary Criticism*, edited by Brian A. Connery and Kirk Combe, 1–15. New York: St. Martin's.

Connolly, S. J. 1992. *Religion, Law, and Power: The Making of Protestant Ireland*. Oxford: Clarendon.

Conyers, Dorothea. 1920. *Sporting Reminiscences.* London: Methuen.

Corbett, Mary Jean. 1992. *Representing Femininity: Middle-Class Subjectivity in Victorian and Edwardian Women's Autobiographies.* New York: Oxford Univ. Press.

Culler, A. Dwight. 1985. *The Victorian Mirror of History.* New Haven: Yale Univ. Press.

Cunningham, Bernadette, and Máire Kennedy. 1999. *The Experience of Reading: Irish Historical Perspectives.* Dublin: Rare Books Group of the Library Association of Ireland.

Curtis, L. Perry. 1996. *Apes and Angels: The Irishman in Victorian Caricature.* Rev. ed. Washington, D.C.: Smithsonian Institution Press.

Daly, Gabriel. 1970. "Church Renewal, 1869–1877." In *Irish Anglicanism, 1869–1969,* edited by Michael Hurley, S.J., 23–38. Dublin: Allen Figgis.

Davis, Gwen, and Beverly A. Joyce. 1989. *Personal Writings by Women to 1900: A Bibliography of American and British Writers.* Norman: Univ. of Oklahoma Press.

Dawe, Gerald, and Edna Longley. 1985. Introduction to *Across a Roaring Hill: The Protestant Imagination in Modern Ireland,* edited by Gerald Dawe and Edna Longley, i-xiii. Belfast: Blackstaff.

Deane, Seamus. 1986a. *A Short History of Irish Literature.* London: Hutchinson.

———. 1986b. "Swift and the Anglo-Irish Intellect." *Eighteenth-Century Ireland* 1: 9–22.

———. 1987. *Celtic Revivals: Essays In Modern Irish Literature, 1880–1980.* Winston-Salem, N.C.: Wake Forest Univ. Press.

———. 1991. "Autobiography and Memoirs, 1890–1988." In *The Field Day Anthology of Irish Writing,* edited by Seamus Deane, 3:380–83. Derry, Northern Ireland: Field Day.

de Man, Paul. 1979. "Autobiography as De-Facement." *Modern Language Notes* 94: 919–30.

De Stacpoole, George Stacpoole, Duke. 1922. *Irish and Other Memories.* London: A. M. Philpot.

Devas, Nicolette. 1966. *Two Flamboyant Fathers: Reminiscences of Francis MacNamara and Augustus John.* London: Collins.

———. 1978. *Susannah's Nightingales.* London: Collins and Harvill.

de Vere, Aubrey. 1897. *Recollections of Aubrey de Vere.* New York: Edward Arnold.

de Vere, Joan. 1990. *In Ruin Reconciled: A Memoir of Anglo-Ireland, 1913–1959.* Dublin: Lilliput.

de Vere White, Terence. 1972. *The Anglo-Irish.* London: Victor Gollancz.

Devlin, Edith Newman. 2001. *Speaking Volumes: A Dublin Childhood.* Belfast: Blackstaff.

Dunraven, Fourth Earl of. 1922. *Past Times and Pastimes.* 2 vols. London: Hodder and Stoughton.

Eakin, Paul John. 1992. *Touching the World: Reference in Autobiography.* Princeton: Princeton Univ. Press.

Edgeworth, Maria. 1965. *Castle Rackrent.* 1800. Reprint. New York: W. W. Norton.

———. 1989. "The Limerick Gloves." 1800. Reprint. In *The Oxford Book of Irish Short Stories,* edited by William Trevor, 27–51. New York: Oxford Univ. Press.

Edgeworth, Richard Lovell. 1969. *Memoirs of Richard Lovell Edgeworth*. 1820. Reprint. Shannon: Irish Univ. Press.

Edgeworth, Richard Lovell, and Maria Edgeworth. 1979. *Essay on Irish Bulls*. 1803. Reprint. New York: Garland.

Everett, Katherine. 1949. *Bricks and Flowers: Memoirs of Katherine Everett*. London: Constable.

Fingall, Elizabeth, Countess of. 1939. *Seventy Years Young*. 1937. Reprint. New York: E. P. Dutton.

Fitzgerald, Mary. 1987. "Perfection of the Life': Lady Gregory's Autobiographical Writings." In *Lady Gregory: 50 Years After*, edited by Ann Saddlemyer and Colin Smythe, 45–55. Gerrards Cross, England: Colin Smythe.

Fitzgibbon, Theodora. 1985. *Love Lies a Loss, an Autobiography, 1946–1959*. London: Century.

Fleishman, Avrom. 1983. *Figures of Autobiography: The Language of Self-Writing in Victorian and Modern England*. Berkeley and Los Angeles: Univ. of California Press.

Fleming, Lionel. 1965. *Head or Harp*. London: Barrier and Rockliff.

Foster, John Wilson. 1985. " 'The Dissidence of Dissent': John Hewitt and W. R. Rogers." In *Across a Roaring Hill: The Protestant Imagination in Modern Ireland*, edited by Gerald Dawe and Edna Longley, 139–60. Belfast: Blackstaff.

———. 1991. "The Topographical Tradition in Anglo-Irish Poetry." In *Colonial Consequences: Essays in Irish Literature and Culture*, 9–29. Dublin: Lilliput.

Foster, R. F. 1988. *Modern Ireland, 1600–1972*. New York: Penguin.

———. 1993. *Paddy and Mr Punch: Connections in Irish and English History*. New York: Penguin.

Frazier, Adrian. 2000. *George Moore, 1852–1933*. New Haven: Yale Univ. Press.

Frowde, Neville. 1767. *The Life, Extraordinary Adventures, Voyages, and Surprising Escapes*. London: J. Brown.

Gagnier, Regenia. 1991. *Subjectivities: A History of Self-Representation in Britain, 1832–1920*. New York: Oxford Univ. Press.

Gibbon, Monk. 1968. *Inglorious Soldier*. London: Hutchinson.

———. 1982. "Am I Irish?" In *The Crane Bag Book of Irish Studies (1977–1981)*, edited by M. P. Hederman and Richard Kearney, 113–14. Dublin: Blackwater.

Gill, Richard. 1972. *Happy Rural Seat: The English Country House and the Literary Imagination*. New Haven: Yale Univ. Press.

Glendinning, Victoria. 1977. *Elizabeth Bowen: Portrait of a Writer*. London: Phoenix.

Glover, Lady. 1923. *Memories of Four Continents*. London: Seeley, Service.

Gogarty, Oliver St. John. 1994. *As I Was Going Down Sackville Street*. 1937. Reprint. Dublin: O'Brien.

Gordon, Lady. 1934. *The Winds of Time*. London: John Murray.

Greene, Gayle. 1991. "Feminist Fiction and the Uses of Memory." *Signs* 16: 290–332.

Gregory, Anne. 1970. *Me and Nu: Childhood at Coole*. Gerrards Cross, England: Colin Smythe.

Gregory, Lady Augusta. 1971. *Coole*. 1931. Reprint. Dublin: Cuala; Shannon: Irish Univ. Press.

———. 1973. *Seventy Years: Being the Autobiography of Lady Gregory*. Edited by Colin Smythe. Gerrards Cross, England: Colin Smythe.

———. 1978. *Lady Gregory's Journals*. Edited by Daniel J. Murphy. 2 vols. New York: Oxford Univ. Press.

———. 1996. *Lady Gregory's Diaries, 1892–1902*. Edited by James Pethica. New York: Oxford Univ. Press.

———. Papers. Robert W. Woodruff Library. Emory Univ., Atlanta.

Gregory, Sir William. 1894. *An Autobiography*. London: John Murry.

Griffin, Dustin. 1994. *Satire: A Critical Reintroduction*. Lexington: Univ. Press of Kentucky.

Grubgeld, Elizabeth. 1994. *George Moore and the Autogenous Self: The Autobiography and Fiction*. Syracuse: Syracuse Univ. Press.

Gwynn, Stephen. 1926. *Experiences of a Literary Man*. London: Thornton Butterworth.

Hall, S. C. 1883. *Retrospect of a Long Life from 1815 to 1883*. New York: Appleton.

Hamilton, Elizabeth. 1954. *A River Full of Stars*. New York: W. W. Norton.

Hamilton, John. 1894. *Sixty Years' Experience as an Irish Landlord*. London: Digby, Long.

Hamilton, Mary. 1948. *Green and Gold*. London: Wingate.

Hayton, David. 1987. "Anglo-Irish Attitudes: Changing Perceptions of National Identity among the Protestant Ascendancy in Ireland, ca. 1690–1750." In *Studies in Eighteenth-Century Culture*, edited by John Yolton and Leslie Ellen Brown, 145–58. Lansing, Mich.: Colleagues Press.

———. 1988. "From Barbarian to Burlesque: English Images of the Irish, c. 1660–1750." *Irish Economic and Social History* 15: 5–31.

Heather, Alannah. 1993. *Errislannan: Scenes from a Painter's Life*. Dublin: Lilliput.

Hemans, Felicia. 1865. *The Poetical Works of Felicia Hemans*. Boston: Crosby and Ainswroth; New York: O. S. Felt.

Henderson, Heather. 1989. *The Victorian Self: Autobiography and Biblical Narrative*. Ithaca: Cornell Univ. Press.

Henn, T. R. 1980. *Five Arches: A Sketch for an Autobiography*. Gerrards Cross, England: Colin Smythe.

Herbert, Dorothea. 1929. *Retrospections of Dorothea Herbert*. London: Gerald Howe.

Hewitt, John. 1987. *Ancestral Voices: The Selected Prose of John Hewitt*. Edited by Tom Clyde. Belfast: Blackstaff.

Higonnet, Anne. 1998. *Pictures of Innocence: The History and Crisis of Ideal Childhood*. New York: Thames and Hudson.

Hill, Jacqueline. 1989. "The Meaning and Significance of 'Protestant Ascendancy,' 1787–1840." In *Ireland after the Union*, edited by Lord Blake, F.B.A., 1–22. Oxford: Oxford Univ. Press.

Hogan, Rebecca. 1991. "Engendered Autobiographies: The Diary as a Feminine

Form." In *Autobiography and Questions of Gender*, edited by Shirley Neuman, 95–107. London: Frank Cass.

Homans, Margaret. 1986. *Bearing the Word: Language and Experience in Nineteenth-Century Women's Writing*. Chicago: Univ. of Chicago Press.

Huff, Cynthia. 1985. *British Women's Diaries: A Descriptive Bibliography of Selected Nineteenth-Century Women's Manuscript Diaries*. New York: AMS Press.

———. 1988. "Private Domains: Queen Victoria and Women's Diaries." *Auto/Biography Studies: a/b* 4, no. 1: 46–52.

Hussey, Samuel. 1904. *The Reminiscences of an Irish Land Agent*. London: Duckworth.

Hutcheon, Linda. 1985. *A Theory of Parody: The Teachings of Twentieth-Century Art Forms*. New York: Methuen.

Jenkins, Brian. 1986. *Sir William Gregory of Coole: The Biography of an Anglo-Irishman*. Gerrards Cross, England: Colin Smythe.

Jones, Joan Gwynn [Joan de Vere]. 1983. *The Abiding Enchantment of Curragh Chase*. Cork: Clo Duanaire.

Kaplan, Caren. 1992. "Resisting Autobiography: Out-Law Genres and Transnational Feminist Subjects." In *De/Colonizing the Subject: The Politics of Gender in Women's Autobiography*, edited by Sidonie Smith and Julia Watson, 115–38. Minneapolis: Univ. of Minnesota Press.

Keane, Molly [M. J. Farrell, pseud.]. 1981. *Good Behaviour*. New York: Alfred A. Knopf.

Kelly, John. 1987. " 'Friendship Is the Only House I Have': Lady Gregory and W. B. Yeats." In *Lady Gregory: 50 Years After*, edited by Ann Saddlemyer and Colin Smythe, 179–257. Gerrards Cross, England: Colin Smythe.

Kelsall, M. M. 1993. *The Great Good Place: The Country House and English Literature*. New York: Harvester Wheatsheaf.

Kenneally, Michael. 1989. "The Autobiographical Imagination and Irish Literary Autobiographies." In *Critical Approaches to Anglo-Irish Literature*, edited by Michael Allen and Angela Wilcox, 111–31. Totowa, N.J.: Barnes and Noble.

Kennedy, Dennis. 1988. *The Widening Gulf: Northern Attitudes Toward the Independent Irish State, 1919–49*. Belfast: Blackstaff.

Kiberd, Declan. 1995. *Inventing Ireland*. Cambridge: Harvard Univ. Press.

Kinahan, Timothy. 1995. *Where Do We Go from Here? Protestants and the Future of Northern Ireland*. Dublin: Columba.

Kohfeldt, Mary Lou. 1985. *Lady Gregory: The Woman Behind the Irish Renaissance*. New York: Atheneum.

Kreilkamp, Vera. 1998. *The Anglo-Irish Novel and the Big House*. Syracuse: Syracuse Univ. Press.

Langer, Susanne. 1953. *Feeling and Form*. New York: Charles Scribner's Sons.

Larkin, Philip. 1989. *Collected Poems*. Edited by Anthony Thwaite. New York: Farrar, Straus, and Giroux.

Lawless, Emily. 1901. *A Garden Diary*. London: Methuen.

Leadbeater, Mary. 1862. *The Leadbeater Papers*. Vol. 3. London: Bell and Daldy.

Leigh, David J. 2000. *Circuitous Journeys: Modern Spiritual Autobiography*. New York: Fordham Univ. Press.

Leonardi, Susan J. 1989. *Dangerous by Degrees: Women at Oxford and the Somerville College Novelists*. New Brunswick: Rutgers Univ. Press.

Leslie, Anita. 1981. *The Gilt and the Gingerbread: An Autobiography*. London: Hutchinson.

———. 1983. *A Story Half Told: A Wartime Autobiography*. London: Hutchinson.

Leslie, Shane. 1908. Letter to Elsie Hope, 23 July. Shane Leslie Papers. Lauinger Library, Georgetown Univ. http://gulib.lausun.georgetown.edu/dept/speccoll/index.htm.

———. 1916. *The End of a Chapter*. New York: Charles Scribner's Sons.

———. 1938. *The Film of Memory*. London: Michael Joseph.

———. 1966. *Long Shadows*. Wilkes-Barre, Pa.: Dimension.

Lewis, C. Day. 1960. *The Buried Day*. London: Chatto and Windus.

Lloyd, David. 1993. *Anomalous States: Irish Writing and the Post-Colonial Moment*. Durham: Duke Univ. Press.

Lubbock, Lady Sybil. 1939. *The Child in the Crystal*. London: Jonathan Cape.

Lubbock, Lady Sybil, and the Earl of Desart. 1936. *A Page from the Past: Memories of the Earl of Desart*. London: Jonathan Cape.

Lummis, Trevor, and Jan Marsh. 1990. *The Woman's Domain: Women and the English Country House*. London: Viking.

Lutton, Anne. 1883. *Memorials of a Consecrated Life*. London: T. Woolmer.

Lynch, Hannah. 1899. *Autobiography of a Child*. New York: Dodd, Mead.

Lyons, F. S. L. 1979. *Culture and Anarchy in Ireland, 1890–1939*. Oxford: Clarendon.

Lysaght, Sidney Royse. 1925. *My Tower in Desmond*. London: Macmillan.

MacNeice, Louis. 1965. *The Strings Are False: An Unfinished Autobiography*. London: Faber and Faber.

———. 1967. *The Collected Poems of Louis MacNeice*. New York: Oxford Univ. Press.

Malcomson, A. P. W. 1982. *The Pursuit of the Heiress: Aristocratic Marriage in Ireland, 1750–1820*. Belfast: Ulster Historical Foundation.

Malin, Jo. 2000. *The Voice of the Mother: Embedded Maternal Narratives in Twentieth-Century Women's Autobiographies*. Carbondale: Southern Illinois Univ. Press.

Malleson, Constance. 1931. *After Ten Years: A Personal Record*. London: Jonathan Cape.

Martin, Augustine. 1970. "Anglo-Irish Literature." In *Irish Anglicanism, 1869–1969*, edited by Michael Hurley, S.J., 120–32. Dublin: Allen Figgis.

Mason, Mary. 1980. "The Other Voice: Autobiographies of Women Writers." In *Autobiography: Essays Theoretical and Critical*, edited by James Olney, 207–35. Princeton: Princeton Univ. Press.

Maxwell, Constantia. 1954. *The Stranger in Ireland: From the Reign of Elizabeth to the Great Famine*. London: Cape.

McConville, Michael. 1986. *Ascendancy to Oblivion: The Story of the Anglo-Irish*. London: Quartet.

McCormack, W. J. 1985a. *Ascendancy and Tradition in Anglo-Irish Literary History from*

1798 to 1939. Oxford: Clarendon.

———. 1985b. " 'The Protestant Strain'; or, A Short History of Anglo-Irish Literature from S. T. Coleridge to Thomas Mann." In *Across a Roaring Hill: The Protestant Imagination in Modern Ireland*, edited by Gerald Dawe and Edna Longley, 48–78. Belfast: Blackstaff.

———. 1992a. "Irish Gothic and After (1820–1945)." In *The Field Day Anthology of Irish Writing*, edited by Seamus Deane, 2:831–949. Derry, Northern Ireland: Field Day.

———. 1992b. "Setting and Ideology: With Reference to the Fiction of Maria Edgeworth." In *Ancestral Voices: The Big House in Anglo-Irish Literature*, edited by Otto Rauchbauer, 33–60. Hildesheim, Germany: Georg Olms Verlag.

———. 1993a. *Dissolute Characters: Irish Literary History Through Balzac, Sheridan Le Fanu, Yeats, and Bowen*. Manchester: Manchester Univ. Press.

———. 1993b. *The Dublin Paper War of 1786–1788: A Bibliographical and Critical Inquiry*. Dublin: Irish Academic Press.

———. 1994. *From Burke to Beckett: Ascendancy, Tradition, and Betrayal in Literary History*. Cork: Cork Univ. Press.

McDiarmid, Lucy. 1996. "The Demotic Lady Gregory." In *High and Low Moderns: Literature and Culture, 1889–1939*, edited by Maria DiBattista and Lucy McDiarmid, 212–34. New York: Oxford Univ. Press.

McDiarmid, Lucy, and Maureen Waters. 1995. Introduction to *Selected Writings*, by Lady Gregory. New York: Penguin.

McDowell, Henry. 1992. "The Big House: A Genealogist's Perspective and a Personal Point of View." In *Ancestral Voices: The Big House in Anglo-Irish Literature*, edited by Otto Rauchbauer, 279–93. Hildesheim, Germany: Georg Olms Verlag.

McGuire, Martin. 1995. "The Church of Ireland and the Problem of the Protestant Working-Class of Dublin, 1870s–1930s." In *As by Law Established: The Church of Ireland since the Reformation*, edited by Alan Ford, James McGuire, and Kenneth Milne, 195–204. Dublin: Lilliput.

McHugh, Mary Frances. 1931. *Thalassa: A Story of Childhood by the Western Wave*. London: Macmillan.

McNally, Patrick. 1999. " 'The Whole People of Ireland': Patriotism, National Identity, and Nationalism in Eighteenth-Century Ireland." In *Ireland in Proximity: History, Gender, Space*, edited by Scott Brewster et al., 28–41. New York: Routledge.

Mercier, Vivian. 1962. *The Irish Comic Tradition*. Oxford: Clarendon.

———. 1982. "Victorian Evangelism and the Anglo-Irish Literary Revival." In *Literature and the Changing Ireland*, edited by Peter Connolloy, 59–102. Gerrards Cross, England: Colin Smythe.

Miller, Kristine A. 1999. " 'Even a Shelter's Not Safe': The Blitz on Homes in Elizabeth Bowen's Wartime Writing." *Twentieth Century Literature* 45, no. 2: 138–58.

Moore, George. 1887. *Parnell and His Island*. London: Sonnenschein, Lowrey.

———. 1942. *Letters of George Moore*. Edited by John Eglington [W. K. Magee]. Bournemouth, England: Sydenham.

————. 1972. *Confessions of a Young Man*. Edited by Susan Dick. Variorum ed. Montreal: McGill-Queen's Univ. Press.

————. 1985. *Hail and Farewell*. 1911–1914. Reprint. Gerrards Cross, England: Colin Smythe.

————. 1988. *George Moore on Parnassus*. Edited by Helmut E. Gerber. Newark: Univ. of Delaware Press.

Moynahan, Julian. 1995. *Anglo-Irish: The Literary Imagination in a Hyphenated Culture*. Princeton: Princeton Univ. Press.

Murphy, William. 1978. *Prodigal Father: The Life of John Butler Yeats (1839–1922)*. Ithaca: Cornell Univ. Press.

Napier, Taura. 2001. *Seeking a Country. Literary Autobiographies of Twentieth-Century Irishwomen*. Lanham, Md.: Univ. Press of America.

Nilson, Don. 1996. *Homer in Irish Literature: A Reference Guide*. Westport, Conn.: Greenwood Press.

Neuman, Shirley. 1992. "Autobiography: From Different Poetics to a Poetics of Differences." In *Essays on Life Writing: From Genre to Critical Practice*, edited by Marlene Kadar, 213–30. Toronto: Univ. of Toronto Press.

Ni Chuilleanain, Eilean. 1996. "The Voices of Maria Edgeworth's Comedy." In *The Comic Tradition in Irish Women Writers*, edited by Theresa O'Connor, 21–39. Gainesville: Univ. Press of Florida.

nic Shiubhlaigh, Marie. 1987. "At the Abbey Theatre." In *Lady Gregory: 50 Years After*, edited by Ann Saddlemyer and Colin Smythe, 23–25. Gerrards Cross, England: Colin Smythe.

O'Connell, Mrs. Morgan John. 1887. *Glimpses of a Hidden Life: Memories of Attie O'Brien*. Dublin: M. H. Gill and Son.

O'Connor, Ulick. 1963. *Times I've Seen: Oliver St. John Gogarty, a Biography*. New York: I. Obolensky.

O'Dea, Patrick. 1994. *A Class of Our Own: Conversations about Class in Ireland*. Dublin: New Island Books.

O'Hart, John. 1969. *The Irish and Anglo-Irish Landed Gentry*. 1884. Reprint. New York: Barnes and Noble.

Olney, James. 1984. "The Uses of Comedy and Irony in Autobiographies and Autobiography." In *Yeats: An Annual of Critical and Textual Studies*, edited by Richard J. Finneran, 198–208. Ithaca: Cornell Univ. Press.

Origo, Iris. 1970. *Images and Shadows: Part of a Life*. New York: Harcourt Brace Jovanovich.

Ormsby, Frank, ed. 1987. *Northern Windows: An Anthology of Ulster Autobiography*. Belfast: Blackstaff.

Orpen, Sir William. 1925. *Stories of Old Ireland and Myself*. New York: Henry Holt.

Pakenham, Lord. 1953. *Born to Believe: An Autobiography*. London: Jonathan Cape.

Pakenham, Mary. 1938. *Brought Up and Brought Out*. London: Cobden-Sanderson.

Palmeri, Frank. 1990. *Satire in Narrative*. Austin: Univ. of Texas Press.

Pascal, Roy. 1960. *Design and Truth in Autobiography*. Cambridge: Harvard Univ. Press.

Peterson, Linda H. 1986. *Victorian Autobiography: The Tradition of Self-Interpretation*. New Haven: Yale Univ. Press.

———. 1999. *Traditions of Victorian Women's Autobiography: The Poetics and Politics of Life Writing*. Charlottesville: Univ. Press of Virginia.

Pethica, James. 1987. "A Woman's Sonnets." In *Lady Gregory: 50 Years After*, edited by Ann Saddlemyer and Colin Smythe, 98–122. Gerrards Cross, England: Colin Smythe.

Powell, Violet. 1960. *Five Out of Six: An Autobiography*. London: Heinemann.

———. 1976. *Within the Family Circle: An Autobiography*. London: Heinemann.

Prior, Thomas. 1991. "From 'A List of the Absentees of Ireland.' " In *The Field Day Anthology of Irish Writing*, edited by Seamus Deane, 1:898–99. Derry, Northern Ireland: Field Day.

Procida, Mary. 2002. "The Greater Part of My Life Has Been Spent in India." *Biography* 25, no. 1: 130–50.

Quarton, Marjorie. 2000. *Breakfast the Night Before: Recollections of an Irish Horse Dealer*. Dublin: Lilliput.

Rendall, Jane. 1997. " 'A Short Account of My Unprofitable Life': Autobiographies of Working Class Women in Britain, c. 1775–1845." In *Women's Lives/Women's Times: New Essays on Auto/Biography*, edited by Trev Lynn Broughton and Linda Anderson, 31–50. Albany: State Univ. of New York Press.

Review of *A Lady's Child*, by Enid Starkie. 1941. *Irish Times* (20 Dec.): 5.

Review of *A Lady's Child*, by Enid Starkie. 1942a. *Dublin Magazine* 17, no. 2: 64.

Review of *A Lady's Child*, by Enid Starkie. 1942b. *Listner* (22 Jan.): 121–22.

Rich, Adrienne. 1976. *Of Woman Born: Motherhood as Experience and Institution*. New York: W. W. Norton.

Richardson, Joanna. 1973. *Enid Starkie*. New York: Macmillan.

Roberts, Elizabeth. 1984. *A Woman's Place: An Oral History of Working-Class Women, 1890–1940*. Oxford: Blackwell.

Robinson, John A. 1992. "Autobiographical Memory." In *Aspects of Memory*, edited by Michael Gruneberg and Peter Morris, 223–51. London: Routledge.

Robinson, Lennox. 1942. *Curtain Up: An Autobiography*. London: Michael Joseph.

Ross, Ellen. 1993. *Love and Toil: Motherhood in Outcast London, 1870–1918*. New York: Oxford Univ. Press.

Rousseau, Jean-Jacques. 1953. *The Confessions*. Translated by J. M. Cohen. New York: Penguin.

Russell, Thomas. 1991. *Journals and Memoirs of Thomas Russell, 1791–5*. Edited by C. J. Woods. Dublin: Irish Academic Press.

Ryan, Mary, Sean Browne, and Kevin Gilmour, eds. 1995. *No Shoes in Summer*. Dublin: Wolfhound.

Said, Edward. 1983. *The World, the Text, and the Critic*. Cambridge: Harvard Univ. Press.

Sanders, Valerie. 1989. *The Private Lives of Victorian Women.* New York: St. Martin's.

Seidel, Michael. 1979. *Satiric Inheritance: Rabelais to Sterne.* Princeton: Princeton Univ. Press.

Shaw, G. B. 1965. *Collected Letters, 1874–1897.* Edited by Dan H. Laurence. New York: Dodd.

———. 1967. *Shaw on Religion.* Edited by Warren Sylvester Smith. London: Constable.

———. 1970. *Shaw: An Autobiography, 1856–1898.* Edited by Stanley Weintraub. London: Max Reinhardt.

Showalter, Elaine. 1990. *Sexual Anarchy: Gender and Culture at the Fin-de-Siècle.* New York. Viking.

Sloan, Barry. 2000. *Writers and Protestantism in the North of Ireland: Heirs to Adamnation?* Dublin: Irish Academic Press.

Smith, Paul. 1988. *Discerning the Subject.* Minneapolis: Univ. of Minnesota Press.

Smith, Sidonie. 1987. *A Poetics of Women's Autobiography: Marginality and the Fictions of Self-Representation.* Bloomington: Indiana Univ. Press.

———. 1993a. *Subjectivity, Identity, and the Body: Women's Autobiographical Practices in the Twentieth Century.* Bloomington: Indiana Univ. Press.

———. 1993b. "Who's Talking/Who's Talking Back? The Subject of Personal Narratives." *Signs* 18: 392–407.

Somerville, E[dith] O., and Martin Ross [Violet Martin, pseud.]. 1893. *Through Connemara in a Governess Cart.* London: W. H. Allen.

———. 1946. *"Happy Days!" Essays of Sorts.* London: Longmans, Green.

———. 1978. *The Big House of Inver.* 1925. Reprint. London: Quartet.

———. 1989. *The Selected Letters of Somerville and Ross.* Edited by Gifford Lewis. London: Faber and Faber.

Spalding, Morid. 1942. Review of *A Lady's Child,* by Enid Starkie. *Life and Letters of To-Day* 32: 141–42.

Stacpoole, Henry de Vere. 1942. *Men and Mice, 1863–1942.* London: Hutchinson.

Stallworthy, Jon. 1995. *Louis MacNeice.* New York: W. W. Norton.

Starkie, Enid. 1941. *A Lady's Child.* London: Faber and Faber.

Stuart, Francis. 1934. *Things to Live For: Notes for an Autobiography.* London: Jonathan Cape.

Stunt, T. C. F. 1989. "Evangelical Cross-Currents in the Church of Ireland, 1820–1833." In *The Churches, Ireland, and the Irish,* edited by W. J. Sheils and Diana Wood, 215–22. Oxford: Basil Blackwell.

Suleiman, Susan Rubin. 1985. "Writing and Motherhood." In *The Mother Tongue: Essays in Feminist Psychoanalytic Interpretation,* edited by Shirley Nelson Garner, Claire Kahane, and Madelon Sprengnether, 352–77. Ithaca: Cornell Univ. Press.

Synge, John Millington. 1982. "Autobiography." In *Collected Works: Prose,* edited by Alan Price, 2:3–15. Gerrards Cross, England: Colin Smythe.

Todorov, Tzvetan. 1994. "Fictions and Truths." In *Critical Reconstructions: The Relation-*

ship of Fiction and Life, edited by Robert M. Polhemus and Roger B. Henkle, 21–51. Stanford: Stanford Univ. Press.

Trench, William. 1868. *Realities of Irish Life.* London: Longmans, Green.

Trevor, William. 1993. *Excursions in the Real World: Memoirs.* New York: Penguin.

Trodd, Colin, Paul Barlow, and David Amigoni, eds. 1999. *Victorian Culture and the Idea of the Grotesque.* Brookfield, Vt.: Ashgate.

Tyrrell, George. 1912. *Autobiography and Life of George Tyrrell.* Edited by Maud Dominica Mary Petre. London: Arnold.

Walvin, James. 1982. *A Child's World: A Social History of English Childhood, 1800–1914.* New York: Penguin.

Waters, Maureen. 1984. *The Comic Irishman.* Albany: State Univ. of New York Press.

Watson, Julia. 1996. "Ordering the Family: Genealogy as Autobiographical Pedigree." In *Getting a Life: Everyday Uses of Autobiography*, edited by Sidonie Smith and Julia Watson, 297–323. Minneapolis: Univ. of Minnesota Press.

Whaley, Thomas. 1906. *Buck Whaley's Memoirs, Including His Journey to Jerusalem, Written by Himself in 1797 and Now First Published from the Recently Recovered Manuscript.* Edited by Sir Edward Sullivan. London: A. Moring.

Wideman, John Edgar. 1994. *Fatheralong.* New York: Vintage.

Woodward, Kathleen. 1988. "Simone de Beauvoir: Aging and Its Discontents." In *The Private Self: Theory and Practice of Women's Autobiographical Writings*, edited by Shari Benstock, 90–113. Chapel Hill: Univ. of North Carolina Press.

Woolf, Virginia. 1985. *Moments of Being.* New York: Harcourt Brace Jovanovich.

Wynne, Maud. 1937. *An Irishman and His Family: Lord Morris and Killanin.* London: John Murray.

Yeats, John Butler. 1971. *Early Memories: Some Chapters of Autobiography.* 1923. Reprint. Shannon: Irish Univ. Press.

Yeats, W. B. 1961. "What Is Popular Poetry?" In *Essays and Introductions*, 3–12. New York: Macmillan.

———. 1962. *Explorations.* New York: Macmillan.

———. 1965. *The Autobiography of William Butler Yeats.* New York: Macmillan.

———. 1972. *Memoirs.* Edited by Denis Donaghue. London: Macmillan.

———. 1983. *W. B. Yeats: The Poems.* Edited by Richard J. Finneran. New York: Macmillan.

———. Papers. National Library of Ireland, Dublin.

Index

Yeats, William Butler: as autobiographer, xix, 77–78, 133, 151, 155; on childhood, 18; as influence on T. R. Henn, 23; on nationality, 24; and mother, 63, 68; on Lady Gregory's autobiography, 70; race theories of, 12–14, 27, 100n. 6, 147; on Robert Gregory, 71; father's similarities with, 63, 116, 116n. 10; on Synge, 112; views of the Anglo-Irish, xiii, xvi, 2–3, 40, 55, 88, 127